# Growing Up With
# MUSIC

## A GUIDE TO
## THE BEST RECORDED
## MUSIC FOR CHILDREN

# Growing Up With
# MUSIC

## A GUIDE TO
## THE BEST RECORDED
## MUSIC FOR CHILDREN

## Laurie
## Sale

AVON BOOKS ◆ NEW YORK

To June and Sam Sale for lighting the fire
and
to Aaron and Jorge Flores for keeping it aglow.

GROWING UP WITH MUSIC is an original publication of Avon Books. This work has never before appeared in book form.

AVON BOOKS
A division of
The Hearst Corporation
1350 Avenue of the Americas
New York, New York 10019

Copyright © 1992 by Laurie Sale
Cover illustration by Elizabeth Hathon
Published by arrangement with the author
Library of Congress Catalog Card Number: 92-15150
ISBN: 0-380-76211-0

Library of Congress Cataloging in Publication Data:

Sale, Laurie.
    Growing up with music : a guide to the best recorded music for children / Laurie Sale.
        p.    cm.
    Includes index.
    ISBN 0-380-76211-0
    1. Children's songs—Discography.  I. Title
ML156.4.C5S24    1992                                    92-15150
016.78242'083'0266—dc20                                  CIP
                                                         MN

First Avon Books Trade Printing: October 1992

AVON TRADEMARK REG. U.S. PAT. OFF. AND IN OTHER COUNTRIES, MARCA REGISTRADA, HECHO EN U.S.A.

Printed in the U.S.A.

OPM   10  9  8  7  6  5  4  3  2  1

# Contents

# *Acknowledgments*

This book could not have been written without the help and support of many wonderful friends. Thanks: to David Hoffman for lunch and getting this started . . . to my wonderful and supportive agent and friend, Patti Breitman . . . to my editors Mark Gompertz and Lisa Considine who are definitely the best! . . . to Norman Josephs for his love and support . . . to Bob Garza who helped with research . . . to Judy Zerbe and Scott Krause who gave me time to work on this project . . . to Natalie Glaser and Judi Williams for their unconditional love . . . to Josh Sale for his patience . . . to all the people in the children's music business who responded so graciously to my incessant requests and questions . . . and finally to all the wonderful performers who have enriched my life with their music and friendship.

# Introduction ♫..

Some of my oldest and fondest memories are of songs that members of my family sang to me and with me as a child, some in Russian, some in Yiddish and some in English. I remember listening to my parents and grandparents humming, singing and listening to music. It surrounded me and was an integral part of my existence. We sang at home, in school and later on at hootenannies, where people would gather specifically to sing folk songs. No one in my family was particularly musical, but everyone seemed to understand that sharing some musical time with each other was a pleasurable and nurturing experience. When my brother and sister and I were infants, we were sung to while we were being rocked to sleep, while we were being driven in the car (imagine . . . a car that didn't have a tape deck in it), while we were being dressed, and at other shared moments in the day. Music was something I associated with pleasure.

My parents bought me a record player when I was two, and this allowed me to select those songs I wanted to hear again and again. I had a wonderful selection of children's music with which I could sing and dance. I grew up with Woody Guthrie, Pete Seeger, The Weavers, Tom Glazer, Leadbelly, and Danny Kaye. Is it any wonder that I still recommend these artists to parents today? Those performers taught me to feel good about singing and moving and brought me hours of entertainment and joy. Like most children, I loved to hear things over and over again, and so I literally wore through several copies of the new 33⅓ recordings that represented the recording industry's latest technological advancement.

Early musical experiences are important for children. They allow children to develop language and listening skills, as well as their motor and coordination skills. Children learn new vocabulary and language patterns through age-appropriate music. The melodic and verbal repetition in many children's songs greatly enhances the learning experience. Because music is so conducive to learning language, many people learn a foreign language through listening to music from other cultures.

Children's music became diversified and more commercially successful about twenty years ago, when material was being developed for schoolroom use. Over the years, schools have typically been the major benefactors of the music available for children. Nursery schools have traditionally had a wide variety of recordings available for their use, since a vast majority of the music was being geared to preschoolers. The elementary schools used recordings in the classroom to teach basic skills and music appreciation, to enhance the physical education program, and to teach English to children as a second language. When I taught school in Mexico and in the United States, I relied heavily on recordings to help children learn language skills, motor and movement skills, and listening skills as well as for the pure excitement of mastering the music and being able to sing along with it. Parents, on the other hand, had fewer recordings specifically geared to individual and home use.

The last five to ten years have seen a renewed interest in producing quality music for children. Interestingly enough, much of the popular music that is now familiar to parents comes from Canada. Although Canada's population is sizably smaller than that of the United States, Canadians place tremendous importance on music and fine arts for children. The government subsidizes children's music and sponsors festivals and television programs. The U.S. government has a lot to learn from our neighbors to the north.

For the last seventeen years, I have been fortunate enough to be the owner of one of the few outlets in the United States for quality children's music. The Children's Book and Music Center (originally called the Children's Music Center) was started in the late 1940s to help parents and teachers find quality recordings for the children in their lives. Happily my family shopped there and made Woody, Pete, Tom, Danny and Leadbelly my first musical friends and heroes. When I moved to Mexico in 1969 and finally had children of my own, I frequently returned to Los Angeles to buy records from the only place I knew that sold children's music. When we returned to the U.S., my ex-husband took a job at the store, and eventually we decided to buy and expand it. In 1975, we became the new owners of the Children's Music Center and proudly renamed it the Children's Book and Music Center. The market has expanded tremendously since those days, but some of my heroes are still sharing their musical wealth with children. Some recordings have disappeared, but equally delightful ones have emerged to carry on wonderful traditions.

When I was living in Mexico City in the late 1960s with my new young son, I bought a sturdy record player and a dozen records from the Children's Music Center, that subsequently lasted through a second son and several moves. In fact, I've saved those first records for my children to use with their children (who will probably *Never* see a record player). My children, who are grown now, still can sing their favorite "first songs." As a nursery school and later elementary school teacher in Mexico, I used recordings by Hap Palmer and Ella Jenkins, among others, to help the children learn English, and later when I taught elementary school in Los Angeles, I used other records to help the students learn Spanish. Over the years, I've spent many hours enjoying new material sent to me for preview and recommending long-time favorites as well as new releases to our customers.

With so many recordings available now, adults are often overwhelmed when trying to buy musical and spoken-word recordings for their children. Although we offer customers the ability to listen to the material before they purchase, we can't do that for people who live far away. It is difficult to read the copy on a recording cover and make a decision, especially if there are no familiar songs listed. I've been helping parents, grandparents, teachers, librarians and others interested in children choose audio recordings for more than seventeen years. It seems many would benefit from a guide to help them choose age-appropriate music for their children.

# Using This Guide ♫..

As children progress through various stages of mental and physical growth, their musical attitudes will change and grow. The first four chapters focus on different age groups and discuss child development in terms of music and movement. They include information on what to look for when choosing recordings for each particular age. Additional chapters concentrate on holiday, classical, Spanish and French recordings for kids. There is a review section in each chapter, arranged alphabetically by artist, where recordings are listed; explained; and reviewed for content, style and age-appropriateness. In attempting to make review sections complete, but not overwhelming, I've chosen material that I feel is most interesting and accessible. I've starred my first choice selections, which I feel are the most outstanding. There may appear to be an excessive number of starred selections, but I really love those recordings (I guess that's why I'm in the business). These starred selections have also been endorsed over the years by our customers, who are parents, teachers and librarians.

Entries in the review sections list the most up-to-date information available on which companies produce which recordings, but as in many other businesses these days, the only thing you *can* count on in the music industry is change. Musicians change labels and companies change their own names, both potentially frustrating the consumer's search for a particular selection. Fortunately, many problems of this nature can be cleared up by a knowledgeable sales clerk in your local music store. Please note that I've listed album and song titles as they appear on the recording company's literature, so there is some variation in the spelling of some songs.

It is important to remember that music is a pleasurable

activity and shouldn't be forced on any child. It can be used for activity time, for driving in the car, for doing daily chores, and for quiet times as well as for many other times throughout the day. Don't be afraid to sing, even if you can't carry a tune. Try making up new words to favorite melodies, words that relate to what you are doing with your child. Make your child feel extra special by inserting his name into a familiar song. Use different words that rhyme with your child's name, and create your own tunes. The more you experiment and create, the more fun you'll have with your child.

I encourage you to share the musical experience with the children in your life. It is both enjoyable and rewarding. Whether you are listening to music, singing along, or making up your own, this is a wonderful and lifelong gift to give to your children.

It was a dilemma as to whether I should use "he," "she" or "it" throughout the book when referring to children. For my own selfish reason, I've decided to use "he" since I have proudly raised two sons and many of these recordings remind me of wonderful hours spent together listening and singing.

# *Lullabies and Quiet Time Music (For All Ages)* ♫..

One of the first sensory experiences we have, even before birth, is the rushing sound of our mother's heartbeat. This rhythmic pattern is something we carry with us throughout life, imitating and transforming it as we grow and change. At birth, some families choose to let newborns listen to recordings that simulate those rhythmic sounds and make the transition from the womb to the outside world less traumatic. These slow, steady, defined sounds are calming and soothing to infants. In fact, we use slow, steady rhythmic motions when we rock a baby to soothe him or to help him get to sleep. We find it relaxes us as well!

Lullabies were created to calm and relax a child, to prepare him to go to sleep. They are both a great way to go from activity to quiet time and the perfect introduction to music for children. What should you look for in good lullaby music? The same words keep appearing: steady rhythm, soft accompaniment and soothing lyrics. Look for clear, simple, and not overly-orchestrated music. You want the child to hear clear pronunciations and sound. If it is a vocal recording, it helps if the singing is not too highly pitched. Orchestral music is wonderful, and any favorite classical pieces are highly recommended. Musical tastes vary and you, as the caregiver, must also enjoy what you and the child are listening to. Let yourself go. Who cares if you can or can't carry a tune? Sing or hum along with the music as you are holding or rocking your child. He will come to associate music with pleasurable times and bonding. Music is a wonderful way to share joy, happiness and love.

Although no specifically ethnic recordings are listed here, I feel that music from different cultures is great to use with children of all ages, starting at birth. Go to your favorite record store and look for music from Greece, Latin America, Israel, Scotland, Ireland, the Balkans. This doesn't need to specifically be children's music; any recordings that you can find will do. Traditional music from these countries tends to have strong, repetitive rhythms, and the instruments from different countries are interesting and seductive.

These repetitive and rhythmic sounds have a wonderful effect on children. It's wonderful to expose children to cultural diversity. My own kids listened to Israeli and Greek music endlessly. Share your ethnic heritage with your child from the time he is an infant. There are many companies that produce ethnic recordings but, unfortunately, the only outlets that seem to carry them are the larger stores and some mail-order houses, but you might also want to check bookstores in ethnic neighborhoods. (See Resources for Children's Recordings for a list of mail-order companies.)

I've always felt that lullabies were wasted on bedtime. Why not use them throughout the day? Sing your favorite lullaby to your child while dressing him or while driving in your car. Lullabies are for relaxing as well as sleeping. We all need relaxing time during our waking hours, and some of the recordings are pleasurably helpful for reducing tension during a hectic day. Even though my children are grown, I keep my favorite lullaby tape in my car for those long drives home after long days at work. It really helps! A good lullaby recording can be used for many years and on many occasions. We are never too old for quiet time music.

Parents often ask whether lullabies should begin to be used at any particular age. One mother was concerned that her infant wouldn't "understand the lyrics." Lullabies are a way for your child to begin to hear the rhythms in language. He may not understand the lyrics but will sense the calm and relaxing sounds. He will learn to identify this music with "quiet" time. Because children, including babies, can pick up on our moods, you may often wish to use this music to put yourself into a relaxed state, and pass that on to your child. Another frequently asked question is at what age does a child outgrow lullabies? The answer to that is "Never!" Babies as well as adults can benefit from soothing music.

Select recordings that reflect your own taste. In my family, we have established the tradition of listening to classical music on Sunday mornings, or whenever we just need to "chill out." As your child gets older, let him verbalize his taste and partake in the music-listening choices.

## DO:

- Hold your child while singing to him, when possible.
- Look for clear, rhythmic music.
- Use your favorite ethnic recording.
- Use these recordings at rest time and bedtime.
- Use these recordings at different times during the day.
- Use your favorite classical recordings.
- Pass on your cultural heritage through lullabies and other music.
- Enjoy yourself when using music with your child.
- Encourage your child to tell you about his personal favorites.
- Look through other chapters as many recordings appeal to a broad age range.

## DON'T:

- Be afraid to sing or hum along.
- Use recordings with high-pitched voices.
- Use recordings that are overly orchestrated or have cluttered sounds.
- Be afraid to enjoy these recordings on your own.
- Pack lullaby recordings away just because your child is no longer an infant.

## EARTH MOTHER LULLABIES FROM AROUND THE WORLD VOLS. I, II AND III
**Pamela Ballingham**
**Earth Mother Productions**
**Cassette**
**Lyrics included**
**Infant–5**

These recordings, with their fascinating view of the world through lullabies, provide a truly multicultural experience. Ballingham's lovely voice melds with harp, guitar, flute, bells, mandolin, drums and other instruments to produce a universal sound. The songs are diverse and you will surely find something from your own heritage. Done in a folk-song style, these recordings will appeal to people who want variety in culture and musical styles. Teachers will find them useful as part of their multicultural units. Helpful lyric sheets are included.

*Volume I* includes "Arrorro, Mi Niño" (Latin America), "Sleep My Baby" (Russia), "Sleep Little One" (Japan), "Ho, Ho Watanay" (Iroquois) plus six more. *Volume II* includes "Tum-Balalayka" (Yiddish), "Gaelic Cradle Song" (Ireland), "Tulleri Lull" (Sweden), "O Mother Glasco" (Afro-American) and six more. *Volume III* includes "Bedtime Song" (England), "Comes the Sandman" (Poland), "Spanish Lullaby" (Spain), "Twilight Song" (Norway), "Time Sends a Warning Call" (England), "Night Herding Song" (United States), "I Gave My Love a Cherry" (United States), "Moon, Sun" (Germany), "O Do Not Cry" (Nigeria) and "Tender Shepherd" (United States).

## MAGICAL MELODIES
**Pamela Ballingham**
**Earth Mother Recordings**
**Cassette**
**No lyrics included**
**Infant–10**

Music adapted from Broadway melodies is increasingly popular and easy to find. I know of four recordings released since the beginning of 1990. Ballingham has joined in with her special collection of tunes from Broadway shows and motion pictures.

Her voice is very alluring and her orchestral arrangements varied and well-suited to the quality of her voice. Although this is listed in the lullaby section, don't keep this on the shelf because it's not bed or rest time. This recording is great for all times of the day. Don't be surprised to catch yourself singing along. These famous and not-so-famous songs include "Over The Rainbow" (*Wizard of Oz*), "Rainbow Connection" (*The Muppet Movie*), "Anyone Can Whistle" (*Anyone Can Whistle*), "No One Is Alone" (*Into the Woods*), "Never Never Land" (*Peter Pan*), "If We Hold On Together" (*The Land Before Time*), "Flying Dreams" (*The Secret of NIMH*) and "Never Ending Story" (*Never Ending Story*).

### A TREASURY OF EARTH MOTHER LULLABIES
**Pamela Ballingham**
**Earth Mother Productions**
**C.D.**
**Lyrics included**
**Infant–10**

This recording, available only in the compact disc format, represents some of the most popular songs from the *Earth Mother Lullabies Volumes I, II, and III*. It is a very popular recording in our store. The fourteen selections are: "Tender Shepherd" (United States), "I Gave My Love a Cherry" (United States), "Arrorro Mi Niño" (Latin America), "Ho Ho Watanay" (Iroquois), "Abiyoyo" (South Africa), "All The Pretty Little Horses" (Afro-American), "Tum-Balalayka" (Yiddish), "The Mockingbird Song" (Appalachian), "Moon, Sun" (Germany), "Bedtime Song" (England), "O Mother Glasco" (Afro-American), "Though Shadows Dark" (Aboriginal), "Little Red Bird" (Isle Of Man) and "Night Herding Song" (United States). This is a great collection of lullabies from around the world, and a great buy, provided you have a C.D. player.

**VOYAGE FOR DREAMERS**
**Pamela Ballingham**
**Earth Mother Productions**
**Cassette**
**Lyrics included**
**Infant–Adult**

This recording isn't just for children. Most of the original lyrics are complex, but the music is restful and calming. The guitar, piano and keyboard accompaniments and Ballingham's lyric voice give it a rhythmic and soothing sound. If you like the sound of New Age music, this will appeal to you. The songs include "When Nighttime Sweeps the Land," "Many the Flowers," "Moon Spirit," "Shadow of a Life," "After the Rain Falls," "Crystal in the Night," "Far Off Shore" and three more. A very pleasant recording.


★★★     **LULLABY MAGIC VOLS. I AND II**
**Joanie Bartels**
**Discovery Music**
**Cassette**
**Lyrics included**
**Infant–6**

These are two of the most popular lullaby recordings on the market, and with good reason as they are produced by people who are very creative and keep getting better. Take some wonderfully familiar songs and mix them with an incredible vocal and musical style, and the result is great music to listen to any time of the day or night. Contemporary songs, including "Close Your Eyes" (written by James Taylor) and "Goodnight" (by Paul McCartney and John Lennon) are combined with such old favorites as "Somewhere over the Rainbow" and "When You Wish upon a Star." One side is vocal and the other is instrumental. *Lullaby Magic Volume I* includes "Twinkle, Twinkle Little Star," "Goodnight," "Lullaby and Goodnight," "Goodnight My Someone," "Hush Little Baby," "Close Your Eyes" and four more. *Volume II* includes "Dream a Little Dream of Me," "Goodnight Sweetheart," "Sleep Song" (written by Graham Nash), "Love Me Tender," "Russian Lullaby," and five more. Be sure to see other recordings by Joanie Bartels on pp. 35, 58–60, and 217.

**LULLABIES FROM AROUND THE WORLD—**
**Caring Music for Expectant Mothers,**
**Crying Babies and Children**
**Steve Bergman**
**Steve Bergman Productions**
**Cassette**
**No lyrics included**
**Infant–6**

Bergman's orchestral arrangements of favorite lullabies from around the world can be enjoyed by children, tearful or not, and adults, pregnant or not. This is the style of music you can use when you just want to lay back and dream or if you need to relieve tension while doing your tax returns! The instrumentation is varied and maintains the listener's attention. Some may call this New Age music, but I prefer to think of it as "All Age music." The ten songs include "Brahms' Lullaby" (Germany), "Soli, Soli, Sittali" (Switzerland), "Golden Slumbers" (England) and an original lullaby by Steve Bergman.

★★★   **MARCIA BERMAN SINGS LULLABIES—**
**And Songs You Never Dreamed Were**
**Lullabies**
**Marcia Berman**
**B/B Records**
**LP/Cassette**
**Lyrics included**
**Infant–8**

Marcia Berman has been entertaining and singing for children in schools and in concerts for over twenty years. She travels extensively, collecting songs from other cultures, and openly shares her musical wealth. In this, one of her finest recordings, the arrangements are rich and full, and the musical styles are varied and always interesting. She uses a wide variety of instruments and back-up voices, so you will experience something new each time you listen to this recording. Included in the twelve selections are "My Little Buckaroo" (originally sung by Bing Crosby), "Lullaby of Birdland," "Russian Lullaby," "Raisins and Almonds" (sung in English and Yiddish) and "Lullaby of Broadway." Marcia's voice is clear, soft and inviting, truly appropriate to this nostalgic feast of songs. Be sure to see Marcia Berman's other recordings on pp. 62–64 and 133.

★ ★ ★   **LULLABIES OF BROADWAY**
**Mimi Bessette**
**Music for Little People**
**Cassette/C.D.**
**Lyrics included**
**All Ages**

I have listened to this recording four times, and each time I visualize Mimi Bessette standing centerstage, singing her heart out to an audience of children and adults. Her voice is powerful enough for any Broadway musical, and yet there is a soft, lulling element that engages and warms listeners. Most of the songs from Broadway musicals on this recording are well-known. Many of them were not written as lullabies per se, but Bessette's performance transforms the tunes into quiet time songs. The collection includes "Lullaby of Broadway/Never-Never Land" (originally from a film called *Goldiggers of 1935*, but most recently from the 1980 opening of *42nd Street* and from *Peter Pan*, which opened in 1954), "Blueberry Eyes" (from *Gone with the Wind*, 1970), "Castle on a Cloud" (my favorite from *Les Miserables*, 1980), "Not While I'm Around" (from *Sweeny Todd*, 1979), "Edelweiss" (from *Sound of Music*, 1959), "Count Your Blessings" (from the movie *White Christmas*, 1954), "Jenny Rebecca" (a love song to a new daughter from composer/lyricist Carol Hall), "My Broth of a Boy" (from an unproduced film of 1943, written by Cole Porter) and "New Words" (from a yet unproduced play called *One, Two, Three, Four Five*, music and lyrics by Maury Yeston). This is a marvelous, magical collection of songs to soothe even the oldest bodies.

**GOLDEN SLUMBERS—**
**Lullabies from Near and Far**
**Oscar Brand, Pete Seeger and others**
**Caedmon Records**
**Cassette**
**No lyrics included**
**Infant–8**

This is a time-tested favorite. These lullabies have been sung the world over and passed down from generation to generation. The arrangements are clear and uncomplicated. The performers are both male and female, exposing the child to different tonal qualities and pitches. Several songs are sung in languages other than English and represent a variety of cultures. Recorded over twenty years ago, this does not have the quality of some of the newer offerings; however, its lasting content and appeal have rendered it a bestseller for years. Enjoy Pete Seeger singing "All the Pretty Little Horses," "Bye'n Bye" and "Hush Little Baby." Oscar Brand sings "Petit Chat Noir," "Kiowa Lullaby" and "Twinkle, Twinkle Little Star." Jean Ritchie sings "Dance to Your Daddy," and Elizabeth Knight sings "Golden Slumbers" and "Sleep, Baby, Sleep." Also included are "Raisins and Almonds," "Bye, Baby Bunting" and thirteen more.

**BABES, BEASTS AND BIRDS**
**Pat Cafra**
**Lullaby Lady Productions**
**LP/Cassette**
**Lyrics included**
**Ages 2–5**

This is by far the best of the series from Pat Cafra, the Canadian Lullaby Lady. Its collection of songs appeals to toddlers as well as older children. The arrangements are simple, and Pat Cafra's voice is lively. The Dozing Off songs are diverse, and some are sung in French. The selection of Quiet songs and Wide Awake songs will give you many opportunities to use this recording. The Dozing Off songs include "Baby's Huggle," "Over in the Meadow," "By'N'Bye," "Ally Bally," "La Poulette Grise," and seven more. The Wide Awake songs include "Little

White Duck," "Bear Hunt," "Skip to My Lou," "Had a Little Rooster," "A La Queue," and five more. Some of the Wide Awake songs are "add a verse" songs, where the child can insert his own version of the song. There is such a diversity of music here that it is difficult to say at what age your child would get the most from this recording. It really touches many levels, and I recommend it for a wide age range.

**LULLABIES AND LAUGHTER—**
  **with the Lullaby Lady**
**Pat Cafra**
**Lullaby Lady Productions**
**LP/Cassette**
**Lyrics included**
**Infant–3**

Pat Cafra here accompanies herself on the guitar and sings thirty-three songs for children. There are lullabies on one side and rhymes and playsongs on the other. Some of the songs have an unnecessary introduction, which makes repeated listening unappealing, but all in all, Cafra offers a wide selection of music. Her clear, well pitched voice is inviting. Because of the variety of music and different languages and activities on this recording, it will have a wide range of uses. Lullabies include "Morningtown Ride," "Turn Around," "All Through the Night," "Wynken, Blynken and Nod" and "My Curly Headed Baby." The rhymes and playsongs include "Pop Goes the Weasel," "Eensy, Weensy Spider," "This Little Piggy," "Down by the Station," "The Marvelous Toy" and "Follow the Leader."

**SONGS FOR SLEEPYHEADS AND**
  **OUT-OF-BEDS!**
**Pat Cafra**
**Lullaby Lady Productions**
**LP/Cassette**
**Lyrics included**
**Infant–3**

This is the second in a Canadian import series by the Lullaby Lady in Canada. Cafra sings a gigantic selection of quiet time and activity time songs with simple guitar accompaniment. The variety of lullabies includes "Go To Sleep Now," "My Pumpkin" (also sung in French), "Owl and the Pussycat," "Golden Slumbers," "Sunrise, Sunset" and "Fais Dodo." The finger plays and activity songs include "Everybody Knows I Love My Toes," "When I Was A Baby," "Sally Go Round the Sun," "I Have a Little Shadow" and "Aiken Drum." Although it contains a good collection of songs, this recording is musically uninteresting.

★★★ **LULLABIES GO JAZZ**
**Jon Crosse**
**Jazz Cat**
**LP/Cassette**
**No lyrics**
**Infant–10**

Imagine lulling a child to sleep with the sounds of a cool jazz saxophone. This, one of the most tender, loving, warm and refreshing lullaby recordings, permits you to do that. Jon Crosse's smooth jazz renditions of favorite lullabies are a perfect way to close the day or just have some quiet, relaxing time. This instrumental treasure is not just for children, since many adults, including myself, listen to it when they want to unwind. Simple and clear, this is a unique recording that is sure to please adults and turn many children into future jazz buffs. The eight songs include "Hush Little Baby," "Twinkle, Twinkle Little Star," "Rockabye Baby," "Brahms' Lullaby" and others.

**NITEYNITE—**
 **Tender Melodies for a Beautiful Bedtime**
**Patti Dallas and Laura Baron**
**Golden Glow Recordings**
**Cassette**
**No lyrics included**
**Infant–6**

Baron and Dallas have lovely voices that meld together in beautiful harmonies. The musical arrangements, using harp, guitar, recorder, flute and keyboard, are perfect accompaniment to their voices, and never overpower them. This collection of mostly traditional songs will definitely have a calming effect. A few of the songs are instrumental pieces. The twenty-two lullaby and quiet-time songs include "Oh How Lovely Is the Evening," "Edelweiss," "Tender Shepherd," "Hush-A-Bye," "White Coral Bells," "Greensleeves," "Mary Had a Little Lamb," "Michael Row Your Boat Ashore," "Little Boy Blue," "Little Doggie" and more. For songs that Baron and Dallas sing for active times see pp. 38–39.


**MICKEY DOLENZ PUTS YOU TO SLEEP**
**Mickey Dolenz**
**Kid Rhino**
**Cassette/C.D.**
**Infant–10**


Many will remember Mickey Dolenz from the sixties group, The Monkees. Before I heard this recording, I couldn't quite figure out what a Monkee could bring to a children's recording of lullabies. After the first track, I was very pleasantly delighted. Dolenz's voice stands the test of repeated listenings. The musical arrangements are never repetitive and reflect varied musical eras. Dolenz has chosen some eclectic songs by famous performers that might not sound like lullabies, but his presentations are lilting and very relaxing. I particularly like "Beautiful Boy," the John Lennon song. Also by Lennon and McCartney are "Blackbird," "Fool on the Hill" and "Goodnight." "Lullaby To Tim" is a Graham Nash piece that encourages a child's imagination. "St. Judy's Comet," by Paul Simon, is about a child who is resisting sleep. "Sugar Mountain" is a Neil Young song about a land of dreams. Other songs are "The Porpoise Song," "Remember," "The Moonbeam Song" and "Pillow Time." This is a fine recording that will relax both nostalgic parents and sleepy children.

★★★     **BABY ROAD**
         **Floyd Domino, Edgar Meyer and Mark**
            **Howard**
         **Golliber Records**
         **LP/Cassette**
         **No lyrics**
         **Infant–8**

Imagine the cover to the Beatles album *Abbey Road*. Next, imagine the same cover, but with four toddlers in diapers crossing the road. Now, imagine all your favorite Beatles tunes as a soothing lullaby recording for your children. Three talented musicians, using piano, upright bass and guitar, perform such classics as "Hey Jude," "Yesterday," "Michelle," "In My Life" and eight more quietly wonderful instrumental pieces. There is one original song called "Baby Road." This recording, great all hours of the day or night, contains the kind of music you can use as background for dinner parties, lazing on a quiet morning, or a hectic drive to take your children to school. It is never intrusive.

★★★     **THE WHITE ALBUM**
         **Floyd Domino, Chris O'Connell, Maryann**
            **Price, Mitch Watkins and Spencer Starnes**
         **Golliber Records**
         **LP/Cassette**
         **No lyrics included**
         **Infant–8**

The Beatles are back and so are "twelve songs peacefully arranged to help you and your little one through a hard day's night"—this album's cover says it all. This second recording by the creator of *Baby Road* has six vocal selections on one side by Chris O'Connell and Maryann Price, accompanied by guitar. The selections include "I Want to Hold Your Hand," "Love Me Do," and "All My Loving." The instrumental side, which in my opinion is the stronger side, has six selections including "I'll Follow the Sun," "A Hard Day's Night," "It's Only Love" and one non-Beatles song, "Golden Slumbers." The arrangements are simple, clear and interesting, and are faithful to the Beatles sound without the full rock 'n' roll volume.

★★★ **A CHILD'S GIFT OF LULLABYES**
**Vocals by Tanya Goodman**
**A Child's Gift Of Lullabyes**
**Cassette/C.D.**
**Lyrics included**
**Infant–6**

A collection of original songs may not appeal to traditionalists, but this is a very nice change from the standard lullabies. Goodman's voice is full and evenly pitched so that anyone can sing along. The melodies are simple, yet very inviting, and the kind that you'll find yourself humming long after turning off the tape player. Side A has vocals, while Side B is solely instrumental. The vocal side is infinitely more interesting and shows Goodman's first-class voice. The instrumentations are full, but never overwhelm her beautiful singing. Original songs include "Someday Baby," "Hushabye Street," "Appalachian Lullaby," "I L.O.V.E. Y.O.U.," "Lullaby for Teddy" and four more. A Spanish edition, *Un Regalo De Arrullos*, is discussed on page 242.

**THE ROCK-A-BYE COLLECTION**
**Vocals by Tanya Goodman**
**A Child's Gift of Lullabyes**
**Cassette**
**Lyrics included**
**Infant–6**

This Grammy Award-winning sequel to *A Child's Gift of Lullabyes* is unfortunately not as interesting as the first volume because the lyrics seem more appropriate for adults than children. Tanya Goodman's voice is vibrant. The arrangements are lilting and beautifully surround her singing. Again, Side A has vocals, and Side B is instrumental only. This collection includes "Rock-A-Bye (Mallory's Song)," "Teeter Totter," "Waltzing Down Lullaby Lane," "Lullaby and Goodnight," "May All Your Dreams Come True" and "Dreamland Concerto."

**SWEET DREAMS—**
**Restful Music for Quiet Times**
**Vocals by Diane Green**
**Kimbo**
**LP/Cassette**
**No lyrics included**
**Infant–5**

Green's lovely, lilting voice makes this recording an excellent choice. It is a fabulous collection of well-produced favorite songs. One side offers vocal selections and the other side is instruments alone. One can't help but feel warm and cozy listening to this music. The vocals are clear and orchestrations are rhythmic, although they utilize synthesizers. I personally would rather hear the real instruments playing, but this recording is tastefully done. The nine vocal songs include "Over the Rainbow," "Brahms' Lullaby," "Hush Little Baby," and "Rockabye Baby." The seven instrumental selections include "Imagine," "Greensleeves," "Scarborough Fair" and "Claire de Lune."

★★★ **STAR DREAMER—**
**Nightsongs and Lullabies**
**Pricilla Herdman**
**Alacazam Records**
**Cassette**
**Lyrics included**
**Infant–6**

Pricilla Herdman's voice is reassuring and caring in this eclectic collection of songs that is perfect for quiet and sleep time and sure to bring you and your children many years of pleasurable, relaxing music. The vocal harmonies are superb, with Herdman's voice always clear, and the musical arrangements are simple and inviting. Although many of the songs are not well-known, they are wonderful for young and not-so-young ears. Side One includes the Nightsongs: "Waltzing the Bears," "Matthew, Mark, Luke & John" (sung a cappella), "Autumn to May" (a Peter Paul and Mary song), "Moon upon the Lift," "The Moon" (words by Robert Louis Stevenson and music by Pricilla Herdman), "Goodnight, Irene" (this piece is worth the price of the recording) and "Twinkle, Twinkle Little Star" (with some new, additional lyrics). The Lullabies include "Time To Sleep" (a loving lullaby by children's performer Marcy Marxer), "Lullaby For Teddy-O," "Douglas Mountain," "First Lullaby," "Bush Lullaby" (an Australian song), "Close Your Eyes," (from "Brahms' Lullaby"), "The First Star Lullaby" (a beautiful song filled with love and hope for the future) and "Thanks A Lot" (written by Raffi and sung by Herdman accompanied only by the sound of her in her rocking chair). A very satisfying recording!

> **SNUGGLE UP COZY—**
> **Lullabies for Little Ones**
> **David Jack**
> **Golden**
> **Cassette**
> **No lyrics included**
> **Infant–5**

This is a collection of original material written and performed by David Jack. Although you probably won't recognize these songs, you'll grow to enjoy them. The combination of male and female voices is pleasant and soothing. "Mookie Pookie Lullaby," featuring David Jack's trademark character, is inventive and catchy, and "When Daddy Says Goodnight" is a nice, fresh song for Dads. This tape seems to be targeted at ages ranging from infant through four or five years old. The eleven songs include "Mama's Lullaby," "All the Things We'll Do Tomorrow," "Naptime," "I Like Us," "Uh-Oh" and "Sleepies." Other recordings by David Jack appear on pp. 79–80.

> **LULLABY BERCEUSE**
> **Connie Kaldor and Carmen Campagne**
> **Music for Little People**
> **Cassette**
> **Lyrics included**
> **Infant–8**

This lovely recording features Connie Kaldor singing lullabies in English on one side, and Carmen Campagne singing other lullabies in French on the other side. This is a very refreshing recording, even for those of us who don't understand French. Kaldor's voice is deep and very robust. Campagne's voice is lilting and soft. It was originally recorded in Canada, where many children are familiar with both languages. Most of the songs are original and written by the performers, with a couple of traditional songs included. Some of the songs were jointly composed. Kaldor's songs include "All Thru the Night," "Prairie Lullaby," "Dream Baby," "I've Been Told," "Dream Baby" (sung in French) and my favorite, "I Have You." I can picture a parent singing this love song to a child as he or she is changing diapers, giving a bath or putting the child to sleep. Campagne's songs include "Bonne Nuit" (melody by Brahms), "Petit Bébé," "Berceuse Pour Emanuel Reuben James," "Isabeau," the beautifully melodic "Maman Fait Dodo" and more. A very soothing recording.

**WHEN YOU WISH UPON A STAR**
**Daniel Kobialka**
**Li-Sem Enterprises**
**Cassette**
**No lyrics included**
**Infant–6**

Violinist Daniel Kobialka plays some lovely classical pieces that are perfect for quiet time listening. Other instruments include oboe, English horn, flute, mandolin, keyboard and synthesized guitar. Some of the songs have a very "new age" feeling to them, while others present a more traditional orchestral sound. This is a very soothing recording, sure to lull you and your child into a peaceful sleep. Although these songs are not all necessarily lullabies, they are perfect for relaxation. Included are "When You Wish upon a Star," "Angels Sleep" (Bach), "Children's Sonata" (Mozart), "Hush Little Baby," "Silki," "The Riddle Song," "Oh, How Lovely Is the Evening" and "The Future Is Beautiful."

★★★     **GOOD MORNING, GOOD NIGHT—**
          **Musical Poems and Lullabies for the Whole**
          **Family**
          **Kathi and Milenko, Nancy Rumbel and Friends**
          **Music for Little People**
          **Cassette**
          **Lyrics included**
          **Infant–8**

In this very different and special recording Kathi and Milenko
Matanovic have chosen some well-loved English poetry to put
to music. Their own vocal talent is augmented by additional,
extraordinary musicians. Children's voices are nicely inter-
mixed. This recording won't be for everyone, but is a rare find
for those seeking something unique. Side One has Good
Morning songs that are a bit faster in tempo and more appro-
priate for singing along than the quieter, more soothing Good
Night songs on Side Two. My favorite is "When It's Dark in the
Night" sung by a young girl named Katya Matanovic. Her voice
and the song's lyrics are very appealing. The eight Good
Morning Songs include "Block City" (Robert Louis Stevenson),
"General Store" (Rachel Field), "Written in March" (William
Wordsworth), a kolo dance from Yugoslavia and "The Secret
Song" (Margaret Wise Brown). Good Night songs include
"Ladybird, Ladybird" (Emily Brontë), "Seal Lullaby" (Rudyard
Kipling), "Land of Nod" (Robert Louis Stevenson) and three
more. This creative and unusual recording will give you many
years of listening and singing enjoyment.

          **FRANCINE SINGS A KEEPSAKE OF NURSERY**
               **SONGS AND LULLABIES**
          **Francine Horvath Lancaster**
          **Lancaster Horvath Productions**
          **Cassette**
          **No lyrics included**
          **All Ages**

Although packaged in a lovely oversized box with a color rep-
resentation of a mother and child, this recording leaves one
very dissatisfied. The collection of Nursery Songs on Side A is
fabulous, but Lancaster's voice is extremely high pitched and

overly theatrical. Such a voice makes it difficult for children to
sing along. Side B also has a wonderful selection of lullabies
sung in an operatic fashion. I personally find this recording
unappealing, but if you're looking for something in the operatic mode, perhaps this will please you. Lullabies include
"Twinkle, Twinkle Little Star," "All Through the Night," "Sleep,
Baby, Sleep," "Hush Little Baby," "Rockabye Baby" and five
more. The Nursery Songs include "Frère Jacques," "The Mulberry Bush," "This Old Man," "Old King Cole," "Jack and Jill,"
"Mary Had a Little Lamb," "Row, Row, Row Your Boat" and
nine more.

### G'NIGHT WOLFGANG—
#### Classical Piano Solos for Bedtime
#### Ric Louchard
#### Music for Little People
#### Cassette/C.D.
#### Infant–adult

This is a truly lovely recording of piano pieces by Mozart and
other composers, beautifully played by Ric Louchard. It is the
kind of recording that will relax even the most active child or
adult. Although great for nap or sleep time, or anytime when
you just want to clear your head, I wouldn't suggest playing
this in the car late at night on a dark highway. The pieces are
Adagio from Sonata in F Major (Mozart), Adagio Sostenuto from
Sonata Quasi Una Fantasia Op. 27, No. 2 ("Moonlight") (Beethoven), Sarabande from French Suite No. 5 in G Major (Bach),
Sarabande from French Suite No. 3 in B Minor (Bach), Prelude
I from *The Well-Tempered Clavier*, Vol. 1 (Bach), "Trois Gym-
nopedies": Lent et Douloureux, Lent et Triste and Lent et
Grave (Satie), Andante from Sonata in C Major (Mozart), and
Scenes of Childhood, Op. 15: "From Foreign Lands and
People," "Child Falling Asleep" and "The Poet Speaks" (Schu-
mann). This fine recording is a wonderful way to share clas-
sical music with your child.

**G'MORNING JOHANN—**
   **Classical Piano Solos for Morning Time**
**Ric Louchard**
**Music for Little People**
**Cassette/C.D.**
**No lyrics included**
**Infant–adult**

Although the title says these songs are for mornings they are really great for any time. Louchard is a fine pianist who presents an interesting selection of classical music. Side A features quieter and more passive pieces. Side B is brighter, more lively music. This can be used as a lullaby recording and as a way to introduce classical music to your children. Selections on Side A are: Aria (from Goldberg Variations by Bach), Adagio Cantabile (from Sonata in C Minor by Beethoven), Solace (Joplin), Sarabande (from Partita #4 in D Major by Bach) and Sonata in E Major (Scarlatti). Side B includes Antante Grazioso (from Sonata in A Major by Mozart), Prelude #9 in E Major (from Well-Tempered Clavier by Bach), Courante (from French suite #5 in G Major by Bach), Gique (from Partita #1 in B Flat Major by Bach), and three more.

**SLEEPY TRAIN**
**Michael Mish**
**Mish Mash Music**
**Cassette/C.D.**
**Lyrics included**
**Ages 2–5**

A delightful collection of original songs and a story is sung, told and orchestrated by Michael Mish. When he sings, his voice is reassuring and gentle. When he tells his story, his voices are funny and captivating. Mish is a very talented and diverse artist. Although the music is appropriate for all ages, the story ("The Princess Story," an original tale with a contemporary message of love) is for children over two. The songs include "Sleepy Train," "The Princess Song," "Boogie Woogie Lullaby," "Dreamland," "Good Night, Sleep Tight" and two more. Other refreshing and satisfying recordings by Michael Mish are discussed on pp. 164–166.

**NOCTURNE—**
   **Lullabies for the Family**
**Metropolis**
**Project Nocturne**
**Cassette**
**Lyrics included**
**Infant–10**

Favorite lullabies and quiet songs are sung a cappella by four
excellent male singers in this very soothing and enjoyable cassette. The selection includes many well-known lullabies, plus
some that are not necessarily lullabies such as "Time Sends a
Warning Call" and "The Coventry Carol," all with original
arrangements. If you're looking for an innovative cassette, this
could be for you, although it may be hard to find (see
Resources for Children's Recording). The selections include
"Golden Slumbers," "Brahms' Lullaby," "All Through the
Night," "Now the Day Is Over," "Rock-A-Bye Baby" and five
more.

**WARM AND TENDER**
**Olivia Newton-John**
**Geffen Records**
**Cassette/C.D.**
**Lyrics included**
**All Ages**

Olivia Newton-John has dedicated this collection of lullabies
and love songs to her three-and-a-half-year-old daughter. While
many of these songs at first glance may seem inappropriate to
sing to babies, after listening to the warm and lilting arrangements, you'll find that the recording is very relaxing and good
for quiet moments. Newton-John's voice is soft, but sometimes
too full of emotion. The orchestrations are flush and interesting. Some of the more eclectic songs include "You'll Never
Walk Alone" (Rodgers and Hammerstein), "The Way You Look
Tonight," "Over the Rainbow," "When You Wish upon a Star,"
"The Twelfth of Never" and "Reach Out for Me." The traditional lullabies include "Brahms' Lullaby," "Sleep My Princess
(Mozart's Cradle Song)," "Rock-A-Bye Baby," "All The Pretty
Little Horses" and several more. The recording is very profes-

sionally done, but one sometimes feels that the intended audience was adults rather than small children. The liner notes
describe in great detail Newton-John's work with ecology and
environmental issues. She includes ten helpful hints as to how
we can all participate.


**THE ROCK-A-BYE COLLECTION VOLUME II**
**Vocals by Diana Rae and David Lehman**
**A Child's Gift of Lullabyes**
**Cassette**
**Lyrics included**
**Infant–6**

Unlike other recordings on this label, this has both male and
female voices singing original lullabies. The voices are very soft
and soothing; the orchestral arrangements are full but never
overwhelming. This recording, like the others from this company, is a bit more expensive than most, perhaps because of
the unique packaging and inclusion of a full-color booklet. It is
a really beautifully produced recording, with words that are
easy to learn. Side A has vocals and Side B is instrumental
only. The seven songs are "Drift Away," "Nightlights," "Rhap-
sody in Baby Blue," "I'll Love You Forever," "Dreamship,"
"Loving My Baby Goodnight" and "Sweet Serenade."


★★★     **LULLABIES AND OTHER CHILDREN'S SONGS**
**Nancy Raven**
**Pacific Cascade Records**
**LP/Cassette**
**Lyrics included**
**Infant–10**

My children enjoyed and used this recording for many years.
Nancy Raven's lovely, deep voice and simple guitar accompaniment have a calming effect on the listener. Her pronunciation is clear and precise. The multicultural collection of songs
are not all specifically lullabies, so this recording has a multitude of uses. This is not a slick or high tech recording, having
been recorded over twenty years ago, but rather one that
approximates having Nancy Raven singing live for you and

your children. You can get a lot of mileage with this recording, since some of the songs can be used with children three to six (they are longer and have more sophisticated language). The nineteen songs include "Mockingbird," "Hush-a-bye," "Raisins and Almonds," "Up in a Balloon," "Arroz con Leche," "Old Joe Clarke," "Mary Wore Her Red Dress" and other folk favorites.

### PERCHANCE TO DREAM
**Carol Rosenberger**
**Delos International**
**Cassette/C.D.**
**Information sheet included**
**Infant–100**

This is a fine collection of short classical piano pieces by famous composers played by Carol Rosenberger. The music is very soothing and is a wonderful way to introduce your child to the pleasures of classical music. The pieces are "My Dear Little Mother" (Tchaikovsky), "A Short Story" (Kabalevsky), Andante from Sonata in C (Mozart), Prelude Op. 28, No. 7 in A Major and Mazurka Op. 68, No. 2 in A Minor (Chopin), Berceuse Op. 56, No. 1 (Faure), Adagio from Sonata in F Major (Haydn), Sinfonia V in E-Flat Major, Prelude 1 in C Major from *The Well-Tempered Clavier*, Aria in G Major from the "Goldberg Variations" (Bach), Andante from Sonata in A Major Op. 120, D. 664 (Schubert), Intermezzo Op. 117, No. 1 (Brahms), Bagatelle Op. 119, No. 11, Adagio Cantabile from Sonata Op. 13 (Beethoven), "Errinerung," "Sehr Langsam," "Abendlied," "Schlummerlied," "Mignon" and "Des Abends" (Schumann). This is a very popular recording at our store.

### ★★★    LULLABIES FOR LITTLE DREAMERS
**Kevin Roth**
**Sony Kids' Music**
**Cassette/C.D.**
**Lyrics included**
**Infant–5**

The gentle sound of a mountain dulcimer accompanying Kevin Roth's calming voice make this an ideal choice for restful music. Familiar and original songs, such as "Quiet Time," show Mr. Roth's outstanding talent as a musician and composer. The warm sounds of this recording will make it a favorite for many years to come. After hearing Kevin's comforting voice, I think you'll want to have some of his other cassettes in your child's library. Because they are great for all ages at all times of the day or night, we never seem to be able to order enough of these tapes for our store. The fourteen songs on this one include "All Through the Night," "Hush Little Baby," "When You Wish upon a Star" and "Bye 'n Bye" and "Brahms' Lullaby" (orchestral). More of Kevin Roth's music can be found on pp. 101, 191–193 and 224.

> **THE SANDMAN—**
> **Lullabies and Night Time Songs**
> **Kevin Roth**
> **Marlboro Records**
> **Cassette**
> **Lyrics included**
> **Infant–4**

With simple arrangements, Roth's beautiful voice in this collection of mostly original lullabies and quiet time songs will help you or your children relax. Some of the songs are quite humorous, such as "Quit That Snoring, Mr. Bed Bug" (wishing the bed bug good night and hoping that the people won't bite) and "It's Time To Go To Bed." The title song, "The Sandman," is a stellar example of beautiful lyrics. Roth has incorporated such classics as "Dream, Dream, Dream" (made famous by the Everly Brothers), a medley of "Little Boy Blue/The Cow Jumped Over the Moon/Star Lite, Star Brite" and "Rock-a-Bye-Baby."

> **LULLABIES FOR A NEW AGE**
> **Jonathan Sprout**
> **Sprout Recordings**
> **Cassette**
> **Lyrics included**
> **Infant–6**

Jonathan Sprout has created some original lullabies that have a very New Age feel to them. The arrangements use lots of keyboards and the lyrics are about love, dreams, starry skies and feelings. Many of the songs express adult feelings, and therefore are not necessarily for children. The melodies are relaxing and if this type of music appeals to you, you'll probably enjoy this recording. The songs include "The Heart Inside of Me," "Forever," "Sweet Dreams," "Close Your Eyes," "Angel," "Waves," "Malibu," "Midnight," "Peace," "Heaven," "Brahms' Lullaby," "Someway, Somehow" and "Nightlights." More recordings by Jonathan Sprout are on pp. 200–201.

**MOONBEAMS AND GENTLE DREAMS**
**Various artists**
**Music for Little People**
**Cassette**
**Lyrics included**
**Infant–6**

If you'd like to sample some lullabies by different recording artists, this is the perfect choice. These twelve songs represent selections from various recordings put out on the Music for Little People label. It's a wonderful way to add some variety to your musical diet; styles and vocals are unique. You can read in more detail about each track, as all of the artists are reviewed individually throughout this book. The pieces are: "When It's Dark in the Night" (by Kathi, Milenko and Friends from *Good Morning, Good Night*), "Poulette Grise" (in French by Connie Kaldor and Carmen Campagne from *Lullaby Berceuse*), "Melancholy Baby" (still one of my favorites by Maria Muldaur from *On the Sunny Side*), "The Poet Speaks" (classical piano by Ric Louchard from *G'night Wolfgang*), "Lavender's Blue" (by the Barolk Folk from *Girls and Boys, Come Out to Play*), "Little Brown Dog" (by Taj Majal from *Shake Sugaree*), "Not While I'm Around" (by Mimi Bessette from *Lullabies Of Broadway*), "Bonne Nuit" (a French version of "Brahms' Lullaby" by Connie Kaldor and Carmen Campagne from *Lullaby Berceuse*), "Give My Heart Ease" (by Judy Bowen from *Shake It to the One That You Love the Best*), "Child Falling Asleep" (by Ric Louchard from *G'night Wolfgang*) and "Matthew, Mark, Luke and John" (by the Barolk Folk from *Girls and Boys, Come Out to Play*).

★ ★ ★     **SWEET DREAMS**
            **Various Artists**
            **CBS Records**
            **Cassette**
            **All Ages**

*Sweet Dreams* is an incredible collection of classical music that is perfect for any time of the day or night. This treasure is presented by various well-known orchestras led by such renowned conductors as Eugene Ormandy, Andre Kostelanetz and Bruno Walter. The composers represented include Brahms ("Lullaby"), Debussy ("Clair de Lune"), Chopin ("Nocturne, Op. 9, No. 2"), Bach ("Sheep May Safely Graze"), Gershwin ("Summertime" from *Porgy and Bess*), Schumann ("Traumerei"), Mozart (Andante from "Eine Kleine Nachtmusik") and Mendelssohn (Nocturne from Incidental Music to *A Midsummer Night's Dream*). This recording is a wonderful way to expose your child to the richness of classical music.

**CRACK IN THE DOOR—**
            **Lullabies to Light the Night**
      **Lois Young**
      **Sony Kids' Music**
      **Cassette/C.D.**
      **Lyrics included**
      **Ages 2–5**

In this original collection of quiet songs by Lois Young, some are written especially for infants while others are definitely for preschool-age children and older. This recording should give you a lot of mileage for your money. The production quality is excellent, and the soft, clear orchestration combines beautifully with Young's lovely vocals. Her voice is clear and her vocal range is attainable for young children. Lois sings extensively in family concerts and school settings, and these songs represent her ability to captivate and encourage children to sing along. These may not be titles that are familiar, but they are full of love and tenderness. The twelve songs include "Hey Little One," "You Are Love," "Purr and Snuggle," "Night Sounds" and "Magic Carpet Ride." More of Lois Young's music is discussed on pp. 119–120.

# Songs and Activities for Infants and Toddlers (Ages 0–2) ♫..

Early musical experiences are important for children, allowing them to develop language and listening skills as well as motor and coordination skills. Children learn new vocabulary and language patterns through age-appropriate music. The melodic and verbal repetition occurring in many children's songs paves the way for children to enhance their speech. Because music is so conducive to learning language, many people learn a foreign language through listening to music from that culture.

As stated earlier, it is never too soon to share music with your children. Activity songs come in all different ages levels, so it is important to choose a recording with the age and development of your child in mind. With very young children, look for clarity in voice and accompaniment, short songs with repetitive verses, a steady beat, and activities that are age appropriate. Infants and toddlers also enjoy animal sounds. Age-appropriateness allows the child to feel successful participating, that the activity is not too advanced for his motor or social skills. It is important to expose children to all types of musical styles, not just the contemporary sounds or the most technologically-sophisticated formats. Some of the finest recordings for very young children were done years ago and have pleased parents and children for several generations.

It is important to preserve our folk heritage, and some of

the recordings listed below are folk music classics. Music also allows us to pass our cultural heritage from one generation to another. Many of our favorite songs were sung to our great-great-grandparents as children.

As with all musical activities, there will be times when you can playfully participate in the songs and there will be other times that are just for listening. If you have an infant and the song says to "move your legs," you can lay the baby on his back and gently move his legs for him. It is imperative that you never force your baby's body when exercising. This is also the time to brush up on the multitude of fingerplays that you learned when you were a child. One of the objectives of fingerplay is the interaction between adult and child. To be able to perform many fingerplays effectively, a child's fine motor skills must be relatively advanced, so you can do "Eency Weency Spider" for your child or along with him, but it won't be until much later that the child will actually be able to do all the finger movements by himself. Don't get upset with your child if he can't do all the movements correctly. Eventually the mastery will come. My children loved it when I changed the words and added their names to the songs. Children feel loved and very special when you're singing about them. I would encourage you to personalize music anytime you can.

Many parents who work outside the home or who leave their children with a childcare provider find that music becomes a way for children to adjust to new surroundings. If there's a particular favorite song of yours, why not record yourself singing and give the tape to the childcare provider to play for your child when you're not there or when separation seems to be a problem? The familiar sound of someone singing, either the recording artist or you yourself, is often very soothing to a child.

In all the years I've been selling recordings of children's music, I've never had anyone say that they're buying for an "average" child. This is a nation of "gifted" and "advanced" children. By far the most common customer we have in the store is the parent who needs to give his children everything right from the beginning. We encourage parents not to rush . . . there are plenty of weeks, months and years to expose your child to music. Children love to hear things over and over again; it gives them a sense of comfort and accomplishment. Even if you get sick and tired of hearing a particular recording, that doesn't necessarily mean that your child feels the same

way. I remember one father who bought two or three tapes
every month or so for his eighteen-month-old son. Apparently
the father got bored with the music and felt he needed to keep
buying more. I was pleased that he was purchasing so much,
but I pointed out to him that an eighteen-month-old probably
couldn't digest that many songs in such a short time. I suggested that he go back and let his child listen to the age-appropriate tapes in the house, and the father listen to his own tapes
in the car. I explained how children learn through repetition,
and he walked away satisfied.

## DO:

• Try different styles of music with your child.

• Personalize the songs and activities.

• Look for clear pronunciation and lots of word repetition as
  vocabulary boosters.

• Look for simple yet appealing arrangements.

• Look for activities that coincide with your child's physical
  and emotional development.

• Share your favorite music with the childcare provider.

• Share your ethnic heritage with your child.

• Remember to look at other chapters as many recordings
  appeal to children of all ages.

## DON'T:

• Be afraid to try music that may not seem or sound like the
  top ten pop recordings.

• Be afraid to sing along, even if you're not Frank Sinatra.

• Get bored playing only one recording over and over. Vary
  the selection.

• Go crazy if your child wants to hear one thing over and
  over; it's O.K. He'll move on when he's ready. Make the
  experience pleasurable.

**GIRLS AND BOYS, COME OUT TO PLAY**
**The Barolk Folk—Featuring Madeline MacNeil**
**and Barbara Hess**
**Music for Little People**
**Cassette/C.D.**
**Lyrics included**
**Ages 3–6**

This recording uses the baroque style of music to present familiar Mother Goose songs. Many of these 17th and 18th century melodies come from dance and ballad melodies. Baroque music uses dulcimers, treble viol, recorders, piano, guitar and synthesizer, and has very repetitive, rhythmic sounds. You can almost imagine people in full costume dancing to these melodies. The vocals are very pleasant. I found this recording too repetitive, but I know some people who think it's great. Let your own tastes be the ultimate guide. The songs and rhymes include "Humpty Dumpty/Hunson House," "Hickory Dickory Dock/Haste to the Wedding," "Do You Know the Muffin Man?/The Shepherd's Lamb," "Dance To Your Daddy," "Oh How Lovely Is the Evening/Oranges and Lemons/Christchurch Bells," "Lavender's Blue/Menuet De La Cour," "Sing a Song of Sixpence/The Touchstone," "Matthew, Mark, Luke and John" and more. Definitely unique.

**MORNING MAGIC**
**Joanie Bartels**
**Discovery Music**
**Cassette**
**Lyrics included**
**Ages 2–5**

Looking for a recording to play during your morning routine? This, a fabulous collection of ten songs that salute the morning, is the perfect solution. Moreover, your child will enjoy this recording for many years. I've put it in the very young section because the songs are short and so clearly sung and orchestrated that they hold a toddler's attention. The songs come from various musical sources: "Rise and Shine" (Raffi), "Morning Has Broken" (Cat Stevens version), "Time to Rise" (Robert Louis Stevenson), "Oh What A Beautiful Morning"

(Rodgers and Hammerstein's *Oklahoma*), "Good Day Sunshine" (John Lennon and Paul McCartney), "Put On a Happy Face" (from *Bye Bye Birdie*) and "59th Street Bridge Song" (Paul Simon). A catchy activity song, "Wake Up Toes" (by Uncle Ruthie Buell), wakes up toes, feet, legs, arms, hands and head. "Easy Going Day" greets the sun, clouds and friends. As with the *Lullaby Magic* recordings (see page 11), one side is vocal and the other is solely instrumental. Bartels' voice is full and alluring. The arrangements are lively and animated. The Bartels collection of recordings is always a good buy!

**WEE SING**
**Pamela Conn Beall and Susan Hagen Nipp**
**Price Stern Sloan**
**Cassette**
**Lyric and Activity Book included**
**Ages 1–4**

This innovative series uses adult's and children's voices to entertain children with a plethora of entertaining activity songs. The first in the series (for more, see Recordings for Pre-schoolers, Music for School-Age Children and Holiday Recordings) presents fingerplays and games that can be used with children from infancy through preschool. Beall and Nipp have taught children and music for many years and have cleverly compiled their songs into a format that both parents and children enjoy. The songs are short, to keep a young child's attention, and the voices are uncluttered. The book that is included explains how to do the fingerplays and gives the melody line and words. This complete package is worth every penny spent. The sixty-minute cassette is sure to give you and your child many hours of interactive fun. The songs include "Eentsy Weentsy Spider," "Clap Your Hands," "Here Is the Beehive," "Jack and Jill," "This Old Man," "Little Peter Rabbit," "Bingo," "Old MacDonald Had a Farm," "1, 2 Buckle My Shoe," "The Alphabet Song," "Twinkle, Twinkle Little Star," "Looby Lou," "Jimmy Crack Corn," "Ring Around the Rosy" and sixty more. A wonderful way to learn all the fingerplays that young children love so much!

**WEE SING NURSERY RHYMES AND**
  **LULLABIES**
**Pamela Conn Beall and Susan Hagen Nipp**
**Price Stern Sloan**
**Cassette**
**Lyric and Activity Book included**
**Ages 1–4**

Using a simple story line, the narrator takes young children through a nursery rhyme adventure. Children's and adults' voices are used to present this vast array of favorite songs for young children. The story may be hard for very young children, but the music is well presented and the children's voices are clear and pleasant. As in all of the recordings from this series, you really get your money's worth, because each cassette contains sixty minutes of entertainment. The nursery rhymes include "Hickory Dickory Dock," "Jack and Jill," "Mary Had A Little Lamb," "Six Little Ducks," "Baa, Baa, Black Sheep," "Twinkle, Twinkle Little Star," "There Was an Old Woman," and forty-eight more. The lullabies include "All Through The Night," "Armenian Lullaby," "Golden Slumbers," "Hush Little Baby" and eighteen more. The booklet contains the music's melody line and words.

**CAR SONGS**
**Dennis Buck/Vocals by Al Dana**
**Kimbo Educational**
**LP/Cassette**
**Lyrics included**
**Ages 2½–5**

Al Dana is accompanied by children in this collection of twenty-two familiar children's songs. You certainly get your money's worth of material with this recording, but the flavor of this music is very ordinary. The instrumentation is unimaginative and the vocals lack energy. The songs include "Car Car Song," "The Wheels on the Bus," "Going to the Zoo," "If I Had A Hammer," "He's Got the Whole World in His Hands," "It's a Small World," "Puff the Magic Dragon," "Twinkle, Twinkle Little Star," "Bingo," "Skinnamarink" and more.

### GOOD MORNING SUNSHINE—
#### Songs for a Day Full of Wonder
**Patti Dallas and Laura Baron**
**Golden Glow Recordings**
**Cassette**
**No lyrics included**
**Ages 2½–5**

Dallas and Baron beautifully harmonize their way through eighteen delightful songs. They are accompanied by a hammer dulcimer, recorder, oboe, drums, trombone, guitar and other instruments. Some of the songs are original and others are well-known nursery songs. This is a very ear-pleasing recording that can be both for active participation and passive listening. The songs are: "ABC Song," "Come Follow" (a beautifully sung round), "Ash Grove" (using a harp), "London Bridge," "Sing a Song of Sixpence," "If You're Happy," "The Eensey Weensey Spider," "Pop! Goes the Weasel," "This Old Man," "Hokey Pokey," "Irish Jig," "Did You Ever See a Lassie" and more. For more delightful recordings by this enchanting duo, see pp. 16–17.

### PLAYTIME PARADE—
#### Musical Magic To Brighten A Child's Day
**Patti Dallas and Laura Baron**
**Golden Glow Recordings**
**Cassette**
**No lyrics included**
**Ages 2½–5**

A collection of mostly traditional songs performed with harmonies by Patti Dallas and Laura Baron, accompanied by children's voices. These songs are sung clearly and slowly enough for small children to be able to follow along vocally and with hand movements. This duo uses interesting combinations of instruments on their recordings, and this time they chose hammer dulcimer, sax, oboe, tuba, trombone, keyboard and more. The nursery rhymes and songs include "Where Is Thumbkin," "Little Teapot/Pat-A-Cake," "Mulberry Bush," "Down By The Station," "This Little Light," "Shoo Fly," "The More We Get Together," "Hear," "Shoulder," "Knees and

Toes," "Mother Goose Medley" and lots more. A very satisfying recording.


## DISNEY RECORDINGS

This book was written to help people select recordings for their children, since there are few stores that actually let you listen to the music before you buy it. There are certain recordings that need no explanation and I include the recordings from Disney among them. The songs are all familiar, and the music has an immediately recognizable sound (that is, if you've ever been to Disneyland or Walt Disney World). I've decided to list two series of the most popular Disney recordings that we sell in our store. There are many other recordings available, but these are the ones that seem to have a strong presence and visibility in the marketplace.


### DISNEY CHILDREN'S FAVORITES
**Larry Groce and the Disneyland Children's
    Sing-Along Chorus
Walt Disney Records
Cassette/C.D.
Lyric booklet included
Ages 2½–6**

This collection of favorite children's songs is presented with all the pizzazz that is typical of Walt Disney projects, and are probably some of the most predictable recordings I've listened to. For those of you who have been to Disneyland or Walt Disney World, or even watched the Disney programs, you can almost see the people who are singing these songs. These recordings have been around for years, and have had several incarnations. They are very popular because they contain the most well-known songs, and they are moderately priced. The lyric book includes some color illustrations, but no melody line. There are several songs on these recordings that I feel are in poor taste, but Disney has used them for many years, and seems insensitive to promoting stereotypes. Hopefully when it comes time for the next incarnation, they'll eliminate some of these offensive songs and add others.

**40**        *GROWING UP WITH MUSIC*

VOLUME 1—"Old MacDonald," "This Old Man," "I've Been
Working On the Railroad," "Oh, Susanna," "Home On the
Range," "Mary Had a Little Lamb," "Take Me Out to the Ball-
game," "The Hokey Pokey," "She'll Be Comin' Round the
Mountain," "Ten Little Indians" (this song is considered inap-
propriate by many Native Americans, and there is no reason
to keep using it on recordings), "Pop! Goes the Weasel,"
"Dixie," "Twinkle, Twinkle Little Star," "The Green Grass Grew
All Around" and more.

VOLUME 2—"The Farmer in the Dell," "Yankee Doodle," "On
Top of Old Smoky," "Camptown Races," "Shortnin' Bread,"
"John Jacob Jingleheimer Schmidt," "The Bear Went Over the
Mountain," "Skip to My Lou," "Swanee River," "London
Bridge," "Bingo," "There Was an Old Lady," "When the Saints
Go Marching In" and more.

VOLUME 3—"If You're Happy and You Know It," "Shoo Fly,"
"Don't Bother Me," "Hush, Little Baby," "Clementine,"
"Michael, Row the Boat Ashore," "Alouette," "Sweet Betsy
from Pike," "Alphabet Song," "Down in the Valley," "Waltzing
Matilda," "Good Night, Ladies," "Over the River and Through
the Woods," "Did You Ever See a Lassie" and more.

VOLUME 4—"The Wheels on the Bus," "Do Your Ears Hang
Low?," "The Wabash Cannonball," "Froggie Went A-Courtin',"
"Big Rock Candy Mountain," "You Are My Sunshine," "It's a
Small World," "There's a Hole in My Bucket," "I'm a Little
Teapot," "He's Got the Whole World in His Hands," "Go In and
Out the Window," "The Marvelous Toy," "Mickey Mouse
March," "Git Along, Little Dogies" and more.

**THE DISNEY COLLECTION—**
**Best Loved Songs from Disney Motion**
**Picture, Television, and Theme Parks**
**Disneyland Records**
**Cassette/C.D.**
**No lyrics included**
**Ages 2½–10**

The tracks in this collection of songs are from original soundtrack recordings, some done over 50 years ago. If you're a

nostalgia buff, these are for you. Listening to these recordings is a walk down memory lane for many adults. The cassettes contain 18 songs each. The C.D.s contain twenty-four.

VOLUME 1—Eighteen songs include "Zip-A-Dee-Doo-Dah" (*Song of the South*, 1946), "Whistle While You Work" (*Snow White and the Seven Dwarfs*, 1937), "Chim Chim Cher-ee" (*Mary Poppins*, 1964), "You Can Fly, You Can Fly, You Can Fly" (*Peter Pan*, 1953), "Who's Afraid of the Big Bad Wolf?" (*Three Little Pigs*, 1933), "It's a Small World" (Disneyland, 1966), "The Mickey Mouse Club March" (*The Mickey Mouse Club*, 1955), "Winnie the Pooh" (*Winnie the Pooh and the Honey Tree*, 1966), "The Siamese Cat Song" (*Lady and the Tramp*, 1955), "Baby Mine" (*Dumbo*, 1941) and "Love Is a Song" (*Bambi*, 1942).

VOLUME 2—Eighteen songs include "When You Wish Upon a Star" (*Pinocchio*, 1940), "He's a Tramp" (*Lady and the Tramp*, 1955), "Heigh-Ho" (*Snow White and the Seven Dwarfs*, 1937), "The Ballad of Davy Crockett" (*Davy Crockett*, 1954), " Super-califragilisticexppialidocious" (*Mary Poppins*, 1964), "Bibbidi-Bobbidi-Boo" (*Cinderella*, 1950), "Yo Ho-Ho-A Pirate's Life For Me" (Disneyland, 1967), "Best of Friends" (*Fox and the Hound*, 1981), "Someday My Prince Will Come" (*Snow White and the Seven Dwarfs*, 1937) and more.

VOLUME 3—Eighteen songs include "Part of Your World" (*The Little Mermaid*, 1989), "So This Is Love" (*Cinderella*, 1950), "When You Wish Upon a Star" (*Pinocchio*, 1940), "Casey Junior" (*Dumbo*, 1941), "Jolly Holiday" (*Mary Poppins*, 1964), "One Song" (*Bambi*, 1942), "Bella Notte" (*Lady and the Tramp*, 1955), "Candle on the Water" (*Pete's Dragon*, 1977) and more.

★ ★ ★    **MUSIC FOR 1'S AND 2'S**
            **Tom Glazer**
            **Gateway Records**
            **Cassette**
            **No lyrics included**
            **Infant–2**

This is probably one of the most appropriately named record-ings available. Tom Glazer's recording has been around for over forty years, and several generations of parents have shared it with their children, rendering it a true, time-tested favorite. The concepts are simple, the songs are short, the accompaniments are clear and the activities are all age appropriate. If you're looking for razzmatazz and rock-type style, this is not for you. Glazer accompanies himself on the guitar, and his voice and intonation are folksy and inviting. The songs titles show the devotion to this particular age. "Where Are Your Eyes?," "What Does Baby Hear?" (all the familiar sounds one might hear during the day), "Clap Hands," "Bye, Bye," "Baby's Bath" and seven more. This really is the perfect first activity recording for very small children. A songbook published by Doubleday of the same name is available in most bookstores.

**SONGS TO GROW ON FOR MOTHER AND
        CHILD**
**Woody Guthrie**
**Smithsonian/Folkways**
**Cassette/C.D.**
**Lyrics included**
**Infant–2**

This collection of Woody Guthrie's songs is a "very first" recording. It includes songs and games that he wrote for his daughter. There are a few chanting-type songs that use repetition and a drum to emphasize the beat. One perceives that Woody is having as much fun singing as the children who are listening. Because of the chanting style and the intense repetition, some adults do not enjoy hearing this recording repeatedly, but small children really like it. This is not a recording for everyone; however, it can be stimulating for hearing impaired children and children with special needs. "Washy, Wash Wash," "Who's My Pretty Baby" and "Why Oh Why" are three of my favorites. Other titles include "Grow, Grow, Grow," "I Want My Milk," "1 Day, 2 Days, 3 Days Old," "Make A Bubble," "Rattle My Rattle," "Pick It Up," "Goodnight Little Arlo" and nine more. This recording now contains some of the songs from the previous recording entitled *Why Oh Why*.

★★★     **SONGS TO GROW ON—NURSERY DAYS**
        **Woody Guthrie**
        **Smithsonian/Folkways**
        **Cassette/C.D.**
        **Lyrics included**
        **Infant–3**

Woody Guthrie was one of America's foremost folksinger/
songwriters. He also wrote wonderful songs for children, some
of which are included here. "Put Your Finger in the Air" is the
classic song that identifies body parts. "The Car Song" asks
Daddy to "take me ridin' in your car, car" and is accompanied
by some realistic and humorous automobile sounds. "Clean O"
is a great bath time song, "Sleepy Eyes" helps lull your child
to sleep, and an important social issue is discussed in "Don't
You Push Me Down." The other fourteen songs include "Wake
Up," "Dance Around," "My Dolly," "Come See," "Howdido"
and "Race You Down the Mountain." This recording contains
three newly released tracks: "Jig Along Home," "My Little
Seed" and "All Work Together." Woody accompanies himself
on the guitar and harmonica. His voice may not appeal to
everyone, but his recordings have been popular for over forty
years and have helped raise more than one generation of children. The recordings were done years ago and don't sound as
sophisticated as current releases, but the songs are always creative and the lyrics and melodies have enough repetition to
hold young children's attention. Woody is an American treasure, and his recordings should be in every child's and adult's
library. This recording now has some of the songs that originally appeared on *Why Oh Why*.

        **FINGERPLAYS AND FOOTPLAYS—**
            **For Fun and Learning**
        **Rosemary Hallum, Ph.D. and Henry "Buzz"**
            **Glass**
        **Educational Activities, Inc.**
        **LP/Cassette**
        **Lyric and Activity Booklet included**
        **18 months–4 years**

Although this recording was made for the educational market,
it can definitely be used by a parent or playgroup leader.

Hallum and Glass have produced and recorded many albums together over the years and are highly respected by teachers. Dr. Hallum is an Early Childhood specialist, and Mr. Glass is a national consultant in movement and dance. This collection of activities gives thorough instructions on how to do all the movements and provides a pleasing musical format to learn and interact with your child. Some of the more traditional songs are "I'm a Little Teapot," "The Wheels on the Bus," "Where is Thumbkin?" and "Five Little Monkeys." The other activities include "Penguins" (done as a fingerplay, but the package includes suggestions for use as a footplay as well), "Two Little Blackbirds," "Footplay" (sung to "The toe bone's connected to the foot bone . . ."), "Peanut Butter," "New Pease Porridge Hot," "New Shoes," "I Have Ten Little Fingers" and "Johnny Works with One Hammer." This is a wonderful way to acquaint yourself with these movements and a fun way for your child to develop listening and motor skills. This recording is also an excellent tool to use with children who are just learning English as a second language, regardless of their age. "Buzz" Glass and Rosemary Hallum are names you can trust for quality movement activity recordings.

**IT'S TODDLER TIME**
**Carol Hammett and Elaine Bueffel**
**Kimbo Educational**
**LP/Cassette**
**Activity Booklet included**
**18 months–4 years**

These well-designed activities are truly geared to toddlers. Each of the authors has physical education and creative movement background and works extensively with preschoolers. Unfortunately, the recording sounds very institutional. The songs are cute and incorporate safe and fun activities, but the vocal and musical arrangements are unimaginative. Playgroup leaders use this a lot, since it has such classics as "Hokey Pokey," "Head Shoulders, Knees and Toes," "Itsy Bitsy Spider," "If You're Happy and You Know It" plus sixteen more.

**TODDLERS ON PARADE—**
   **Musical Exercises for Infants and Toddlers**
**Carol Hammett and Elaine Bueffel**
**Kimbo Educational**
**LP/Cassette**
**Activity Booklet included**
**Infant–2½**

This recording contains a wide variety of short, safe exercises for very young children by the people who presented *It's Toddler Time*. While still not the most musically rousing, this collection is not as dull as its predecessor. The female vocals are clear, and the accompanying activity ideas are creative and useful for both home and school. Two of the songs are about Halloween and Thanksgiving. The rest explore all the fun ways children's bodies can move, including "Roll Your Hands," "Gifts for Mommy" (making animal sounds), "Hop Like a Bunny," "Grand Old Duke of York" (marching), "Bicycle, Bicycle," "Peek-A-Boo," "Wheels on the Bus" and "Little Bunny Foo-Foo."

**BABY GAMES—6 Weeks to 1 Year**
**Priscilla Hegner**
**Kimbo Educational**
**LP/Cassette**
**Activity Book included**
**Infant–1**

This recording is very similar to *Diaper Gym* (see page 46) and is produced by one of the same authors. It is, however, intended for infants only. The activities are well conceived, but I can't imagine a parent doing too many of them at one time. It's more likely that you'll choose two or three of the ideas your child especially enjoys. The pieces are short, so that neither you nor your child will overdo it, but the musical arrangements tend to become repetitious. The activities are explained in the booklet as well as in the song itself, so you can be gently guided as you play with your child. The songs are based on familiar melodies, such as "Mary Had a Little Lamb" (hand to knee stretch), "Yankee Doodle" (arms high, arms low) and "Singin' in the Rain" (bathing in the tub). Hegner has included lyrics that show great warmth and tenderness, and you can exchange the word "baby" for your child's name. Both male and female singers are featured. I would recommend using this recording in small doses.

### DIAPER GYM—
Fun Activities for Babies on the Move for Children from 6 Weeks to 1 Year
Priscilla Hegner and Rose Grasselli
Kimbo Educational
LP/Cassette
Lyrics and Activity Booklet included
Infant–1

These activities were developed as the Playful Parenting program. A wonderful way to bond and express love to your child, using cuddling, rocking, massage and kisses, is to use these short, well-developed and safe activities. Directions are given in a fully illustrated manual and are sometimes verbally cued on the recording. The music, based on familiar melodies, is soft and uncluttered. The arrangements are lackluster, but provide adequate accompaniment as you create a loving way to play and exercise with your child. Side A if for babies six weeks to seven months, and Side B is for eight months to one year. There are over forty activities. For ages one to three, see *Touch, Teach and Hug a Toddler* below. We were fortunate enough to have Ms. Hegner do a workshop for parents and babies in our store, and everyone raved about the activities.

### TOUCH, TEACH, AND HUG A TODDLER—
For Children from 1 Year to 3 Years
Priscilla Hegner and Rose Grasselli
Kimbo Educational
LP/Cassette
Lyrics and Activity Booklet included
Ages 1–3

This is the sequel to *Diaper Gym*. Using the same format, toddlers and parents can share some fun and safe movement and sensory activities together. The activities are geared to the developmental abilities of toddlers, such as running, stomping and rolling. Children develop listening and language skills as well as small and large muscle skills. The songs are short enough to hold the attention of a small child, and the activities aren't strenuous. Sung by both male and female voices, the music is unfortunately a bit repetitive. Overall, however, this is a very good recording that you can feel very comfortable using with toddlers. Side A is for children one and two years old, and Side B is for children two and three years old. There are over twenty activities on this recording.

★★★ **THERE'S A HIPPO IN MY TUB**
**Anne Murray**
**Capitol Records**
**Cassette**
**No lyric sheet**
**Ages 2½–5**

If you combine the full, rich, lovely voice of Anne Murray and ten favorite children's songs, you'll have this perennial best-selling recording. Murray's vocal range is perfect for young singers. If this is not already in your collection, it's a must! The title song, actually called "Hey Daddy," is a silly song about a hippo in the bathtub, a dragon in the driveway and a grizzly on the lawn. "Animal Crackers" tells of what happens with those animals in your soup. Time-tested favorites include: "Hi-Lilli Hi-Lo," "Teddy Bears' Picnic," "Inchworm" (*Hans Christian Andersen*) and a beautiful lullaby medley of "Hush Little Baby," "Sleep Child" and "Brahms' Lullaby." Murray tries to answer questions such as "Why can't a cow have kittens? . . . why can't a mouse eat a street car?" in a truly wonderful version of Woody Guthrie's song "Why Oh Why." Other songs include "Stars Are the Windows of Heaven," "Sleepytime," and "You Are My Sunshine", "Open Up Your Heart." This is a classic for good reason. Grab this up quickly, as it repeatedly goes in and out of print.

★★★        **BABYSONGS**
**Hap Palmer and Martha Cheney**
**Educational Activities**
**LP/Cassette/C.D.**
**Lyrics included**
**Ages 1–3**

Having worked in schools with children for many years, Hap and Martha know and understand how and to what children respond. The musical arrangements are upbeat, creative and contagious. (I find myself walking around humming the music.) The lyrics are sensitive, clear and fun. The songs include selections about both mothers and fathers. Hap's voice is very inviting and it's easy to sing along with him. "My Mommy Comes Back" is a classic example of the warm and reassuring feelings relayed in this recording. Whether Mommy goes out shopping or to work, whether the child is cared for by a sitter, another family member or in a childcare setting, Mommy will always come back. Another favorite is "Today I Took My Diapers Off." Also included are "Sittin' in a Highchair," "Come Read A Book," "Daddy Be a Horsie," "I Sleep 'Til the Morning" and seven others. This winning combination of songs, along with songs from *More Baby Songs* has been produced as a video with the same name, and has sold so well that there is now a series of videos. See other Hap Palmer recordings on pp. 87–88, 168–173, and 221–222.

★★★        **HAP PALMER SINGS CLASSIC NURSERY**
            **RHYMES**
**Hap Palmer**
**Educational Activities**
**LP/Cassette/C.D.**
**Lyric Sheet included**
**Infant–4**

Very few satisfying recordings of the classic nursery and Mother Goose rhymes are available. This upbeat, classy version fills the gap perfectly. Hap, a movement specialist with a master's degree in Dance Education, has chosen some of the most popular songs and given them a contemporary and inviting sound. His gentle voice makes it easy for young ears to listen attentively, and his clear pronunciation makes this a perfect tool to aid in language development. The musical arrangements are filled with a joyous childhood sound and are often supplemented by an excellent children's chorus. This is a superb recording! The songs are "Ride A Cockhorse," "Mistress Mary," "Old King Cole," "Little Boy Blue," "Little Miss Muffet," "Mary Had a Little Lamb," "Hickory Dickory Dock," "Higglety Pigglety Pop," "Humpty Dumpty," "Twinkle, Twinkle Little Star," "Baa Baa Black Sheep" and more. There are also some fun tongue twisters that will delight the older child: "Moses Supposses," "Peter Piper" and "Swan Swam." You'll get a lot of mileage out of this recording.

★★★    **MORE BABY SONGS**
         **Hap Palmer and Martha Cheney**
         **Educational Activities**
         **LP/Cassette**
         **Lyrics and Activity Ideas included**
         **18 month–3**

Previously called *Tickly Toddle*, this sequel to *Babysongs* is for the toddler. Hap and Martha's respect for children is very apparent when you listen to the warm and caring lyrics that are directed to the experiences of the toddler-aged child. Hap's music is diverse, melodic and alluring. It can be used at home or in small playgroup settings. "Piggy Toes" is one of my favorite songs on this recording. Other songs include, "Rub-A-Dub" (a clever bath-time song), "Family Harmony" (which presents the sounds and names of various instruments), "Wild And Woolly" (a cowboy rodeo song), "Sleepy Time Sea" (a calming lullaby), "So Much To Hear" (lots of sounds heard throughout the day) and seven more.

★ ★ ★        **PEEK-A-BOO—**
            **And Other Songs for Young Children**
**Hap Palmer**
**Hap-Pal Music**
**Cassette**
**Lyric and Activity Booklet included**
**Ages 2–4**

This collection of Hap's musical treasures for infants and toddlers presents some revised and musically updated versions of
popular movement songs that were originally done for the
school market. "Raggedy Rag Doll Friend" (encouraging free-
form movements that a rag doll might make) and "Oh What
A Miracle" (a contagious song that develops positive self-esteem
and explores all the special things that children can do with
their bodies) have been very successful with teachers and now
are available for home use. "Gettin' Up Time" imitates all the
ways different animals greet the morning, and "Peek-A-Boo" is
a song that you can use when playing this game with your
child. "Lovey and Me" talks about those special dolls, bears or
rags to which small children become attached. Other songs
include "Baby's First," "I Can Put My Clothes On by Myself,"
"Merry-Go-Round," "Finger Foods" and four more. There are
numerous movement activities, and the music is always upbeat
and highly original. Many songs have a children's chorus in the
background.


**HARMONY RANCH**
**Riders In the Sky**
**Columbia Records**
**Cassette**
**No lyric sheet included**
**Ages 3–10**

They're back and they're singing some great cowboy songs.
Ranger Doug, Too Slim and Woody Paul harmonize, yodel and
sing some really clever songs. I first heard this recording in
my car with a five and eight year old in the back seat. Before
the tape was over, they had both wanted to hear two of the
songs a second time. My personal favorite, and that of the two
kids, was "How Does He Yodel," which features Ranger Doug

in an all-out fabulous yodel demonstration. After we heard the song twice, we had to turn off the tape so that the kids could practice. I even tried. "One Little Coyote" was the second hit of the afternoon. An ingenious counting song that talks of different kinds of animals one might find in the western plains, complete with sound effects. The melody to this song is very contagious, and we hummed it all weekend long. "The Cowboy's ABC" is a review of things that relate to the Old West and cowboys. "Face the Music" is an interactive piece in which Too Slim literally uses his mouth as an instrument. Riders In the Sky harmonize beautifully, and each song is accompanied by a short, clever introduction. The musical arrangements are inventive and never boring. Other songs include "The Big Corral," "Pecos Bill," "Cody of the Pony Express," "Prairie Lullaby" and more. I must say that I found the random use of language that stereotypes Native Americans in a couple of the songs a bit strange. Some of these lyrics are from old folk songs, but there is no need to perpetuate these terms today. These three extremely talented men could have chosen other songs. The songs they wrote themselves are fabulous.

**BABY FACE—**
   **Activities for Infants and Toddlers**
**Georgiana Liccione Stewart**
**Kimbo Educational**
**LP/Cassette**
**Lyrics and Activities Booklet included**
**Infant–2½**

When you want to be assured of high quality movement activities for children, look for the name of Georgiana Liccione Stewart. She is a dance and special education specialist who is highly respected in the movement education field. Although the songs are sung by various performers, Stewart creates all of the activities. Here is a name you can trust for safe and sound fun. Each song has an activity appropriate for infants and another, more complex activity for toddlers. Each song uses specific motor skills; for example, "Baby's Hokey Pokey" uses arms and legs and "Ring Around the Rosie" is for walking and falling down. Since an infant can't walk yet, you would "circle the baby's arms on Ring Around, and clap their hands up high on Clap Hands. Bring the baby's arms down when you hear All Fall Down." The music is based on familiar songs, but some of the arrangements are unexciting and bland. If you're looking for directed activities to use with infants and toddlers, this is a very worthwhile concept and recording. One side is vocals and the other is solely instrumental. Included are "Baby Take A Bow" (Walking), "Toot, Toot, Tootsie Goodbye" (Wave Bye-Bye), "Put Your Little Foot" (Tiptoe, Stamp), "Rock-A-Bye Baby" (Sway) and four more.

> **MY TEDDY BEAR AND ME—**
> **Musical Play Activities for Infants and Toddlers**
> **Georgiana Liccione Stewart**
> **Kimbo Educational**
> **LP/Cassette**
> **Lyrics and Activities Booklet included**
> **Infant-3**

This is a collection of directed movement activities developed by Georgiana Stewart. Each activity has specific ideas that are appropriate for both infants and toddlers, and each uses a teddy bear as a prop. The movements are well conceived and safe. If your child has a teddy bear, this could be a fun way to do some creative movement. The songs are based on familiar children's melodies, such as "Whee! There Goes Teddy (Pop Goes The Weasel)," "Pokey, Honey and Busy Bear (Old MacDonald)" and "Nosey Bear (Baa Baa Black Sheep)" plus six more. Side A is vocal, and Side B is instrumental only. My only complaint with this recording is that the arrangements are not varied and it becomes repetitive.

> **OVER IN THE MEADOW—**
> **A Silly Sing-Along of Animal Songs**
> **Karen Stokes and the Marrel of Bonkeys Band**
> **Music for Little People**
> **Cassette**
> **Lyrics included**
> **Ages 2½-5**

The cover of the recording says that this is "A flock of eighteen songs full of facts, giggles and fun." There are indeed eighteen songs, and the giggles come from the kids on the recording. The facts consist of one or two lines preceding some of the pieces that briefly explain something about the animals in the song. As for fun, I can recommend the collection of songs, but the overall presentation of them is a bit lackluster and sometimes too cute. The orchestrations are repetitive and overall not very interesting. The songs include: "Little White Duck," "Be Kind To Your Web-Footed Friends," "The Old Grey Mare," "Samba De General," "Five Little Monkeys," "Kookabura Song," "Three Blind Mice," "Five Speckled Frogs," " Bingo," "All God's Creatures," "Turkey in the Straw," "A Fly Walked into a Grocery Store" (the most interesting song on the recording) and more. For silly fun I personally prefer *Wee Sing Silly Songs* and *Sillytime Magic* more.

# Recordings for Preschoolers (Ages 2½–4) ♫..

Believe it! Music stimulates language development. By the time a child is about two and a half, he is rapidly developing verbal skills and wanting explanations for everything. He is stringing words together to form complete sentences and has developed some fine and gross motor skills that allow him to move in such new ways as jumping, running and turning around in circles. These new talents give toddlers the ability to relate to music in a new way. They can hear the music and make their bodies express the music's feeling. Their imaginations begin to flourish as they move to the sounds they hear. They are able to follow some simple musical and movement directions.

Beware of directions and music that are too fast and prevent the child from fully completing one action before another direction is given. Consider tempo, rhythm and clarity when looking for activity recordings for this age group. If the music says to follow directions, is it clear enough to be understood? Does the child have enough time to understand the message and act on it before another idea is presented? Are the rhythm and tempo appropriate for the skills of the child? This sounds like a lot to try to discern when you haven't heard the recording. I'll try to point these things out in the synopses that follow. Some recording artists are known for targeting their music to a positive first movement experience for the child:

people like Hap Palmer, Greg and Steve, Ella Jenkins and many more. These are people who work extensively with children and create music with specific goals in mind.

Not all music needs to create a movement environment. Some is just wonderful to listen to and sing along. You should look for clear lyrics that relate to the child's age. Orchestration can be a little more complex now, and multiple voices are fitting. Funny sounds and words make children giggle and invite response. Kids will also become more insistent about listening to their own favorites. It's important to let them start making choices. I like recordings that have activity songs mixed in with sing-alongs, and also have a quiet song or two. Some kids can get all worked up and need some soothing music to relax them.

The call and response style is a wonderful tool to elicit active participation. This involves calling out or singing a word or a verse of the song, and having the child either repeat what you've just sung or respond to your call in a musical way. Again, I encourage you to add the child's name to your songs whenever possible. You can use your favorite song in a call and response style as a way to personalize the musical experience with your child. Music is a form of communication and anytime you can personalize it, both you and your child will benefit. It's also great for you to join in the fun. Don't worry if you can't move as quickly as your child; he will love the fact that you're interested enough to join him.

It seems that a great portion of children's recordings are geared to this age group, which will give you a phenomenal number from which to choose. Children in this period of their lives are doing and learning many things, and the following recordings have a myriad of songs and activities that will coincide with your child's development. It is important not to rush your child. Each progresses at a different speed, and these activities should be used in a non-stressful way. Parents are often leery of movement activities because they say their children can't sit still long enough to listen. I remember one grandmother who took care of her active three-year-old grandson while his parents worked. She was terrified of "over stimulating" the child. After a long discussion, I convinced her to try a recording that had both active and passive, or quiet time, songs. She returned two weeks later with a huge grin and bought more. The child was so engrossed in the music, that all the hyperactivity got channeled into listening and responding to the recording. The child couldn't wait for the next song to start. When the quiet time music came on, the child very happily got into that frame of mind. Obviously, each child is different and will react differently to outside stimuli. This grandmother, by taking a chance, found that far from over exciting her grandson, these recordings were a wonderful way for him to direct his energies.

## DO:

- Look for music that gives children some simple activities to do.

- Find recordings with clear lyrics that relate to your child's daily experiences.

- Look for activities that are age and developmentally appropriate.

- Mix quiet time and active time music for your child.

- Encourage repetition in music—it really helps language development.

- Personalize songs by using your child's name.

- Encourage active participation by joining in the fun.

- Look at reviews in other chapters as many selections are for children of any age.

## DON'T:

- Force your child to do movement activities that are beyond his physical or emotional development.

- Be afraid to sing or move with your child.

- Ignore your child's verbal or non-verbal cues about what he would like to hear.

- Let your child become frustrated or confused with activity recordings that move too fast.

**THE FARMER'S MARKET**
**Timmy Abell**
**Upstream Records**
**Cassette**
**No Lyrics included**
**Ages 2½–5**

This is a fresh old-fashioned folk music recording. Abell's clear and smooth voice is an open invitation to sing along. The orchestrations includes banjo, dulcimer, fiddle, mandolin, guitars and even an English concertina. The collection of songs includes traditional music such as "Jimmy Crack Corn," "Mail Myself to You" (by Woody Guthrie), "A Place in the Choir," and "The Unicorn Song" (by Shel Silverstein). Abell also includes several of his own upbeat compositions, including "Hi Ho We're Rolling Home," "I Love You," "Farmer's Market," "Away, Mommy, Away" (a very clever Irish Jig about taking a bath) and three more. Needless, to say, there is plenty of variety and fun in this recording.

★ ★ ★     **THE BEST OF THE BABYSITTERS**
**The Babysitters**
**Vanguard Records**
**2 Cassettes**
**No Lyrics included**
**Ages 2½–6**

For those of you old enough to remember them, the Babysitters were a wonderful group that linked the talents of Lee Hays (from the Weavers), the actor Alan Arkin, Jeremy Arkin and Doris Kaplan. The following quotation from the liner notes best summarizes this recording:

"A recording of songs made up at home and in playgrounds. Traditional songs revised by joint experiment of kids and baby sitters singing together. There are new songs for dancing, swinging, counting, climbing stairs; songs for imagining and pretending; songs to go to sleep by; an anti-lullaby, and songs for spells of long quiet listening. Musical accompaniment includes guitar, piano, violin, clarinet, brushes, Armenian drum, child's xylophone, child's piano, autoharp, recorder, pots, pans, bottles, glasses, beer mugs, lamp stands, door bells, whistling, finger snapping, foot tapping, and baby laughter."

This treasure is full of great songs and guarantees many hours of entertainment. It includes "Hush Little Baby," "The Clock Song," "This Old Man," "Ha-Ha Thisaway," "Over in the Meadow," "Take You Riding in the Car," "The Old Sow" (Lee Hays' uncut laughter throughout the song is contagious), "There's a Hole in the Bucket" and thirty-three more. A great folk classic!

**BATHTIME MAGIC**
**Joanie Bartels**
**Discovery Music**
**Cassette**
**Lyrics included**
**Ages 2–5**

With fifteen of the most dazzling songs about bathtime and waterplay that I've ever heard, Joanie Bartels and the Discovery Music team have created another hit recording. Using contemporary and traditional songs, children can sing along in and out of the bathtub. Some of my favorites on this recording are "Bathtime" (written by Raffi), "Rubber Duckie," "Bubble Bath" (sung in a fifties do-wa style), "Splish Splash" (the Bobby Darrin hit from the fifties), "You Can Never Go Down the Drain" (a wonderfully sensitive song by Fred Rogers), "Little White Duck" and "Rub-A-Dub" (written by Hap Palmer and Martha Cheney). Other bubbly songs include "(Wash) Head, Shoulders, Knees and Toes," "There's A Hippo In My Tub" (an original song by Bartels), "Rub-A-Dub/Row Your Boat," "Three Little Fishies," "Yellow Submarine," "Octopus's Garden," "Six Little Ducks" and "Itsy, Bitsy Spider." Sung and arranged with an upbeat sound, this fine collection will make bath time a fun and entertaining experience.

★ ★ ★    **DANCIN' MAGIC**
       **Joanie Bartels**
       **Discovery Music**
       **Cassette**
       **Lyrics included**
       **Ages 2½–6**

This wonderful collection of songs will get your children (and you) up and dancing. Bartels' magical voice delivers some classic rock 'n' roll favorites in a bright, new format perfect for young bodies on the move. This recording is great for use with groups of children, such as parties or playgroups, or alone where a child can explore movement to the different beats and rhythms. The songs include "The Loco-Motion" (one of my favorites), "Dance, Dance, Dance" (made famous by the Beach Boys), "The Peppermint Twist," "Limbo Rock," "The Polka Dot Polka," "Dancing on the Ceiling," "Rockin' Robin," "The Martian Hop," "Barefootin'," "Hokey Pokey" (this song is always a favorite, although done a bit fast here), "Dinosaur Rock 'n' Roll," "Happy Feet" and "La Bamba" (Bartels' Spanish is very good). The musical arrangements are exciting and withstand repeated hearing. This recording is sure to bring delight and a sense of accomplishment to young dancers.

       **SILLYTIME MAGIC**
       **Joanie Bartels**
       **Discovery Music**
       **Cassette**
       **Lyrics included**
       **Ages 2½–5**

In another magical recording, Joanie Bartels presents fourteen songs that are sure to tickle the preschool funnybone. Included are lively and engaging versions of songs that have silly sounding words such as "Supercalifragilisticexpialidocious" (from *Mary Poppins*), "The Witch Doctor" (complete with the famous Chipmunk sound), "Chickery Chick," "The Name Game" ("Joanie Joanie Bo Boanie Banana Fana Fo Foanie Fe Fi Mo Moanie Joanie," etc.), "The Alphabet Song" ("B-a Bay, B-e Bee, B-i Bicky Bi B-o Boe, Bicky Bi Boe B-u Bu, Bicky Bi Boe Bu," etc.) and "Mairzy Doats." Other silly songs include "This Old

Man," "I Like Bananas Because They Have No Bones," "Do Your Ears Hang Low," "Aba Daba Honeymoon," "Animal Crackers in My Soup," "Ya Wanna Buy A Bunny" and "Swinging On A Star." Bartels' voice is clear and delightful. The musical arrangements are upbeat, but have a "synthesized" sound. Kids of all ages like humor, and this fine collection is sure to spark belly laughs. Silly songs are great for language development, as children listen carefully and imitate the sounds they hear. You will derive many years of use from this recording, since some of the songs will have added appeal as your child gets older and understands their lyrics more fully. This is fun recording to keep in your car during short or long trips, or to use with groups (Brownie troop meetings, parties and classrooms).

★★★    **TRAVELIN' MAGIC**
**Joanie Bartels**
**Discovery Music**
**Cassette**
**Lyrics included**
**Ages 2½–5**

As in previous recordings, Joanie Bartels combines songs specifically written for children with songs that weren't, but fit into the musical theme of the recording. The selections are playful and enticing, and expose children to some classic songs that they might not otherwise hear. Some of the traditional children's songs about traveling include, "Car Car" (by Woody Guthrie), "Wheels on the Bus" and "Little Red Caboose." Some of the songs that weren't necessarily written for children include "Side by Side," "Beep Beep (the song from the fifties about a Volkswagon and a Cadillac), "Surrey with the Fringe on Top" (from *Oklahoma*), "On The Road Again" (by Willie Nelson) and "Rolleo Rolling Along" (a great song from the forties). There are two original songs, "On the Road to Where We're Going" and "We're Flying." One side is vocal music and the other is solely instrumental. This format permits children to sense the accomplishment of knowing the lyrics to songs. This wonderful collection of songs is perfect for car, train, boat or plane travel! Also see more Joanie Bartels on pp. 11, 35 and 217–218.

### WEE SING AND PLAY—
#### Musical Games and Rhymes for Children
**Pamela Conn Beall and Susan Hagen Nipp**
**Price Stern Sloan**
**Cassette**
**Lyrics and Activity Book included**
**Ages 2½–5**

The Wee Sing Ladies have compiled another fabulous collection of fun interactive songs for young children. These well-known activity songs are great for parties and playgroups or just for use at home with you and your child. The book gives directions on playing the games as well as melody lines so that you can use your piano, guitar or autoharp. Seventy-two songs are presented in a full sixty-minute cassette, including "London Bridge," "Sally Go 'Round The Sun," "Punchinello, "Hokey-Pokey," "Noble Duke of York," "Muffin Man," "Polly Put the Kettle On," "Head and Shoulders," "Hambone" and "Pease Porridge Hot." Lots of entertainment and fun are to be had with this recording. More Wee Sing recordings are discussed on pp. 36–37, 131–132, and 218.

### WEE SING SILLY SONGS
**Pamela Conn Beall and Susan Hagen Nipp**
**Price Stern Sloan**
**Cassette**
**Lyrics and Activity Book included**
**Ages 3–8**

It's a toss-up as to whether to put this into this age category or with the older children's music. I decided to put it here because many preschoolers love to sing these silly songs and, while many don't understand all the words, they certainly grow into them quickly. The grosser the words (as in "Nobody Likes Me," a song about icky worms), the more kids love the songs. Part of the charm of silly songs is the silliness of their lyrics. As in the other tapes from Wee Sing, these songs are mostly sung by a group of children; this may not appeal to all adults, but kids love to hear other kids sing. The orchestrations are not overdone, so the words are clear and understandable. If you are in doubt, the booklet gives lyrics, melody line, and activity instructions. The forty-seven songs include "Little Rabbit Foo," "The Bear Went over the Mountain," "Do Your Ears Hang Low?," "Michael Finnegan," "A Peanut Sat on a Railroad Track," "There's A Hole In The Middle Of The Sea," "Throw It out the Window," "I'm A Nut," "Ninety-Nine Bottles of Pop," and more.

> **EVERYBODY CRIES SOMETIMES—**
> **Songs for Self-Appreciation and**
> **Self-Expression**
> **Marcia Berman and Patty Zeitlin**
> **Educational Activities**
> **LP/Cassette**
> **Lyric and Activity Book included**
> **Ages 2½–5**

Marcia Berman and Patty Zeitlin have joined forces to give children an opportunity to sing about themselves and their feelings. They in turn are joined by a children's chorus and the wonderful voice of Dave Zeitlin. "Beautiful Arms" tells about all the ways children can move their bodies. "Everybody Says," written by Malvina Reynolds, explains why it's so hard to sit down when your body is "all full of dance around." My favorite is a warm and inclusive song called "Room In The Boat," which uses a gospel music style and lets you add the name of your child and other family members or friends. This recording also includes "Don't You Push Me Down" (by Woody Guthrie), "Scarey Things," "Here's A Song" (you add the name of your child) and six more.

> ★★★   **RABBITS DANCE**
> **Marcia Berman Sings Malvina Reynolds**
> **Marcia Berman**
> **B/B Records**
> **LP/Cassette**
> **Lyric Sheet included**
> **Ages 2½–5**

Malvina Reynolds (1900–1978) was a fabulous songwriter who had a terrific talent for using music to explore emotional and social concepts. Marcia Berman's musical genius presents the best of Malvina's children's music in a varied and inviting format. Her voice is easy to follow, and the musical arrangements are multi-layered and perpetually intriguing. There are so many "favorite" songs on this recording, that I don't know where to start. "Magic Penny" talks about sharing love and giving it to others; "Move Over" incorporates many different children's names and gives the listener the chance to include their own. "Mommy's Girl" tells of all the things a mother loves about her child. "Rabbits Dance" is beautifully accompanied by a Japanese shakuhachi (bamboo flute). "The Pets" is a silly song with wonderful words. "You Can't Make a Turtle Come Out," "I Live in a City," and "Morningtown Ride" are Reynolds' classics. Marcia includes a song about Chanukah called "Eight Candles" and a Christmas song called "In Bethlehem." There are five other treasures on this recording, which was a winner of the Parent's Choice Award. No doubt Malvina would have been proud of the terrific job that Marcia has done. A must!

★ ★ ★    **WON'T YOU BE MY FRIEND?—**
       **Songs for Social and Emotional Growth**
       **Marcia Berman and Patty Zeitlin**
       **Educational Activities**
       **LP/Cassette**
       **Lyrics and Activity Book included**
       **Ages 2½–5**

Marcia Berman and Patty Zeitlin have extensive experience as teachers and music workshop presenters. This recording was made several years ago specifically for nursery school teachers, but the material is excellent for use in the home as well. A wide variety of musical styles and instrumental accompaniments encourage children to participate in the fun. Although these songs are original and written by both women, you will soon find yourself singing along. They are simple yet impressive, with repetitive lyrics. Many songs leave spaces for you to insert the name of your child or other members of your family. "Where's Mary," which lets the listeners play a game using many names, was our family's favorite song to sing in the car. There is a realistic song about twins and an encouraging song called "Everyday You're Growing." On the side with songs about emotional development, the selections include "Angry Song," which every child (and most adults) should learn. It says that it's okay to be angry and shout, but it's not okay to hit or hurt. The tender lyrics in "I'm Afraid" are soothing and address realistic fears. "Won't You Be My Friend" is a touching song for children (and adults) of all ages. Marcia Berman's voice is lovely and full of variety. Often Berman and Zeitlin will sing together, and a couple of songs include male voices as well. This recording has thirteen songs that are fun, reassuring and innovative. More recordings by Marcia Berman are on pp. 12–13.

**HUG-A-LONG SONGS**
**Debby Boone**
**Golden**
**Cassette**
**No lyrics included**
**Ages 3–5**

Debby Boone has a lovely voice, and the recording quality and arrangements are very good. Many of these songs were conceived with young children in mind, but the actual lyrics are clearly for much older children or adults. "I Think You're Growing Up," for example, is a song an adult sings to a child, but not one that a preschool child would relate to. "A Bee Can't Fly" uses words like aerodynamically, theoretically and philosophically, which are giant words with no meaning for young children. This use of adult vocabulary occurs throughout. The songs were obviously written with love, but are really not appropriate for this age. There is a medley of classic children's songs sung by an over-exuberant children's chorus: "Heads And Shoulders," "Bingo," "Old MacDonald" and "The More We Get Together." Original songs include "Me and My Blanket," "Possibilities," "Shooting Star," "Just as You Are" and "My Favorite Toy." The title song, "Hugs," is repeated three times. This is a very unsatisfying recording.

**MORE HUG-A-LONG SONGS**
**Debby Boone**
**Golden**
**Cassette**
**No Lyrics included**
**Ages 3–5**

This recording contains more overdone songs that were intended for very young children. The title song "Hugs," used on the first recording, is again repeated three times. There is a medley of "John Brown's Body," "Row, Row, Row," "Eentsy-Weentsy Spider" and "I've Been Working on the Railroad" sung by the same group of children whose singing was as forced on the last recording as it is here. There are two songs with a religious theme, "Hello, God," and "Count Your Blessings." Other songs are "J'Ever Have A Funny Dream," "Shooting Star" (an instrumental version of the same song on the first recording), "Flying," "Goodbye Dirt" and more. You really don't get very much for your money with this recording or its predecessor.

**GOOD**
**Frank Cappelli**
**A&M Records**
**Cassette**
**No Lyrics included**
**Ages 2½–4**

Frank Cappelli sings new original songs plus two old favorites. "Swinging On A Star," which has a very full orchestration, sounds like a Broadway production. Another classic song is "The Garden Song (Inch by Inch, Row by Row)." "Mom," a salute to mothers, and "Roberto," a salute to baseball star Roberto Clemente, are a bit contrived. Other Cappelli recordings seem better suited to young children, focusing more on their language and physical abilities. This product is more forced and consequently not as much fun to listen to. The six other songs are "All Aboard the Train," "Slap Me Five," "Brush-A Your Teeth," "The Colors," "I Am a Fine Musician" and "Down by the River."

**LOOK BOTH WAYS**
**Frank Cappelli**
**A&M Records**
**Cassette**
**No Lyrics included**
**Ages 2½–5**

Frank Cappelli's voice is pleasing and clear and his musical arrangements are diverse and interesting. Although his songs are fairly long, Cappelli's lyrics are full of repetitive refrains, which gives young children the power to learn the words and join the singing. Many of the songs encourage active participation, while others are more appropriate for educational use. "I'm Smiling, You're Smiling" gets kids moving their hands and arms and "Good Old Farmer Brown" imitates the sounds of the barnyard animals. "Gather In A Circle" is an activity song for large groups, but can be adapted for two children. Some of Cappelli's concept songs include "Look Both Ways" (crossing the street), "I've Got One" (a counting song to five), "Washing My Face" and "Growing Up" (a song full of questions for children to answer). Other songs include "Gramma Comes to My House Today" and "You and Me" (a song about friends).

**ON VACATION**
**Frank Cappelli**
**A&M Records**
**Cassette**
**No lyrics included**
**Ages 2½–4**

Here are more lengthy, original songs from Frank Cappelli. The concepts on this recording are for very different age groups. "One Dollar" is about the different coins we use, which is an advanced numerical concept for small children. "Golf," while interesting to act out, uses terms that won't be familiar to most non-golfers and "The Alphabet Song" may be confusing to very young children, since the vowels and their sounds are introduced. Two of the more interesting songs are "Rat-A-Tat-Tat," an introduction to the orchestra and its various sections and instruments, and "Head-Shoulders-Hips-Knees-Toes," a fun song about body parts. Other songs include "In the Jungle," "On

Vacation," "Sun Shine Down on Me," "Lindsey's Bakery" and
"Oh, I Love the Circus."


**YOU WANNA BE A DUCK?**
**Frank Cappelli**
**A&M Records**
**Cassette**
**No lyrics included**
**Ages 2½–4**

This is an interesting collection of songs, some original and
some familiar. Cappelli engages children with lyrics that
encourage participation. "Over in the Meadow" makes animal
sounds, "You Wanna Be A Duck?" will have small children
waddle and quack, and "Swan Song" turns them into beautiful
swans (a three-part round that also introduces some classical
instruments). Traditional songs include "Oh, Susanna" and
"When You Wish upon a Star." You can learn about different
fruit in "The Fruit Market" and go and prepare a pizza in
"Making A Pizza." Other songs include "My Yellow Truck,"
"Let's Make a Circle" and "Giuseppi's My Boy."


**10 CARROT DIAMOND**
**Charlotte Diamond**
**Diamond Records**
**LP/Cassette**
**Lyrics included**
**Ages 2½–5**

Charlotte Diamond is another bright and exciting recording
artist from Canada, as demonstrated in this collection of eighteen singable, lovable songs. Diamond has a clear, pleasing
voice and the musical arrangements are interesting and varied.
One of my favorite songs is "Four Hugs A Day" ("that's the
minimum, not the maximum"). A French version of this song
is also included. The other French song is "J'ai Perdu le 'Do'
de ma Clarinette." She also sings "La Bamba" in Spanish. "May
There Always Be Sunshine" ("May there always be sunshine,
blue skies, Mama, Papa and me") is beautifully sung in English,
Russian, French, Spanish, German and Cantonese. There are

spoken rhymes: "Stella, Stella Oga," "Looking for Dracula" (a version of "We're Going on a Bear Hunt") and "Zing Zing, Zing." Some of the sillier songs include "Octopus," "I Am a Pizza" (with some verses in French), "Why Do I Have to Have a Sister?" and the extra-silly "10 Crunchy Carrots." Other songs include "Love Me for Who I Am," "Each of Us Is a Flower," "The Garden Song" ("Inch by inch, row by row"), "I Wanna Be A Dog," "Spider's Web" and "Sasquatch." This is a marvelous collection of musical fun from a gem of Diamond.

**THE FOUR TOTS**
**Piano by Floyd Domino—Vocals by Christine**
**Albert, Chris O'Connell, Maryann Price**
**and Tish Hinojosa**
**Golliber Records**
**LP/Cassette/C.D.**
**No lyrics included**
**Ages 2–5**

If you enjoy nostalgia and want to share some of the most popular and famous hit songs of the fifties and sixties with your children, then this is the recording for you. The same musicians who brought you *Baby Road* and *The White Album* (see the first chapter) have again joined forces to present this enjoyable recording. Although the songs and lyrics don't relate well to children, the arrangements are true to the originals, but with a softened edge. The female singing is lovely. This could be a wonderful recording to keep in your car, because you'll be able to sing along with the songs. The vocal side includes "Locomotion," "Up on the Roof," "The Way You Do the Things You Do," "What a Wonderful World This Would Be," "My Girl" and "You Send Me." The instrumental side includes "Baby Love," "You Really Got a Hold on Me," "You Can't Hurry Love," "How Sweet It Is to Be Loved by You" and "I Hear a Symphony." This recording is good for sing along or rest time.

**HELP YOURSELF**
**Cathy Fink and Marcy Marxer**
**Rounder Records**
**Cassette/C.D.**
**Lyrics included**
**Ages 3-5**

This recording contains twelve songs that promote self-esteem
and self-confidence. The two dynamic musicians and singers
have written original songs with great messages and delightful
musical arrangements. Their voices blend beautifully together
and are equally delightful when singing solos. Marxer's voice
is melodious and mellow, while Fink's voice is hearty and
robust. As in their other recordings, Marxer and Fink keep the
arrangements interesting by using a variety of musical styles.
The songs include "Stop, Look and Listen," "When My Shoes
Are Loose," "Help Yourself!" (all the things that kids at this age
are learning to do on their own such as getting dressed, etc.),
"You Are What You Eat," "I Believe in Myself," "Read a Book,"
"Nobody Else Like Me," and "The Name And Address Song."
"I've Got A Secret" and "Never Talk To Strangers" are songs
that many teachers and playgroup leaders will find appealing.
This is a recording that withstands repeated listenings.

**WHEN THE RAIN COMES DOWN**
**Cathy Fink**
**Rounder Records**
**LP/Cassette**
**Lyrics and Activity Booklet included**
**Ages 3-6**

Stylistically, this varied recording has a wide audience appeal.
Fink's voice invites listeners to join the singing, and her
arrangements are interesting and very pleasing. Although the
targeted age range is varied, many of the songs are ageless.
Some of the younger songs include a rollicking "Alphabet
Boogie," "Uncle Noah's Ark," "Skip to My Lou" (accompanied
by a mouthbow) and a rap-type song called "Cookies." Fink
also does a wonderful tongue twister called "Betty Botter."
"Rock, Old Joe (Old Joe Clark)," "Magic Penny" (Malvina Rey-

nolds' song "Love is something if you give it away you end up having more"), "Whoever Shall Have Some Good Peanuts" (a song to which you can add your own verses and that requires a good memory), "When The Rain Comes Down" ("whether rich or poor, big or small, comes down on us all"), "Seven Days to Rock" (all the days of the week), "Banjo Song" (showing off Cathy's magical banjo playing), "Happy Trails" (yes! the Dale Evans and Roy Rogers theme song), "Martin Luther King" and three more songs will delight children (and adults). It's a fun and musically exciting recording. For more recordings by Cathy Fink see pp. 145–146.


**THERE'S NOBODY ELSE LIKE YOU**
**Caren Glasser**
**Kid Rhino Music**
**Cassette/C.D.**
**Lyrics included**
**Ages 3–8**

If you're looking for a recording that is full of original songs about positive self esteem, this will fit the bill. Glasser has a warm inviting voice, and the musical arrangements are never overpowering. Children often accompany Glasser. The title song is an upbeat song about how we are all distinctive. Glasser's version of "Free to Be a Family" is delightful. "Make Your Own Kind of Music" is about maintaining your individuality. "We'll Show The World" is about saving electricity and water. One of my favorite songs is "One Step At A Time," which is about doing things little by little, a song that even adults should listen carefully to. This could easily become a theme song for the "stressed-out generation." Glasser even includes a song about self-esteem for dogs called "Dogs Need Love Too." This is a fine recording that both parents and teachers can use. Glasser has a powerful energy. Hope she'll do more.

**LET'S SING FINGERPLAYS**
**Tom Glazer**
**Gateway Records**
**Cassette**
**No lyrics included**
**Ages 2½–4**

Although this recording contains the most popular fingerplays, it may only have limited use. Tom Glazer's musical presentations are clear with simple instrumentation; however, many songs have spoken instructions either preceding or within them. While this may be helpful for the parent or teacher, children will, over many uses, find it uninteresting, especially if they have learned the movements. The rest of the recording is fine. Glazer's voice is pleasant and perfect for children's language development. The fingerplays include "Bingo," "The Bus Song (Wheels on the Bus)," "Eentsy Weentsy Spider," "Eye Winker, Tom Tinker, Chin Chopper," "Five Little Ducks," "Go in and out the Window," "He's Got the Whole World in His Hands," "Here Is the Church" and five more. This is a good choice for playgroup settings and for children learning English as a second language.

**CAN YOU SOUND JUST LIKE ME?**
**Red Grammer**
**Children's Group**
**Cassette/C.D.**
**No lyrics included**
**Ages 2½–5**

This is a marvelous collection of thirteen original songs, fingerplays and activity songs for children. Grammer's musical arrangements, enticing singing, and age-appropriate lyrics make this a wonderful recording for young children. "My House" describes rooms, furniture and other things found in a home. "Counting Song" is a cumulative song that counts up to ten. "Doggie" lets kids pretend to be dogs, sniffing, licking and sleeping. The title song gives children the opportunity to make many kinds of sounds with their voices, and "Big Brass Band" encourages them to imitate instruments. "Ready Set" is a movement song wherein children listen and then move to the music. Other songs include "Beautiful Morning," "Squeep Doodle A De Doaw," "I'm Lucky," "Monster," "Let's Go Riding" (based on the Woody Guthrie song, "Car Car"), "I Love To See You" and "Fingerplay." Since there is no lyric sheet, there are no written instructions for the song "Fingerplay."

### DOWN THE DO RE MI
### Red Grammer
### Children's Group
### Cassette/C.D.
### No lyrics included
### Ages 2½–5

Red and Kathy Grammer have written some new imaginative and fun songs for kids that, supplemented with some traditional tunes, are featured on this recording. Red's voice is inviting and excellently pitched for young listeners to join them in singing. The musical accompaniments are enticing and accentuate Grammer's melodic voice. "Heading Down to the Barn" uses different animal sounds, and "The ABC's of You" is a darling song that describes all the wonderful things a child is. "Down by the Sea" relates the pleasurable things to do at the seashore. There is a rollicking version of "Place In The Choir." "Rattlin' Bog" is a traditional song with cumulative verses (fly on the flower, flower on the leaf, leaf on the twig, etc.). "Two Hands Four Hands" is a lively hand-clapping song in which you will work up a sweat if you keep time with the music. "Musical Animal" is a clever piece about playing different instruments. Other songs include "Me and the Morning," "Land of the Silver Birch," "Grandfather's Clock," "Dreamtime Rendezvous" and a beautiful song called "Brothers and Sisters" where children of all cultures are celebrated. This upbeat, hearty recording is sure to bring hours of listening and singing pleasure.

★★★          **TEACHING PEACE**
             **Red Grammer**
             **Children's Group**
             **Cassette/C.D.**
             **No lyrics included**
             **Ages 3–6**

Red Grammer has the special gifts of a phenomenal voice and
a great sense of children's preferences. He and his wife Kathy
have written a recording full of clever songs with upbeat and
cheery musical arrangements. The songs are both engaging
and thought provoking. "Places in the World" names a plethora of cities and countries around the world, and "Rapp
Songs" teaches children how to say "hello" in several languages. "Barnyard Boogie" is a clever song about the animals
on a farm. Grammer sings several songs about interpersonal
relationships and making the planet a better place to live:
"Hooray for the World," "Use A Word," "Teaching Peace,"
"Shake Your Brains" (about thinking things through), "I Think
You're Wonderful," "Listen" (to the heartbeat and laughter of
the family of man), "Say Hi!," "With Two Wings" and "See Me
Beautiful." This is the type of recording that withstands
repeated hearing; the songs are catchy and easy to learn, and
Grammer's voice is spectacular. Children's voices are utilized
on many of the songs.

★★★          **GREG AND STEVE PLAYING FAVORITES**
             **Greg and Steve**
             **CTP/Youngheart Records**
             **LP/Cassette/C.D.**
             **Lyrics included**
             **Ages 2½–6**

Greg and Steve's love of music and children is apparent in this
delightful recording of classic songs. The songs may be traditional, but the arrangements and lyrics are not always as you
might remember them. "Join into the Game" uses children's
voices as Greg and Steve get kids to snore, giggle and clap to
this lively rendition. Every verse gets progressively faster in
"Ain't Gonna Rain." There is a very clever "blues" version of
"Three Little Pigs." "Heavenly Music" is a rollicking piece about

all the sounds that animals make, but my favorite is "We've Got the Whole World in Our Hands," based on the traditional song but with an ecological message. Greg and Steve (previously known as Youngheart) have put music to the popular book *Brown Bear, Brown Bear* by Bill Martin, Jr. Other songs on this upbeat and energetic recording are "I've Been Working on the Railroad," "This Old Man," "Down by the Bay," "Did You Ever See A Lassie/The More We Get Together," "Put Your Finger In The Air" and "Zip-A-Dee-Do-Dah." Greg and Steve have included many participation songs, which are great for children learning English as a second language. The addition of kids' voices enhances this fun recording. Watch for this dynamic duo in your town. Their show is professional, invigorating and upbeat! Everytime I see them perform I'm reminded of what quality children's music is all about!

**KIDDING AROUND (WITH GREG AND STEVE)**
**Greg and Steve**
**CTP/Youngheart Records**
**LP/Cassette**
**Lyrics included**
**Ages 3–8**

This is another rockin' and swingin' recording from Greg and Steve, full of new songs and activities to enhance language development, motor skills and feelings of positive self-esteem. "Believe in Yourself" and "The Hugging Song" are filled with love and caring. "Safety Break," done in rap style, is a clever way to learn safety tips. The rock 'n move songs include "The Body Rock" (kids really love this song), "The Hokey Pokey" and "Copy Cat." Their version of "Jimmie Crack Corn" is a square dance-type song suitable either for a group of children or one child alone. This song is recommended for children over four since it utilizes more complex coordination skills, but younger children can enjoy it to the best of their capabilities. There's a call and response called "Rhyme Time" where children are asked to respond with words that rhyme.

★★★     ON THE MOVE WITH GREG AND STEVE
        **Greg and Steve**
        **CTP/Youngheart Records**
        **LP/Cassette**
        **Lyrics and Activity Sheet included**
        **Ages 2½–5**

This recording fulfills the title's promises. Children are delightfully activated by Greg and Steve's fun and inviting music.
Here is one of the best all-around movement activity recordings available. "Rock to the Music" creates an environment in
which kids can move and boogie, and "Scat Like That" is an
innovative song that encourages children to imitate the funny
sounds and tempos that Greg creates. A children's chorus helps
kids learn "How Many Days?" (in the months of the year) and
about "Friends." A wonderful imagination piece, called "An
Adventure in Space," presents a story for children to act out.
This is a great activity for all kids, but can be particularly stimulating for children who are learning English. "Warmin' Up" is
a safe and fun way to exercise little bodies, one version with
ques and the other with music only. For sports fans, there's a
cute exercise song called "'The Sports Dance," where children
can move as if they were playing different sports. The title
song, "On The Move," explores movements that different animals make. "Shoo Fly," adapted from the folk song, encourages children to jump like a kangaroo, wiggle like a worm, and
swim like a fish. All of these activities have been tested with
young children, and the movements are physically safe for
young bodies. This recording can also be used with children
who have physical and learning disabilities. If you're looking
for music with hours of active participation, this will fill the bill.


★★★     WE ALL LIVE TOGETHER—VOLUME I
        **Greg and Steve**
        **CTP/Youngheart Records**
        **LP/Cassette**
        **Lyrics included**
        **Ages 2½–5**

Steve Millang and Greg Scelsa, previously known as Youngheart, are definitely the dynamic duo of children's music. Their

sound is upbeat, lively and energetic. Their voices are clear, animated and spirited. Their message is love and global understanding. Who can resist this combination? With vast musical backgrounds and extensive work in the schools with children, Greg and Steve bring the right mix of styles, rhythms and movement activities into your home or classroom. Teachers and librarians throughout the country have been reaping the benefits of their recordings since the mid-1970s. Their kinetic energy is contagious, and kids are absorbed with their music. Children's voices are included in their arrangements. Their recordings contain many movement activities that can be done individually or in a group. These activities are appropriate for children of all ages and can also be used with physically challenged children. The title song, "We All Live Together," is about people in different places, all sharing the planet earth. "ABC Rock," the alphabet sung in a true rock 'n' roll style, has become a classic. "Little Sir Echo" is a call and response song, which is sung in the first version and parts are left open for children's participation in the second version. There are new and very lively versions of "Loop 'D Loo" and "Skip to My Lou," as well as the get down and boogie movement songs, "Round in a Circle," "Wiggle Wobble" and "Rock-A-Motion Choo Choo." Each side of the recording ends with a quiet, resting song, so that kids can unwind after having been active. You can choose any of Greg and Steve's recordings for your children and really get your money's worth. You'll enjoy the music as much as your children.


★★★     **WE ALL LIVE TOGETHER—VOLUME 2**
        **Greg and Steve**
        **CTP/Youngheart Records**
        **LP/Cassette**
        **Lyrics included**
        **Ages 2½–5**

This is one of Greg and Steve's most popular recordings, presenting a fabulous collection of movement, call and response, and fun sing-a-long music. "The World Is a Rainbow," which has become their trademark with its message of love among different cultures and races, is used by teachers across the country in choral groups and assembly programs. Religious groups use it for presentations to their congregations. It's a superspecial song! "The Number Rock" is a rock 'n' roll way to learn to count to ten, and the "Months of the Year" are taught in English and Spanish. The movement songs include "The Boogie Walk," "Listen and Move," a delightful song called "Popcorn," and a follow-along song called "The Freeze" (move around until the music stops, then freeze in that position). Steve sings a wild and woolly new version of "She'll Be Coming 'Round the Mountain" (in call and response format) and "The Muffin Man." There is also a "Resting Song" to help your children do just that. A children's chorus is used in many of the songs. If you ever hear of Greg and Steve performing in your area, be sure to take your children to see them. They put on a wonderful show!!

**WE ALL LIVE TOGETHER—VOLUME 3**
**Greg and Steve**
**CTP/Youngheart Records**
**LP/Cassette**
**Lyrics included**
**Ages 3–5**

Greg and Steve's musical and teaching talents are reflected in "Rock 'Round the Mulberry Bush" (a lively song about hygiene), "Simon Says" (a wonderfully fun way to identify body parts), and "Dancin' Machine" (sure to get kids up and moving). Although the songs "Shapes" and "Disco Limbo" are geared to groups, they can definitely be enjoyed by only one child as well. Greg and Steve have a new and lively version of "If You're Happy and You Know It" and "1, 2 Buckle My Shoe." "Piggy Bank" reveals how many pennies you need to make a nickel, dime, or quarter. A children's chorus performs "Sing a Happy Song," and the quiet instrumental song is called "Nocturne." This is an appealing and entertaining recording.

**WE ALL LIVE TOGETHER—VOLUME 4**
**Greg and Steve**
**CTP/Youngheart Records**
**LP/Cassette**
**Lyrics and Activity Sheet included**
**Ages 3–6**

This volume contains more upbeat songs that encourage active participation and singing. Greg and Steve present movement songs such as "Ballin' the Jack," "Hand Jive" (a clapping song that encourages children to repeat Greg and Steve's clapping patterns), "Just Like Me," "What If" (song for creative dramatics), and "Dance Medley," which includes dances like the swim, the twist and the elephant walk. As in other recordings, there is a beautiful resting song, "Siesta." Listeners can also learn the "Days of the Week" in English and Spanish. The only song that doesn't really work for home use is "Across The Bridge," designed to accompany work on a balance beam but also adaptable for creative movement at home. You can make a balance beam by buying a piece of board and suspending in on top of bricks or blocks of wood. Be sure to supervise your child. See Greg and Steve's holiday recording on pp. 224–225.

**KARAN AND THE MUSICAL MEDICINE SHOW**
**Karan Bunin Huss**
**Medicine Show Music**
**Cassette**
**No lyrics included**
**Ages 2½–5**

I was so pleased when Karan sent me this tape. Her incredibly full, robust and exciting voice is well known on the East Coast, where she performs for family concerts and schools. The musical arrangements are upbeat and dynamic, using a variety of musical styles. Eleven of the twelve songs are Karan's original compositions, many of which are performed with a children's chorus. They include "Be The Best" (a wonderful song about the freedom to aspire to any profession), "The Puddle Song" (a clever counting song), "The Letter Song," "Sam and Max" (about friendship between a frog and a duck), "The Choo Choo Song" (all the people and sounds heard when riding a train—a concept similar to "The Wheels on the Bus"), "Daddy's Coming Home" and "Tickle Bug." Karan also sings a beautiful version of "Puff the Magic Dragon." This recording is one that neither parents nor children will tire of playing.

**WARM FUZZIES**
**Karan Bunin Huss**
**Medicine Show Music**
**Cassette**
**No lyrics included**
**Ages 2½–5**

Karan and the Musical Medicine Show return with a rich collection of mostly original songs. Her voice is robust and contagious, and the musical arrangements by Jeff Waxman are varied and enticing. A children's chorus adds to the fullness of the songs. These are pieces that Karan uses in her frequent shows for schools and families, and they offer a range of themes and ideas. A patriotic motif is presented in songs like "The Story of The Star Spangled Banner" (a brief historical overview followed by the singing of the National Anthem) and "Welcome Home" (written for the troops returning from the Middle East). Songs about feelings include "Talk Talk It Out," "Warm Fuzzies," "The Ping Pong Song" (Dad says to ask Mom, who says to go ask Dad, etc.), "That Makes Me Embarrassed" and "One Hand One Heart." Among the other songs are "Monkey Sing Monkey Do," "Plenty Of Time," "The Lion Sleeps Tonight" and "Rhythm and Blues Train." Karan's musical medicine show is a delight!

**DANCE IN YOUR PANTS**
**David Jack**
**Golden**
**Cassette**
**No lyrics included**
**Ages 3–5**

David Jack's voice is clear and well pitched for little singers. Most of these original songs encourage active participation. There are some great movement songs like "Dance in Your

Pants," "The Cozy Bug Twist," "Rag Doll Rag," "Mookie Pookie Choo-Choo-Choo" and "One Note March." Other songs invite children to sing along: "The Silly Song," "Feelin' Fine (The Elbow Song)," "Making Music," "Making Friends" and "When You Don't Want to Say Goodbye (Hasta Luego)." Jack's musical accompaniments are fun and varied. The concepts in some of the songs are more appropriate for older children, so there is a wide age range that can benefit from this recording. It's a pity there is no lyric sheet included. Other recordings by David Jack appear on pp. 21 and below.

**GOTTA HOP**
**David Jack**
**Golden**
**Cassette**
**No lyrics included**
**Ages 3–5**

More movement and sing-along songs for young children are presented here. This collection of original songs is not as interesting as *Dance in Your Pants* because some of the lyrics are rather lackluster. Jack's voice is very pleasing, as are the instrumental arrangements. His trademark character, Mookie Pookie, has another song on this recording, called "Mookie Pookie Yodelin' Cow." The title song is lively and wonderful for dancing. "Makin' Faces" encourages children to explore ways they can show emotion with their faces. "Walkin' Through the Jungle" is about animal sounds. Other songs are "Wake Up," "The Dinosaur Dip," "When It's Showery," "Miranda the Panda" and "Sunbreak."

**JAMBO—AND OTHER CALL AND RESPONSE**
  **SONGS AND CHANTS**
  **Ella Jenkins**
  **Smithsonian/Folkways**
  **Cassette**
  **Lyrics included**
  **Ages 3–6**

Many of these songs were written by Ella on a trip to Africa; all are in the "call and response" format. This recording is very popular in classroom settings, but also has great value for home use. Ella uses Swahili terms such as *jambo* (hello) and develops a simple rhythmic chant. She has a spoken section of counting in Swahili and a delightful song called "Pole Pole" (go slowly) about all the different animals one might see on a safari. Side Two has songs and chants about life in the U.S. such as "Annie My Cooking Friend," "I Looked In The Mirror," "A Train's-a-Coming" and two more plus a spoken section called "Seasons" which features children's voices, although a bit too long. Overall this is a very worthwhile recording, sharing music and words based on African culture. The format of call and response is monotonous to some adults, but children love repetition and the sense of accomplishment that this style promotes.

### PLAY YOUR INSTRUMENTS AND MAKE A PRETTY SOUND
**Ella Jenkins**
**Smithsonian/Folkways**
**LP/Cassette**
**Lyrics included**
**Ages 3–6**

This is one of the few recordings available for use with rhythm instruments (such as maracas, triangles, rhythm sticks, cowbells, etc.). Side A takes Ella's original song, "Play Your Instruments and Make a Pretty Song," and uses its melody to teach about different instruments. The children can experience other children using designated instruments and hear their sounds as they themselves accompany Ella and her young friends. They are also rhythmically helped to "Put Your Instruments Away" and then "Follow The Leader," making sounds with different parts of their bodies. The various members of a jazz band play their instruments (tuba, clarinet, banjo, snare drum, piano, trumpet and trombone) as they "make a pretty sound." Children are also able to lead the jazz band in waltz, march and jazz beats. Side B introduces the harmonica and includes "No More Pie" (a call and response song) and "Stop and Go," a song to listen and move to. Many teachers over the years have used this in the classroom, but if you supply your child with some commercial or homemade rhythm instruments, this is perfectly wonderful at home as well.

**THIS-A-WAY THAT-A-WAY**
**Ella Jenkins**
**Smithsonian/Folkways**
**LP/Cassette/C.D.**
**Lyrics and notes included**
**Ages 2½–5**

Jenkins' original and traditional songs invite active participation. She always encourages children to sing along in these short, rhythmic selections. Sometimes she is accompanied by a group of young children. "Please Is a Pleasant Expression" teaches how to say "please" in many different languages, and "I Love to Ride" discusses feelings about different forms of transportation. "Miss Sue" tells of different states; "I Like the Way That They Stack the Hay" is a farm counting song. Ella uses simple accompaniment on the baritone ukelele, with occasional help from a fiddle, guitar and kazoo. Although not high-tech or jazzy, this is a valuable recording for vocal participation and language development. Ella's voice is crisp and clear, and adaptations and arrangements are geared for young children.

★★★    **YOU'LL SING A SONG AND I'LL SING A SONG**
**Ella Jenkins**
**Folkways/Smithsonian**
**LP/Cassette/C.D.**
**Lyrics included**
**Ages 1½–4**

This has been a classic in preschools since the mid-1960s. Ella Jenkins is a national treasure who was one of the first to bring music into the educational system. She is known for developing the "call and response" method (calling out a verse and waiting for the children to respond), used here in "You'll Sing A Song and I'll Sing A Song," "Shabot Shalom," "Cadima," "Did You Feed My Cow?," "Miss Mary Mack" and many more. The

wealth of cultural diversity is also an important Jenkins trademark. Ella sings songs that she has written or has learned on
her many trips around the world singing for and with children.
She accompanies herself on a baritone ukelele as she sings
with a delightful children's chorus. The vocals are clear and
wonderful for non-English-speaking children as well as native
speakers. Her music is inviting, enticing and filled with love
and respect for children. This is a must!

★★★   **BOB'S FAVORITE STREET SONGS**
      **Bob McGrath**
      **A&M Records**
      **Cassette/C.D.**
      **Lyrics included**
      **Ages 2½–6**

Any child who has ever watched *Sesame Street* knows Bob
McGrath as just plain Bob. His smiling face and warm personality bring love and comfort to children all over the world. This
delightful recording brings Bob's gentle voice into your home
or car for repeated listening pleasure. Although many of the
songs are from *Sesame Street*, they have new and interesting
arrangements, reminiscent of the Big Band era. Since the pronunciation is crystal clear, this is a perfect recording to give to
a child who is learning English as a second language. Bob performs around the country with live symphony orchestras, and
this recording reflects that full orchestral sound. If Bob is ever
in your town, be sure to see his wonderful show. You may be
sitting far back in the theater, but his warm presence will make
you feel as if he's singing just for you. Bob's favorite street
songs are "Sesame Street Theme," "Hi Friend," "Right in the
Middle of My Face," "Morning Town Ride," "The People in
Your Neighborhood," "Sing," "Somebody Come and Play,"
"Rubber Duckie," "Put Down the Duckie," "Bein' Green," "A
Face" and "See You Tomorrow." This is a fabulous collection
of favorite songs, sung by the one and only Bob.

**SING ALONG WITH BOB—VOLUMES I AND II**
**Bob McGrath**
**Golden**
**Cassette**
**No lyrics included**
**Ages 2½-5**

Bob McGrath of *Sesame Street* sings some of the most popular and recognizable children's songs. These recordings contain more songs (between thirty-two and thirty-four) than most recordings, and are really worth the investment. Bob's voice is clear and pleasant; the orchestrations are clever and never overpower him. These volumes are great for parents who don't know a lot of children's classic songs and want to learn the favorites along with their children. It is also appropriate for children who are learning English.

VOLUME I includes "The Wheels on the Bus," "A, B, C, D," "Incey Wincey Spider," "Skip to My Lou," "When The Saints Go Marching In," "Six Little Ducks," "On Top of Spaghetti," "Happy Birthday," "She'll Be Comin' Round the Mountain," "The Farmer in the Dell," "Dreydel," "Skinnamarink," "If You're Happy And You Know It," "Home on the Range" and more.

VOLUME II includes "Three Blind Mice," "Old King Cole," "You Are My Sunshine," "Hokey Pokey," "Let Everyone Clap Hands Like Me," "Hush Little Baby," "Twinkle Twinkle Little Star," "Oh Susanna," "London Bridge," "We've Got the Whole World in Our Hands," "Mary Had a Little Lamb," "Old MacDonald Had A Farm," "Ha Ha Thisaway," "Put Your Finger in the Air," "Shake My Sillies Out" and more.

★★★   **JUMP CHILDREN**
      **Marcy Marxer**
      **Rounder Records**
      **LP/Cassette**
      **Lyrics and Activity Booklet included**
      **Ages 2½-5**

This is one of my favorite recordings. Not only is Marxer's voice delightful to hear, but she has combined a variety of musical styles that makes this recording interesting listening. All of the songs reinforce either a movement, musical or cognitive skill in a fun and clever way. Many songs include a children's chorus and/or harmonies with Cathy Fink (see Fink's recordings on pp. 69–70 and 145–146). "Jump Children," a lively, upbeat movement song, uses blues and rock 'n' roll styles. "Chickery Chick," contagious, funny and full of great made-up words ("Chickery Chick, Chilla chilla, Chirck-a-la-romi, in a bananica," etc.), is presented in a jazz format. The counting song "10 Cats Down" is performed as rockabilly. Marxer incorporates the reggae sound into one of the most original versions of "Hush, Little Baby" that I've ever heard; it's really tremendous. "Grandpa's Farm" (a song full of animal sounds) uses an old-time string band, and "If You're Happy and You Know It" is in a jazz style. Other fun songs include "Rock-Bye Boogie" (rockabilly), "Use Your Own Two Feet" (rock 'n' roll), "January, February, March" (calypso), "Time To Sleep" (folk), "Ride 'Em High" (old-time string band), "The Star (Twinkle, Twinkle Little Star)" (Celtic), "Skinnamirink" (folk) and "Beautiful Day" (folk/calypso). This wonderful recording will bring your children hours of listening and moving fun. Adults may find themselves singing also!

**CIRCLE TIME**
**Lisa Monet**
**Music for Little People**
**Cassette**
**Lyrics included**
**Ages 2½–5**

Thirty of the most popular songs and rhymes for young children are sung with very simple accompaniment. Monet has a clear voice, although some of the accompanying harmony seems strained. This compendium of early childhood fun includes "If You're Happy," "Thumbkin," "Itsy, Bitsy Spider," "Muffin Man," "Five Little Speckled Frogs," "Fuzzy Wuzzy," "ABC Song," "Head and Shoulders," "Little Red Caboose," "Open/Shut Them" and "This Old Man." A worthwhile recording.

**JUMP DOWN**
**Lisa Monet**
**Music for Little People**
**Cassette**
**Lyrics included**
**Ages 2½–5**

This is a very uneven recording. Monet's voice is nice on most songs, but often sounds off key, and many of the harmonies make listening to this recording less than enjoyable. The collection of twenty-five songs and rhymes is very good and includes "Bingo," "The Bear Went over the Mountain," "Pop Goes the Weasel," "Old Mother Hubbard," "Three Blind Mice," "Little Peter Rabbit" and "Brahms' Lullaby."

**A GARDEN OF GIVING—**
   **Seeds Of Self-Esteem**
**Created by Lisa Marie Nelson with Various**
   **Artists**
**Bright Ideas Productions**
**Cassette**
**No lyrics included**
**Ages 2½–6**

This recording presents a collection of songs about positive self-image from a variety of children's recording artists. Their proceeds are donated to Childhelp USA (a non-profit organization that works to combat child abuse). I like listening to recordings that feature different singers and musicians because they offer a multi-sound experience. Included in the compilation are "The Power" (Robin and Micheal Goodrow from *Amazing*), "Rainy Day Child" (Michael Mish from *Sleepy Time*), "I Can If I Wanna" (Peter Alsop from *Pluggin' Away*), "Mighty Big Plans" (Joe Scruggs from *Bahamas Pajamas*), "With People I Like" (Banana Slug Band from *Dirt Made My Lunch*), "Laugh All Your Blues Away" (by Janet and Judy), and five more. The recording is appropriate for children of various ages (some songs are for very young kids, while others are for much older children). This is a collection of songs that will help kids feel good about themselves.

**CAN A CHERRY PIE WAVE GOODBYE?—**
**Songs for Learning Through Music and**
**Movement**
**Hap Palmer**
**Kids U.S.A.**
**Cassette**
**Lyrics and Activity Booklet included**
**Ages 2½–6**

This Hap Palmer collection of songs for fun and learning, targeted at preschoolers, can be used by either parents or teachers. Hap's musical genius and his dedication to creative movement (he has a masters degree in Dance Education) make this a wonderful way to use musical activities with children. The title song is a clever riddle that will elicit many giggles. "Let's All Clap Our Hands Together" encourages clapping, shaking, bouncing, swinging, swaying and hopping. There are two songs about colors, "Parade of Colors" and "Put A Little Color On You," and two songs about the alphabet, "Bean Bag Alphabet Rag" and "Pocket Full of B's." Other songs include "Following You," "Everyone Can Be a Helper," "Say the Opposite," "Stepping Out on the Town," "Animal Quiz" and "Weekly Rap." For more Hap Palmer recordings please see pp. 48–50, 168–173, and 221–222.

**GETTING TO KNOW MYSELF**
**Hap Palmer**
**Educational Activities**
**LP/Cassette**
**Lyrics included**
**Ages 2½–5**

Although originally for classroom use, this recording is also wonderful for home. A song called "Sammy" is probably one of Hap's best known; teachers throughout the country know and use this movement song. Sammy imagines going to the store by hopping like a bunny, swimming like a fish and crawling like a bug. This, like many of Hap's other songs, speaks of children's self-esteem and encourages them to feel good about themselves. "Feelings" is another sensitive song that encourages children to identify and express emotions such as happy, sad, angry, sleepy and funny. Other songs include "Touch," "Shake Something," "The Circle," "Turn Around Circle Game," "Left and Right," "Be My Friend," "What Do People Do," "The Opposite" and "Change." This is a great recording to use on rainy days at home or for parties and playgroups.

**CIRCLE OF FRIENDS**
**Parachute Express**
**Walt Disney Records**
**Cassette/C.D.**
**Lyrics included**
**Ages 2½–5**

The original music written and performed by the Parachute Express shows an understanding of young children's physical and emotional development. The key in which they sing is easily accessible to young voices, the tempos are appropriate for movement by young bodies, and the lyrics and sense of humor appeal to kids. This collection of movement-oriented songs includes "Circle Of Friends," "Wiggle Your Bones" (sure to evoke giggles and rollicking fun), "Down on the Farm" and "Going On A Lion Hunt." Other contagious songs include "Baby Of Mine," "Walkin' in My Neighborhood," "When You Come over to My House," "Good Morning, Neighbors," "La-La Man," "When I Build My House" (a wonderful song to act out), "Red Means Stop" and an instrumental song called "Circus." This recording is filled with hours of listening and movement fun.

★★★     **FEEL THE MUSIC**
**Parachute Express**
**Walt Disney Records**
**Cassette/C.D.**
**Lyrics included**
**Ages 2½–5**

The Parachute Express has developed a popular following through their association with Gymboree, a nationwide franchise that teaches young children gymnastics and movement activities. Their wonderful music is now available to everyone through Walt Disney Records. The original music is lively and upbeat; the vocals by Donny, Stephen, and Janice are harmonious and retain their interest after repeated listening. Much of their material is movement oriented, so it's wonderful for activity time at home, playgroups and schools. In the title song, children are encouraged to feel the music as they stretch, jump and run. "I Like You" is a darling song about friendship. "Bubbles" shows all the different ways you can pop a bubble. "World of Make Believe" is a creative song about acting and sounding like a train, truck, plane and rocket ship. Other fun songs include "Time to Get Ready to Go," "These Hands," "Good Night, Moon" (a salute to the book by Margaret Wise Brown), "Kickin' the Can" (an instrumental selection), "Put Your Finger On," "Who Am I," "Color Song," "Dance, Puppet, Dance." A very satisfying and entertaining recording.

**HAPPY TO BE HERE**
**Parachute Express**
**Walt Disney Records**
**Cassette/C.D.**
**Lyrics included**
**Ages 2½–5**

Parachute Express' experience in working with children over the years enables them to provide quality and entertaining movement music. The length and content of their songs reflect their dedication to their targeted audience. This offering of their magical recordings contains twelve original songs that invite movement and listening activities with an upbeat, harmonious and contempory sound. The title song allows children to add their own names to the music, and "I Go to School" is a great song about growing up. "What Will I Take to the Moon" is another participatory song in which different things are suggested to take on a journey into space. As each new item is mentioned, it is added to the chorus, which grows delightfully longer and longer. See how well your memory works. "Smooth Movin' Boogie Express" is a dance tune wherein all parts of the body have an opportunity to boogie. Other songs include "The Changing Garden of Mister Bell," "Polka Dots, Checks and Stripes," "Ups and Downs," "My History" (another song about growing up), "Willy Fall Down" (a tongue twister song), "As Long as We're Together" (a loving look at friendship) and "Friendship Chain" ("grab a hand and pass it on"). Even though many of the songs will get your children moving, this is a worthwhile recording to use in your car, as the listening songs are equally engaging. Parachute Express is a group that your children should experience, either on a recording or live. Watch for them in your town.

**SUNNY SIDE UP**
**Parachute Express**
**Walt Disney Records**
**Cassette/C.D.**
**Lyrics included**
**Ages 2½–5**

More delightful music from the ever exciting Parachute Express is found in this treasury of activity and sing-along songs with a contemporary sound and safe movement actions. The group is musically superb, and their voices are always varied and interesting. The instrumental piece on this recording is "Riggedy Jig." "Can You Show Us?" encourages children to be frogs, birds and fish. "Fantasy Automobile" is a silly song in which kids can drive away in their imaginations. "Birthday Cake" is a great way to pretend to do the cracking, pouring, stirring, spreading and blowing required to make and eat one. "Doo-Wacka-Doo" is a very silly song that will make little children giggle every time they hear it. Others include "Around The Block," "Butterfly," "You and Me Parade," "Sunny Side Up," "I Can Do That," "Goo-Goo-Giggly-I-Oh" (about babies), "The Shapes Game" and "Bye-Bye Pizza Pie." This recording provides hours of rewarding listening.

**THE CAT CAME BACK**
**Fred Penner**
**Oak Street Music**
**Cassette/C.D.**
**Lyrics included**
**Ages 2½–5**

This is the first in a series of popular recordings by Fred Penner, a Canadian performer who is finally and deservedly becoming a household name in the U.S. His wit, charm and talent are evident in his recordings. This recording, like others, has songs that cover many age ranges and thus is good for families with more than one child. The orchestrations are folksy and varied. The title song has become Penner's unofficial theme song and is great fun to play. Other songs include "I Had A Rooster" (and the rooster pleased me), "Sandwiches," "Winken, Blinken and Nod," "Ghost Riders in the Sky" (for the older crowd), "It Ain't Gonna Rain No More," "Little White Duck," a very long "Story of Blunder" which involves story and song, and two more. Watch for Fred on cable T.V. More recordings by Penner are on pp. 92–93, 177, 222, and below.

**COLLECTIONS**
**Fred Penner**
**Oak Street Music**
**Cassette/C.D.**
**Lyrics included**
**Ages 2½–6**

This live recording with Fred Penner and his band includes the most popular songs from four of his previous albums. It is great fun and includes plenty of action songs. Since this is a live concert, the sound of children in the background can be conducive to your child's participation. You don't hear the kids during the actual cuts, only between them. The title song about things kids like to collect, is new. Other songs are "The Cat Came Back," "A House Is a House for Me," "Ghost Riders in the Sky," "Marvelous Toy," "Poco," "If I Knew You Were Coming," "Car, Car Song," "Roller-skating," "Sandwiches," "The Bump," "Teagan's Lullaby," "Otto the Hippo" and "Holiday." A worthwhile recording!

**FRED PENNER'S PLACE**
**Fred Penner**
**Oak Street Music**
**Cassette/C.D.**
**Lyrics included**
**Ages 2½–6**

Fred Penner has his own television program with the same name as this recording, produced in Canada, which can now be seen in the U.S. These eighteen selections combine original with traditional songs. Penner's voice is clear and easy to sing with. Some of the more exciting songs include "E Compare" (sung in Italian), "We're Gonna Shine" (sung in English, French and Spanish), "Keemo Kimo" (a song full of funny sounds), "Rhyme a Word or Two" (very clever and fun), "Jim Along Josie," "10 in the Bed" and "Rock A Little, Baby." Some of the songs, such as "I Am The Wind" and "A Father's Song," are really beautiful, but may be hard for a child to identify with. Overall, however, this is a fun and inviting recording.

★★★    **A HOUSE FOR ME**
**Fred Penner**
**Oak Street Music**
**Cassette/C.D.**
**Lyrics included**
**Ages 2½–5**

This is my favorite Fred Penner recording. He presents some original as well as classic children's songs, both with exciting musical arrangements. This collection is specifically directed to preschoolers, and the songs invite singing and active participation. The title song comes from the popular children's book called "A House Is A House For Me." It's a wonderful piece about all those things that are houses for other things: a shoe or a boot is a house for a foot, a book is a house for a story, and so on. "Skip To My Lou" is rousing and exciting. Other well-known favorites, sung with real pizzazz, are "Camptown Races/Oh Susannah," "Grandma's Glasses," "Hush Little Baby," "There's a Hole in the Bottom of the Sea," "This Land Is Your Land," "The Ugly Duckling" (from *Hans Christian Andersen*), "Cowboy's Lament/Home on the Range," "Michael Row The Boat Ashore," and more. A really fun recording.

**POCO**
**Fred Penner**
**Oak Street Music**
**Cassette/C.D.**
**No lyrics included**
**Ages 2½–6**

This second recording previously entitled "The Polka Dot Pony" by Fred Penner is lively and entertaining. The songs are for many age groups and, as in other Penner recordings, individual tracks are for more sophisticated children and others for younger kids. Penner's musical arrangements are very creative and his voice is inviting. "If I Knew You Were Coming, I'd Have Baked a Cake" is a rousing introduction to the recording. "Li'l Liza Jane," although a folk dance, has been beautifully adapted for young children. Penner presents a particularly pleasing arrangement of "Joshua (Fought The Battle of Jericho)" and sings "The Cat Came Back." The story of "Julie Gerond and the Polka Dot Pony" is very long. Other songs include "Piggyback Ride" (a song you can use while giving a piggyback ride to your child), "The Bump," "Poco" (about a dog), an instrumental piece using an African kalimba, "Never Smile At A Crocodile," plus "Roller Skating" and "The Rattlin' Bog," an adapted version of the cumulative Irish song.

★★★     **BABY BELUGA**
**Raffi**
**Shoreline/MCA**
**Cassette/C.D.**
**Lyrics included**
**Ages 2½–6**

Raffi is an incredible success story in children's music. His amazing career began in Canada, where several of his records went "gold" before many people had heard of him in the U.S. His recordings eventually did become available in the U.S., and his immediate success here was hastened by media reviews, word of mouth and timing. Although preceded by other successful children's performers, Raffi's relationship with the media helped propel him into the spotlight. Raffi had performed as an adult folksinger for many years, but when encouraged by his then wife Debi Pike, a teacher, to work in her school with children, he found a new and satisfying career in children's music. With the help of teachers and friends, he collected and wrote some wonderful children's music. His recordings showcase his mellow and inviting voice, simple yet interesting accompaniments, and an exciting variety of songs. Ken Whiteley often accompanies him, additionally creating a dynamic duo. Any Raffi album is a great recording.

This is Raffi's fourth album, and it evinces continued growth and strength of musical accomplishments. The title song, a delightful and loving exploration of this wonderful mammal, has become a classic among young children. "Day O," while not sung with the pizzazz of Harry Belafonte, is fun and catchy. The African lullaby "Kumbaya" and Raffi's original song "Thanks a Lot" are caring and soothing, while "This Old Man" is uplifting and lively. In addition to traditional songs, he concentrates his efforts on newer songs about friendship, ecology and living harmoniously in this world. This recording includes one of my favorites called "All I Really Need" ("is a song in my heart, food in my belly and love in my family"), a song you'll catch yourself singing throughout the day. Another beautiful message is conveyed in "To Everyone in All the World" (sung in English and French). Other songs include "Morningtown Ride," "Joshua Giraffe" (a story song), "Over in the Meadow," "Biscuits in the Oven," "Oats and Beans and Barley" and an instrumental selection called "Water Dance." The message of this recording is love. More Raffi recordings are on pp. 95–98, 183–184, and 223.

**CORNER GROCERY STORE**
**Raffi**
**Shoreline/MCA**
**Cassette/C.D.**
**Lyrics included**
**Ages 2½–5**

This is the third of Raffi's recordings. Although the collection of songs is varied and interesting, the accompaniments and arrangements are less imaginative than on some of his other offerings. Among more interesting songs are "Cluck, Cluck, Red Hen" (with new verses to "Baa Baa Black Sheep" that enumerate the products we receive from the sheep, hen, cow and bee), "Les zombis et les Loups-Garous," (a French call and response song), "Swing Low Sweet Chariot," "Jig Along Home" (a Woody Guthrie song) and "Goodnight, Irene," Leadbelly's famous song with some new verses about where animals sleep. There is no age definition in this recording; again, you'll find some songs for the very young and others for older children. Three more of the eighteen songs are in French, "Frère Jacques," "Y' a un rat" and "Sur le pont d'Avignon." Other songs include "Going on a Picnic," "Corner Grocery Store," an instrumental version of "Rock-A-Bye Baby," "Pick a Bale o'Cotton," "You'll Sing A Song and I'll Sing A Song," "Boom Boom (Ain't It Great to Be Crazy)" and "There Came a Girl from France."

**MORE SINGABLE SONGS**
**Raffi with Ken Whiteley**
**Shoreline/MCA**
**Cassette/C.D.**
**Lyrics included**
**Ages 2½–5**

Raffi's second collection of songs has selections for very young children as well as songs for much older children, which means that you'll use the recording for a long time. This contains Raffi's popular "Shake My Sillies Out" (a wonderful movement song) and "Six Little Ducks." There are the traditional songs (with enticing new arrangements): "Who Built The Ark," "Workin' on the Railroad," "New River Train," "You Gotta Sing (When the Spirit Says Sing)" and the French "Les Petites Marionettes." There's a Brazilian song (sung in English) called "Sambelê" and seven more. Raffi's voice is addictive, and Ken Whiteley's voice and musical accompaniments are delightful.

★ ★ ★          **ONE LIGHT, ONE SUN**
**Raffi**
**Shoreline/MCA**
**Cassette/C.D.**
**Lyrics included**
**Ages 2½–5**

This is one of Raffi's finest collections because the arrangements are varied and exciting, the songs have their roots in
different cultures, and the general message is one of peace and
understanding among people. The recording has a full and satisfying sound. Raffi has never sung better, and the vocal
accompaniments are very pleasing. There isn't one boring song
on this recording. Original songs include "Time to Sing" (a
contagious movement song), "Riding in an Airplane," "The
Bowling Song," "Like Me and You" (Raffi salutes children
around the world by singing their names and different countries of origin) and the title song, which speaks of love and
sharing the planet. Some of the traditional songs include,
"Down on Grandpa's Farm," "Twinkle, Twinkle, Little Star,"
"Tingalyo," "Fais Dodo" (French), "Octopus's Garden" (made
popular by the Beatles), and "Apples and Bananas" (a rollicking song where the sounds of the words change in each
verse by inserting different vowels—for example, using the
letter "e" . . . I like to eet, eet, eet eeples and baneenees). Raffi
has done a super job with "De Colores," one of the most popular Spanish-language children's songs in the world. (I'm proud
to say I taught it to him.) Although sung in Spanish, the lyric
sheet provides the English words. This recording is sure to
thrill you and your children.

★ ★ ★          **RAFFI IN CONCERT**
**Raffi**
**Shoreline/MCA**
**Cassette/C.D.**
**Lyrics included**
**Ages 2½–5**

This collection should really be called "The Best of Raffi," as
it includes his most popular and well known songs. It was
recorded live in concert, so you'll hear the audience partici-

pate (a great encouragement for children who are reluctant to sing along). The recording is well produced and maintains a high quality of sound. The all-time favorite songs include "Time To Sing," "Tingalayo," "Rise and Shine," "Five Little Ducks," "Bathtime," "Apples And Bananas," "De Colores," "Day O," "Knees up Mother Brown," "Like Me and You," "Baby Beluga," "Shake My Sillies Out," "All I Really Need," a medley of "He's Got the Whole World/One Light, One Sun/This Little Light Of Mine" plus "The More We Get Together" and "Everything Grows." If you must choose one Raffi recording, this is probably it. There are so many other great songs on other recordings, however, that you might want them for home use and this one to play in the car. A video of this concert is also available from A&M Records. If your children are Raffi fans, the video and recording are going to be favorites.

**RISE AND SHINE**
**Raffi**
**Shoreline/MCA**
**Cassette/C.D.**
**Lyrics included**
**Ages 2½–5**

Join Raffi and Ken Whiteley in such great participation songs as "I'm in the Mood" (for singing, clapping, whistling and stomping), "Wheels on the Bus," "Walk, Walk, Walk" and "Something In My Shoe." Raffi and a children's chorus also perform a lovely version of "Thumbelina" from *Hans Christian Andersen* as well as "He's Got the Whole World in His Hands." Raffi's ecology song, "Big Beautiful Planet," conveys an important message. The French songs include "Michaud" and "Tête, Epaules" (head and shoulders,) sung in both French and English. He includes such favorites as "Row, Row, Row," "This Little Light of Mine (I'm Gonna Let It Shine)" and "Five Little Ducks." Raffi does a number of "duck" songs, and each is different, so don't be confused by similar titles. The seventeen selections include a "Nursery Rhyme Instrumental" medley. All in all, this recording is appropriate for a wide range of ages.

### SINGABLE SONGS FOR THE VERY YOUNG
**Raffi**
**Shoreline/MCA**
**Cassette/C.D.**
**Lyrics included**
**Ages 2½–5**

*Singable Songs* is Raffi's first recording and one of his most popular. Because of most of the songs' content, we like to recommend this for toddlers to age four. Often his music is bought for newborns because it is the only recording and performer many people know. This recording has some of his most popular songs, including "The More We Get Together," "Down by the Bay" and "Willoughby Wallaby Woo" (a silly song that uses children's names in funny rhymes). There are wonderful versions of "Going to the Zoo" and "Aikendrum." One of my favorites is "Old McDonald Had a Band," a delightful new rendition of the classic children's song. There are even some winter holiday songs, "Must Be Santa" and "My Dreydel." The original songs, "Brush Your Teeth," "I Wonder if I'm Growing," "Peanut Butter Sandwich" and "The Sharing Song," show the concern, humor and love that Raffi's music radiates. This recording also includes "Baa, Baa, Black Sheep," "Bumping Up and Down" (in my little red wagon), "Spider on the Floor," "Mr. Sun," "Five Little Pumpkins" and "Robin in the Rain." Because of the clarity of his voice and music, Raffi's recordings are wonderful for children learning English as a second language.

### MISTER ROGERS NEIGHBORHOOD: YOU ARE SPECIAL, WON'T YOU BE MY NEIGHBOR?, LET'S BE TOGETHER TODAY and A PLACE OF OUR OWN
**Fred Rogers**
**Family Communications**
**LP/Cassette**
**Lyrics included**
**Ages 2–4**

Mister Rogers is an institution in children's television programming. His warm manner and sincere explanations have helped children to grow emotionally over the many years of his show.

Rogers has surrounded himself with top-notch child development specialists, and subsequently his lyrics discuss very real issues that affect young children. These four recordings contain songs from his program. He introduces each one with simple, comforting language, and then presents them in the same uncluttered way they are on the show. My children loved the fact that Mister Rogers offers unconditional love and respect, and I love the fact that things move at a thorough and deliberate speed. These are not high-tech recordings nor do they have an upbeat sound; they are Mister Rogers doing what he does so well—teaching children to respect themselves.

*You Are Special* contains "You Are Special," "Children Can," "You Can Never Go Down the Drain" (very useful for children who are having trouble with potty training), "Just for Once," "You Have to Learn Your Trade," "Hopping and Skipping Music," "Troll Talk," "Days of the Week," "You've Got To Do It," "Marching Music," "We Welcome You Today," and two songs in French, "Il y' avait une fois" and "J'aime prendre un bain."

*Won't You Be My Neighbor?* contains "Won't You Be My Neighbor?" (the theme song from the show), "Some Things I Don't Understand," "Everybody's Fancy," "You're Growing," "Exercise Your Eyes," "Going To Marry Mom," "When the Baby Comes," "Be Brave, Be Strong," "Sometimes People Are Good," "I Like to Take My Time," "It's You I Like," "Tree Tree Tree" and "It's Such a Good Thing."

*Let's Be Together Again* contains "Let's Be Together Today," "The Clown in Me," "Everything Grows Together," "Parents Were Little Once Too," "Alphabet Song," "One and One Are Two," "What Do You Do?" "Please Don't Think It's Funny," "I Hope It Will Rain," "I'm Taking Care of You," "I'm a Man Who Manufactures," "I Like to Be Told" and "Peace and Quiet."

*A Place of Our Own* contains "A Place of My Own," "It's Such a Good Feeling," "You Are Pretty," "A Lonely Kind of Thing," "Wishes Don't Make Things Come True," "You Will Not Go," "A Handy Lady and a Handy Man," "I Did Too," "Wake Up Sounds," "Look and Listen," "Propel Propel Propel Your Craft," "Many Ways to Say I Love You" and "I Need You."

**THE PAW PAW PATCH**
**Phil Rosenthal**
**American Melody**
**Cassette**
**No lyrics included**
**Ages 2½–5**

Phil Rosenthal, a master mandolin and banjo player, presents some of the most popular children's folk music. His voice is inviting and pitched perfectly for little voices. The musical arrangements are full, yet never overbearing. Songs include "Six Little Ducks," "Mary Had a Little Lamb," "Looby Loo," "Polly Wolly Doodle," "I'm a Little Teapot," "This Old Man," "Are You Sleeping?" "Skip To My Lou," "Horsey, Horsey," "When I First Came to This Land" and "Paw Paw Patch." On some songs, Rosenthal is accompanied by very pleasing children's voices. This recording is especially enjoyable because of the mandolin, an instrument many children may not have heard before.

**TURKEY IN THE STRAW—**
   **Bluegrass Songs for Children**
**Phil Rosenthal**
**American Melody**
**Cassette**
**No lyrics included**
**Ages 2½–6**

If you like banjo, mandolin, guitar and wonderful vocals, this recording of mostly traditional children's folk music is for you. Rosenthal is a master musician, with a pleasing voice that is never overpowered by the orchestrations. Among the familiar songs are "Ain't Gonna Rain No More," "Bingo" (with new words by Rosenthal), "Riding in the Buggy," "Twinkle, Twinkle Little Star," "Aiken Drum," "Little Liza Jane" and "Turkey in the Straw." Original material includes "Snowy Day," "Sailing in the Boat" (new words by Rosenthal), "Listen to the Bluegrass" (bluegrass fans will love this piece) and "Open Up the Window, Noah." A very rewarding and fun recording.

**OSCAR, BINGO AND BUDDIES**
**Kevin Roth**
**Marlboro Records**
**Cassette**
**No lyrics included**
**Ages 3–6**

Kevin Roth's voice is full, melodic and inviting. His accompaniments include a mountain dulcimer, piano, guitar, drums and banjo. Put these together and you have a collection of traditional children's music, presented in authentic folk fashion. The collection includes "I've Been Working on the Railroad," "She'll Be Comin' 'Round the Mountain," "It Ain't Gonna Rain No More," "Oh Suzanna," "The Green Grass Grows All Around," "He's Got the Whole World in His Hands," "Animal Fair," "Old McDonald Had a Farm," "Do Your Ears Hang Low," "You Are My Sunshine," "Bingo," "On Top of Old Smokey," "This Old Man" and many more. I am uncomfortable with this recording because of the inclusion of "Ten Little Indians," a racist song by most current standards. There is no reason to include this type of stereotypical song. There is also a song called "Burglar Man," which is an old folk song that basically tells of a burglar entering a house to find an "old maid" who is bald, and wears a glass eye. He says he'd rather die than marry her. While this is from the folk tradition, I find it hard to understand why it was chosen when there are thousands of less offensive songs around. This is a perfectly wonderful recording, aside from the two aforementioned songs.

**UNBEARABLE BEARS**
**Kevin Roth**
**Sony Kids' Music**
**Cassette/C.D.**
**Lyrics included**
**Ages 2½–5**

This is an excellent selection of songs about bears and more bears. Roth's soft, inviting voice is perfectly suited for singing about lovable bears of all kinds. Clear and easy musical arrangements are suitable for active or quiet time listening. I particularly love Roth's version of "Teddy Bear's Picnic" because the rhythm and tempo conjure up visions of marching bears. "That Bear Makes Me Crazy" is about a mischievous bear at school, and the only non-bear song, "The Garden," is based on Arnold Lobel's story about Frog and Toad. Other songs include "Honey Bear," "Oh Let Me Be Your Teddy Bear," "The Show Biz Bear," "The Bear You Loved," "You Are You" and five more. Everyone needs songs about bears, and this is the best collection yet. More recordings by Kevin Roth are discussed on pp. 28–29, 191–193 and 224.


★ ★ ★     **LATE LAST NIGHT**
          **Joe Scruggs**
          **Educational Graphics Press**
          **LP/Cassette**
          **Lyrics included**
          **Ages 3–8**


This is one of those recordings that really gives you your money's worth with its eleven creative, innovative and fun-filled songs to delight you and your children. Scruggs' warm and inviting voice is coupled with imaginative musical arrangements and a sparkling sense of humor. Side A has four original songs that invite active participation. "Late Last Night" inspires children to move like a ballet dancer, ice skater, motorcyclist, cowboy, roller skater, tap dancer and more. "Wiggle in My Toe," one of my favorites, is a cumulative song about not being able to sit still because you have a wiggle in your tummy, knee, seat, feet, and toe. I find myself singing this catchy song at very strange times. "Ants in My Pants" is a long song that evokes many kinds of amusing movements. Other whimsical songs include "Grandma's Sleeping in My Bed Tonight," "Please Don't Bring a Tyrannosaurus Rex to Show and Tell," "Grape Jelly Cure," "The Other Shoe" (about that chronic lost shoe), "Peanut Butter" and "Belly Button" ("I found a button, but it's not from a shirt. I found a button, but it's not from a skirt. I found a button: it's a part of me. It's the button in the middle of my tummy"). "What Do They Do with the Children?" is a sensitive song about the fear of getting separated from an adult while in the market or store. Although many of these songs are quite long, small children love the humor and respect that

Joe Scruggs imparts. Many of these songs are great for teachers to use in their preschool or elementary classrooms as group sing-alongs or for choral groups. I recommend his recordings whenever I do workshops for parents and teachers because Scruggs' music is so accessible. Joe Scruggs is a brilliant talent! For more Joe Scruggs recordings, see pp. 195–197, and 225.

**TRAFFIC JAMS—**
>     **Songs for the Car**
**Joe Scruggs**
**Educational Graphics Press**
**LP/Cassette**
**Lyrics included**
**Ages 2½–5**

Joe Scruggs is a man with a wonderful sense of humor and an animated and spirited voice. This collection of mostly original songs is perfect for travel since all the lyrics are about the things that could and do often happen while in a car. Scruggs' wit will tickle funnybones and give children a sense that adults can understand some of their issues. "Buckle Up," sung from a child's point of view, talks about making sure everyone uses their seat buckles, and "Under Your Bed" deals with nightmares in a positive way. "Car Seat Exercise" invites kids to partake in a rock-style movement activity while riding in their car seats. "Big Tow Truck" is sung to the tune of "This Old Man," but is a whimsical fantasy song about a tow truck, a forklift and a pickup truck. Other songs that have new adaptations include "Pat-A-Cake," "This Little Piggy" and my favorite, "The People in the Car" (sung with fabulous sound effects). "Are We There Yet?" is a song that adults and children can relate to, each in their own way. Other fun songs include "Speed Bump Blues," "Raindrops and Lemon Drops," "Evening Breeze Lullaby," "Goo Goo Ga Ga" and "In the Freezer." Joe Scruggs' soft, clear voice combines nicely with varied and interesting musical arrangements.

★★★ **AMERICAN FOLK SONGS FOR CHILDREN**
**Pete Seeger**
**Smithsonian/Folkways**
**LP/Cassette**
**Lyrics included**
**Ages 2–6**

This is the definitive collection of American folk music for children. When Pete sings and plays banjo, love, warmth and a sense of humor are evoked. He asks children to join along and sing with him, and few can refuse the offer. He is such a master banjo player that sometimes you think you hear other voices or instruments, when in fact it's just Pete and his banjo. This treasure includes "Bought Me a Cat" (and the cat pleased me), "Jim Crack Corn," "Train Is A-Coming," "This Old Man," "Frog Went A-Courting" (with great animal sounds), "Jim Along Josie" (a lively movement song), "There Was a Man and He Was Mad" (after he sings the song through the first time, he omits words and invites the kids to insert them), "She'll Be Coming 'Round the Mountain," "Clap Your Hands," "Billy Barlow" and "All Around the Kitchen." This recording has been extremely popular with parents and teachers since it came out in 1954. I can't recommend it highly enough!

**AMERICAN GAME AND ACTIVITY SONGS FOR CHILDREN**
**Pete Seeger**
**Smithsonian/Folkways**
**Cassette**
**Lyrics included**
**Ages 3–5**

In this collection of traditional activity songs, Pete Seeger sings both a cappella and with banjo accompaniment. Some of the songs are young children's games, such as "London Bridge," "Here We Go 'Round the Mulberry Bush" and "Ring Around the Rosy." The lyrics to "Pig in the Parlor," "Jolly Is the Miller" and "Candy Gal" involve calls for square dancing. Hearing them is fun, but children's participation will be difficult if your children are not in a playgroup with other square dancers. These same songs are a bit too long for young children. Other selections include "Yankee Doodle," "Liza Jane," "Shoo Fly" and "Skip to My Lou." The songs that are performed without banjo have Pete accompanying himself clapping, which gives a certain folk sound. While the recording says that these are activity songs for young children, I feel that most of the material will be more appropriate for sing-along with older children. Other recordings by Pete Seeger are much more exciting.

### BIRDS BEASTS BUGS AND BIGGER FISHES
**Pete Seeger**
**Smithsonian/Folkways**
**Cassette**
**Lyrics included**
**Ages 3–6**

This recording contains Pete's famous story/song of "The Foolish Frog," a cumulative tale of how the farmer and all the animals get involved in a song. He also sings about the sad tale of the dog called "Old Blue," "The Fox (Went Out On A Chilly Night)," two cowboy tunes, "Little Dogies" and "Old Paint," "The Keeper and the Doe" (the keeper did a hunting go), "The Little Black Bull," "The Turtle Dove," "The Elephant," "Leatherwing Bat" and more. These songs are longer than those on *Birds Beasts Bugs and Little Fishes* and therefore are more appropriate for slightly older children. The story songs, "Foolish Frog" and "Bear Hunt," are fun to hear because Pete's voice and banjo take on the humor and mood of the stories. If you are a folk music fan, these recordings are a must for your library. They are an authentic part of the American storytelling tradition.

### BIRDS BEASTS BUGS AND LITTLE FISHES
**Pete Seeger**
**Smithsonian/Folkways**
**Cassette**
**Lyrics included**
**Ages 2–5**

Here is a classic collection of animal songs sung by Pete Seeger. Some will be very familiar, such as "I Had a Rooster" (all the sounds of the different barnyard animals can be heard), "I Know an Old Lady (Who Swallowed a Fly)," "Teency Weency Spider," "Frog Went A-Courtin'," "Skip to My Lou," "Fly Through My Window" and "The Grey Goose." The lesser known songs include "Alligator Hedgehog" (a song that lists over forty animals), "My Little Kitty," "Mister Rabbit" (a loving song about how rabbits look and live) and "Raccoon's Got a Bushy Tail." Some of these traditional folk songs discuss how animals end up on the table, such as "The Old Hen," "The Grey Goose" and "Ground Hog." These songs are part of our cultural heritage and have been sung and enjoyed for generations, so don't be alarmed. Pete's voice and banjo are very conducive to singing along. This recording has been a best seller for decades. Some of these songs have very uncomplicated lyrics, while others are a bit more difficult, so you'll be able to enjoy this offering for years as your child grows into the more sophisticated selections.

★★★     **SONG AND PLAY TIME**
**Pete Seeger**
**Folkways/Smithsonian**
**Cassette**
**Lyrics included**
**Ages 2–4**

The master of folk music shares some wonderful selections. He accompanies himself on his magical banjo and sings such classics as "Here We Go Loopy-Loo," "Skip to My Loo," "I've Been Working on the Railroad," "She'll Be Coming 'Round the Mountain" and "Go in and out the Window." He also sings an original song called "I Wonder What Tina Can Do," where you can add the name of your child, "Let Us Come In," and "Birthday Polka" (by Malvina Reynolds), "Goin' to Boston" (by Jean Ritchie) and "Red Bird" (by Leadbelly). The singing is inviting, and the lyrics encourage active participation. Pete has always made listeners feel as if he's giving a private performance for them alone, and this recording is no exception. Every child should own at least one of Pete Seeger's recordings, as his singing is what American culture is all about. Even if the folk tradition has not been part of your experience, I highly recommend this, and any other, Pete Seeger recording.

This is also a great tool for children and adults to learn English as a second language, as the lyrics are uncomplicated and repetitive and the vocals are extremely clear.

★★★     **STORIES AND SONGS FOR LITTLE CHILDREN**
**Pete Seeger**
**High Windy Audio**
**Cassette**
**No lyrics included**
**Ages 2½–6**

This cassette might be called the "Best Of Pete Seeger," as it contains some of Pete's most popular children's songs and stories. The original story songs "Foolish Frog" and "Abiyoyo" are each over seven minutes long, but are engaging and have become classics in American storytelling. "Abiyoyo" is a cumulative story song about a giant, and was one of my favorite stories to listen to as a child. The same was true for my kids. Pete sings "Green Grass Grew All Around," "Mister Rabbit," "Skip to My Lou," "Frog Went A-Courting," "She'll Be Coming 'Round The Mountain," "I Know An Old Lady" and "Raccoon Got A Bushy Tail." His banjo is the only accompaniment. A fabulous collection of Americana is interpreted by Pete Seeger on one magical cassette!

**HAPPY BIRTHDAY**
**Sharon, Lois and Bram**
**Elephant Records/A&M**
**Cassette/C.D.**
**No lyrics included**
**Ages 2½–5**

This popular trio from Canada are probably known best in the U.S. from their appearances on Nickelodeon Television. These extremely talented musicians and performers also have their own television show in Canada and are a delight to hear and even more fun to experience live. The music they sing is interactive and inviting to children. Their recordings have more tracks than most on the market and familiar songs are interspersed with some new or lesser known ones. Their voices and harmonies are wonderfully pleasing, and the wide variety of instruments that they use makes the arrangements exciting and never dull. Their extensive work with children in school settings in Ontario is reflected in their presentation and adaptations of children's music. If you want French songs, you can always count on Sharon, Lois and Bram, as all of their recordings have at least one song in that language.

This wild and wonderful collection of songs primarily relates to birthdays, growing up, and celebration. This group's vocal mastery as well as their animated and spirited arrangements resound with full strength in this recording. There are songs about birthdays: "Happy Birthday to You," four versions of a "Happy Birthday Jig," "The Unbirthday Song," "Birthday Hallelujah" and "Happy Birthday Waltz." Songs about growing up include "Being Five," "I'm Five," "When I Was One" and "Turn Around." There are international birthday songs: "Las Mañanitas," "Charoumena Genethlia," "Sto Lat," "Petit Papa" and "Tsu Dayn Geburtstog." There are fun songs for celebration: "I Had an Old Coat," "Puff the Magic Dragon," "Sarah the Whale," "Boomps-a-Daisy," "Jock-a-Mo" and "We're All Together Again." There are even songs about eating: "If I Knew You Were Coming I'd've Baked a Cake," "Fish and Chips and Vinegar," "Apples, Peaches, Pears and Plums," "Everybody Eats When They Come to My House," and more. All in all, this is an eclectic and fun collection of songs for all kinds of celebratory occasions. For more Sharon, Lois and Bram recordings, see pp. 109–114.

**IN THE SCHOOLYARD**
**Sharon, Lois and Bram**
**Elephant Records/A&M**
**Cassette**
**No lyrics included**
**Ages 3–6**

Although the title has the word schoolyard in it, don't let that keep you from using this recording at home with your children. It has twenty-seven fun fingerplays, tongue twisters, and songs from other cultures. The tongue twisters are performed by children's voices and are great fun to play. Some of the activity fingerplays include "Where Is Thumbkin?" "Pufferbel-

lies," "You Can't Make a Turtle Come Out," "Punchinello 47"
(an English game) and "Stone Games," which requires more
than two people to play (on the beat of the music, stones or
sticks are passed until the music stops). There are songs from
Ghana, Latin America and Trinidad. Sharon, Lois and Bram's
versions of "La Bamba" and "Un Elefante" (Spanish version of
their popular "One Elephant") are wonderful ways to share
songs in Spanish with your child. Some of the songs about love
and friendship include "It's a Small World" and "Love Some-
body/A Bushel and a Peck." A booklet gives a wealth of information about the songs they sing plus activities for you and
your children. Another winner from Sharon, Lois and Bram.

**MAINLY MOTHER GOOSE—**
**Songs and Rhymes for Merry Young Souls**
**Sharon, Lois and Bram**
**A&M Records**
**Cassette**
**No lyrics included**
**Ages 2–4**

Imagine more than forty Mother Goose songs on one
recording! This delightful trio brings new life to some old
favorites by adding new and updated lyrics, by performing
medleys, and by combining music with the spoken word. This
is a fantastic collection of well-known children's songs, mostly
derived from Mother Goose nursery rhymes. The arrangements are innovative, the talent is immeasurable, and charm
is exuded on every song. This is an all-around recording that
can be used again and again. Two of the medleys are "Miss
Muffet/Eensy Weensy Spider," and "Three Little Kittens/Pussy
Cat, Pussy Cat/Hickory, Dickory, Dock/Three Blind Mice." Also
featured are such favorites as "Pop! Goes the Weasel," "Mary
Had a Little Lamb" and "Jack and Jill," plus many, many more.
Some of the songs are sung by children.

**ONE ELEPHANT, DEUX ÉLÉPHANTS**
**Sharon, Lois and Bram**
**Elephant Records/A&M**
**Cassette**
**No lyrics included**
**Ages 2½–5**

This particular cassette was Sharon, Lois, and Bram's first recording and contains some of their more familiar songs, including "Skinnamarink," "Tingalayo" and "One Elephant, Deux Éléphants." Many children accompany Sharon, Lois and Bram in singing "Turkey in the Straw," "Five Little Monkeys," "She'll Be Comin' 'Round the Mountain," "Looby Loo," "Paw Paw Patch," "Candy Man, Salty Dog" and in chanting the playground rhymes "Cookie Jar (Who Stole the Cookies)," "One Potato, Two Potato" and "Going To Kentucky." Some of these playground chants may be too hard to actually do with very young children, but the rhymes are fun for them to learn. There are a total of thirty-two songs and activities for children.

**ONE, TWO, THREE, FOUR, LOOK WHO'S**
**COMING THROUGH THE DOOR—**
  **Live in Concert with the Mammoth Band**
**Sharon, Lois and Bram**
**Elephant Records/A&M**
**Cassette**
**No lyrics included**
**Ages 2½–5**

This is a recording of a 1982 concert in Ontario, Canada. If you have nothing else by Sharon, Lois and Bram, this could be considered a "best of" recording. Many of the songs have appeared on previous recordings, such as "Where Is Thumbkin?" "Skinnamarink," "Little Tommy Tinker," "Candy Man, Salty Dog," "Pufferbellies" and "One Elephant, Deux Éléphants." Since it was recorded live, plenty of directional information is given by the performers, which is a nice detail, but the sound quality is not as clear and crisp as on studio recordings.

SINGING 'N SWINGING
Sharon, Lois and Bram
Elephant Records/A&M
Cassette
No lyrics included
Ages 3–5

The twenty-five international songs and chants on this recording represent fewer familiar songs, but no less exuberant renditions, than on other Sharon, Lois and Bram recordings. "The Cat Came Back," "Waddaly Atcha" (one of their trademark songs) and "Yes Indeed" (a gospel-type song that encourages kids to dance and move) are among my favorites because they typify the diversity of this trio—always new, original and exciting to hear. The group incorporates authentic musical styles from many cultures. "The Very Best Band" singles out the different sounds and instruments of a band (including piccolo, trumpet, drum and tuba), and "The Muffin Man" has a great fiddle accompaniment. As usual, children recite and sing on this recording. These twenty-five songs give many hours of pleasurable music.

★★★  SHARON, LOIS AND BRAM SING A TO Z
Sharon, Lois and Bram
A&M Records
Cassette/C.D.
No lyrics included
Ages 2½–5

Bravo again to Sharon, Lois and Bram for a clever and eclectic collection of songs from A to Z! The children who participate on this recording are stellar and encourage young listeners to join them. The musical arrangements and harmonies are outstanding. When you purchase any recording by this wonderful trio, you can be sure you'll never get bored. They introduce songs and rhymes from different cultures such as "Tzena, Tzena," "'R' Con 'Rr'" (a rhyme in Spanish), "Les Petits Poissons," "Caballito Blanco" (sung in Spanish), and "Kiddy Kum Kimo." Other songs include "Alphabet Medley" ("Alphabet Song," "ABC Jig"), "Spelling Medley" ("Lollipop," "Cute Little Rhyme," "S-M-I-L-E," "W-A-L-K Walk," "Bingo"), "The Name

Game," "Baby Face," "Mairzy Doats," "Little Sir Echo," "On the Sunny Side of the Street," "Down in the Valley," and a rollicking "XYZinnamarink" that uses a xylophone, yodeling, and a zither. This group never becomes tiresome because they keep their music new and varied. A real treat! I was fortunate enough to see them live in concert on their A–Z tour, and they presented one of the most professional and entertaining concerts I have ever seen. They are alive and always in touch with their audience. Watch for them in your town. It's definitely worth a long drive to let your children have the opportunity to experience them in person!

**SHARON, LOIS AND BRAM'S ELEPHANT
SHOW RECORD
Sharon, Lois and Bram
Elephant Records/A&M
Cassette
No lyrics included
Ages 2½–5**

This recording contains twenty-four new (and not so new) songs from Sharon, Lois and Bram's *The Elephant Show*. Except for the traditional "One Elephant Went Out to Play" and "Skinnamarink," these songs are new and delicious. "Jelly, Jelly in My Belly" is an adorable song where kids can add their favorite foods to those already in the song, and "Going To The Zoo," using varied tempi and creative vocal arrangements, describes the animals in the zoo. Other rousing songs include "Ten in the Bed," "Everybody Happy," "Where's My Pajamas?" "Take Me Out to the Ballgame/Bravo, Bravissimo" (with a tricky change of beat) plus "Three Craw," " Ballin' the Jack," "Wheels on the Bus" and more. Some of the quieter songs are "Go To Sleep Now, My Pumpkin" and "There's A Little Wheel A-Turning In My Heart." A wonderful collection, including children's voices, from a wonderful trio.

★★★  SMORGASBORD
Sharon, Lois and Bram
Elephant Records/A&M
Cassette
No lyrics included
Ages 2½–5

This is one of my favorite Sharon, Lois and Bram recordings. The twenty-six songs are singable, laughable, dancable and great fun. As the cover states, this is "a musical feast for the whole family." The title song "Smorgasbord" is a delightful view of foods from different cultures; "Che Che Koolay" is a movement song sung in different African countries; and "Sur le pont d'Avignon" is a traditional French song. "Peanut Butter" is one of the most requested songs in our store. "Rags" is a participation song about a dog called Rags. Their version of Ella Jenkins' "Did You Feed My Cow" is upbeat and lively, and "Jenny Jenkins" is a fun song about colors. This talented trio always sounds like they're having a great time, and that contagious feeling comes through on each of their recordings. Some of the sillier songs include "Michael Finnegan (Begin Again)," "John Jacob Jingleheimer Schmidt" and "Long Legged Sailor." The instrumentation (particularly the drums) and arrangements are superb. As usual, Sharon, Lois and Bram's voices are sublime. They also incorporate each others' names into many of their songs, which encourages kids to add their own. Although you could close your eyes, pick any one of their many recordings and be very happy, this is the one I would say you shouldn't be without!

★★★  STAY TUNED
Sharon, Lois and Bram
Elephant Records/A&M
Cassette
No lyrics included
Ages 2½–5

A collection of twenty-three energetic and rousing songs from *The Elephant Show*. I can't recommend this group strongly enough. Their vocal and musical arrangements are extremely varied, and they have a tremendous range of styles. The gospel sound is magical in "We're Gonna Shine." "How Much Is That Doggie In The Window" uses different dog species as background lyrics in a tremendously clever way. "The Galaxy Song" and "Lots of Worms" are songs about science, and old favorites (with new arrangements) including "Rock Around the Clock," "All Around the Kitchen," "Hot Time in the Old Town Tonight" and "The Hokey Pokey" will make kids (and adults) boogie. "Shoo-Fly Pie" sounds so sweet that you actually may want to bake it. "Breakfast Bowl" is a silly song about what kids might like to have for breakfast. The songs incorporate children's voices and encourage listeners to add their own verses. A happy and intoxicating recording that will be played for hours.

★ ★ ★          **FREE TO BE . . . YOU AND ME**
              **Marlo Thomas and Friends**
              **Arista Records**
              **Cassette/C.D.**
              **Lyrics included**
              **Ages 3–8**

This classic recording should be in every home and school and library in the country. Although recorded many years ago, the songs and stories endure and are important for every generation. Marlo Thomas gathered a fine group of artists to perform original stories and songs about self-discovery, humanity and love among the races and between the sexes. The only negative comment I can make about this recording is that many adults couldn't enjoy and learn from it when we were growing up. The classic Charlotte Zolotow book *William's Doll* is sung by Alan Alda and Marlo Thomas. One of my children's favorites, "It's Alright to Cry," is sung by Rosie Grier. "Boy Meets Girl" is a riotous piece on gender issues told by Mel Brooks and Marlo Thomas. "When We Grow Up" is sung by Diana Ross, and "Housework" is delightfully told by Carol Channing. "Parents Are People" (about all kinds of parents and what they do) is a great song by Harry Belafonte and Marlo Thomas. Other fun and thought-provoking songs and stories include "Free To Be . . . You and Me" (The New Seekers), "Don't Dress Your Cat in an Apron" (Billy De Wolfe), "Helping"

(Tom Smothers), "Dudley Pippen and the Principal" (Billy De Wolfe, Bobby Morse and Marlo Thomas), "Sisters and Brothers" (the Sisters and Brothers), "My Dog Is a Plumber" (Dick Cavett), "Atalanta" (Alan Alda and Marlo Thomas), "Grandma" (Diana Sands), "Girl Land" (Jack Cassidy and Shirley Jones), "Dudley Pippen and His No-Friend" (Bobby Morse and Marlo Thomas) and "Glad to Have a Friend Like You" (Marlo Thomas). A fabulous recording that will get you singing, listening and thinking!

★★★    **FREE TO BE . . . A FAMILY**
       **Marlo Thomas and Friends**
       **A&M Records**
       **Cassette/C.D.**
       **Lyrics included**
       **Ages 3–12**

Marlo Thomas has again produced an exciting collection of poems, stories and songs about modern-day living styles and issues. Some top recording artists and actors have participated in this delightful recording, based on the book with the same title. Christopher Cerf, a bright shining star in creating brilliant projects for children and adults, helped write many of the pieces and collaborated with Thomas on this recording. Their combined talent makes this a winner. There is a sequel to a piece done on *Free to Be . . . You and Me* with Mel Brooks and Thomas as babies who meet in the park. This is a very silly and fun dialogue. Robin Williams tells the story of "The Day Dad Made Toast," a rib-tickling view of non-stereotyped gender roles in a family, and Steve Martin recites one of my favorite poems by Judith Viorst called "Somethings Don't Make Any Sense At All" about a new baby in the house. Whoopi Goldberg performs her own creation called "Doris Knows Everything" about how a young girl and her friend perceive what the welfare office is like. Christopher Reeve, Elaine May and Mike Nichols collaborate on "And Superboy Makes 3" about being adopted. "Another Cinderella" is a feminist view of growing up told by Marlo Thomas, Bea Arthur, Jane Curtin and Gilda Radner. Some of the delightful songs are: "The Stupid Song" sung with great enthusiasm by Ladysmith Black Mambazo; "I'm Never Afraid (To Say What's on My Mind)," my favorite, sung with soul by Bonnie Raitt; "Jimmy Says," a song about peer pressure sung by Pat Benatar; "Yourself Belongs To You," a rap piece by The Fat Boys; "The Turn of the Tide," sung by Carly Simon and many more. Hours of thought-provoking fun and entertainment.


★ ★ ★      **FAMILY FOLK FESTIVAL—**
             **A Multicultural Sing-Along**
             **Various Artists**
             **Music for Little People**
             **Cassette/C.D.**
             **Lyrics included**
             **Ages 2½–8**

An all-star group of performers present a fabulous collection of folk songs from different parts of America, the Caribbean, South America and Africa. Although many of these songs will be unfamiliar, they are easy to learn. John McCutcheon sings a wonderful version of "Skip To My Lou" with a plethora of verses. "Little Red Caboose" (complete with train sounds) and "Ise Oluwa" are sung by Sweet Honey in the Rock. "Humpty Dumpty" is delightfully performed by Taj Majal. Pete Seeger sings "I Had A Rooster" and "I've Been Workin' on the Railroad." Maria Muldaur engages young singers with "The Circus Song" and "The Garden Song (Inch By Inch)." A wild and silly song called "Colors" is sung by Lillian Allen. Doc Watson does a down-home version of "Grandfather's Clock," and "El Gallo Pinto" is beautifully sung by Claudia Gomez. The Smothers Brothers sing a cute song called "Honesty Is the Best Policy," and "Puff the Magic Dragon" is sung by a child named Amber McInnis. This is a great collection of songs by a great collection of performers.


             **GRANDMA'S PATCHWORK QUILT**
             **Various Artists**
             **American Melody**
             **Cassette**
             **No lyrics included**
             **Ages 3–6**

In what is fast becoming a familiar format, several children's performers have combined their talents to present a collection of fun stories and songs. This collection is appropriate for a wide range of ages, so you'll get lots of mileage for your money. The recording features "Zip-A-Dee-Doo-Dah" sung by Cathy Fink, "Three Blind Mice" sung by Jonathan Edwards, "The Pumpkin Man" sung by John McCutcheon, "I'm a Little Cookie" sung by Larry Penn, "A Duck Named Earl" sung by Phil Rosenthal, "Oh Susanna" sung by Jonathan Edwards, "You Can't Make a Turtle Come Out" sung by Cathy Fink, "Down the Mountainside We Go" sung by Naomi Rosenthal, "On My Grandma's Patchwork Quilt" sung by Larry Penn, "The Awful Hilly Daddy-Willie Trip" sung by John McCutcheon, and "Buffalo Gals" sung by Cathy Fink. The artists accompany each other in these musical arrangements, so you really get a feeling of a family kind of recording.

**IN HARMONY—VOLUMES I AND II**
**Various Artists**
**Volume I—Warner Brothers**
**Volume II—Columbia Records/Music for Little People**
**Cassette**
**No lyrics included**
**Ages 2½–6**

This series was one of the first to invite many recording artists to perform on the same album. Volume I was done in conjunction with *Sesame Street*. The musical talent is unequaled, and, although most of the songs were written by the performers and are thus unfamiliar, they are nevertheless terrific. The age ranges of the songs is vast, so you will get lots of mileage from these two recordings. They are upbeat, of high quality, sensitive and fun. If any of these artists appeal to you, than you'll love these recordings.

VOLUME I contains "Wynken, Blynken and Nod" by The Doobie Brothers, "Jelly Man Kelly" by James Taylor, "Be with Me" by Carly Simon, "Blueberry Pie" by Bette Midler (one of my favorites), "Share" by Ernie and Cookie Monster, "One Good Turn" by Al Jarreau, "I Want a Horse" by Linda Ronstadt and Wendy Waldman, "The Sailor and the Mermaid" by Libby Titus and Dr. John, "Pajamas" by Livingston Taylor, "A

Friend for All Seasons" by George Benson and Pauline Wilson, "I Have a Song" by Lucy Simon and "In Harmony" by Kate Taylor and the Simon/Taylor Family.

VOLUME II contains "Nobody Knows but Me" by Billy Joel, "Sunny Skies" by James Taylor, "The Owl and the Pussycat" by Lou Rawls and Deniece Williams, "Reach Out and Touch (Somebody's Hand)" by Teddy Pendergrass, "Ginny the Flying Fish" by Janis Ian, "Here Comes the Rainbow" by Crystal Gayle, "Splish, Splash" by Dr. John, "Some Kitties Don't Care" by Kenny Loggins, "Maryanne" by Carly and Lucy Simon, and the ever popular "Santa Claus Is Comin' to Town" by Bruce Springsteen.

**KIDS IN MOTION**
**Various Artists**
**CTP/Youngheart Records**
**LP/Cassette**
**Lyrics and Activity Sheet included**
**Ages 2½–5**

This is the soundtrack recording from the video of the same name from Playhouse Video. All of the songs are movement oriented and are performed by many talented recording artists. The activities are well conceived and safe for young bodies. Since many of the songs have vocal instructions, the children are also building their listening skills. This is a fun recording that will keep kids on their feet. The title song is sung by the Temptations. Greg and Steve have written and produced many of the songs on this recording, including "The Body Rock," "The Freeze," "Animal Action" and "Shadow Dancing." These are also available on their previous recordings. Other action-packed songs include "Beanbag Boogie," "Tummy Tango," "Count Balance" and "Body Talk." More lively recordings by Greg and Steve are on pp. 73–78 and 224–225.

**MOTHER GOOSE PRESENTS ALL-TIME
   FAVORITES**
**Various Artists**
**Brentwood Music**
**Cassette**
**Lyrics included**
**Ages 2½–5**

This recording features a children's chorus singing some of the
most popular children's songs. It contains a "split track" feature, where you can tune out the voices or the instruments and
hear just one part. The musical arrangements are not very
interesting, but many people like the sound of a children's
vocal group. The recording is generally acceptable, but in
comparison with other versions of the same songs, these are
somewhat lackluster. The songs (repeated in the "split track"
format on Side B) are "London Bridge Is Falling Down," "Skip
to My Lou," "Reuben, Reuben," "The Farmer in the Dell," "The
Muffin Man," "She'll Be Comin' Round The Mountain," "Are
You Sleeping?" "B-I-N-G-O," "Three Blind Mice," "Oh!
Susannah," "Row, Row, Row Your Boat," "This Old Man,"
"Lightly Row," "Itsy, Bitsy Spider" and "Old MacDonald."

**PANCAKES—A Batch of Fun Songs for Kids**
**Lois Young**
**Sony Kids' Music**
**Cassette/C.D.**
**Lyrics included**
**Ages 2½–5**

Lois Young, featured in this collection of fifteen original sing-
along songs, has a high pixie-like voice that is always animated and energetic. The title song will become a favorite of
all those pancake-loving children. "Runny Nose," sung in a fun
nasal style, discusses all those wonderful things that you have
to deal with when you're a child and have a runny nose. "I
Can't Sleep" is about procrastination. "Toot Toot Rumpy Dum
Dum" is a delightful song about playing instruments. Other
songs include "Counting Your Toes," "Feathers" and "Holding
Hands." Young's enthusiasm is sometimes excessive, but overall
this is a professional cassette.

**YOU'RE MY FRIEND**
**Lois Young**
**Pepperpot Children's Productions**
**Cassette**
**No lyrics included**
**Ages 3–5**

This recording contains fifteen more original songs by Lois Young. Her voice has a wide vocal range and is the kind you might hear in a Broadway musical. The musical accompaniments are full and varied. Some of the lyrics are a bit tiresome, but in general the songs are spirited and fun. "Baby Jazz" is a clever scat piece that readily involves children. Some of the other songs include "Mailman's Coming" (in a forced calypso style), "Wake Up" (the trials and tribulations of getting up in the morning), "Blow Me A Kiss," "Excuse Me," "Sharing" and "At The Zoo."

# Music for School-Age
# Children
# (Ages 4–10) ♫..

This age encompasses many social as well as physical changes. Children can now participate in more group activities and as they get older want to take part in more peer activities. They are less self-centered and very much aware of the world around them. Their vocabularies have developed substantially, and their sense of humor now reaches into another sphere. Riddles, tongue twisters and words with double meanings are an endless source of delight, as are word games and coded languages. Their socialization and motor skills are more complex and complete. As they learn to read, their imaginations are given wings. Some can sit for longer periods of time. They have more social consciousness now and want to know and understand things about their environment and the state of the world.

Starting at about age four, the media and advertisers will have a profound effect upon your children. Up until this age (if you're lucky), children will listen to music that you choose for them. Now is the time when your influence could easily be overpowered by the likes of Ninja Turtles or another current fad. It's very important to maintain your own personal direction. Most of the recordings listed in this book will never get media advertising (unless some smart publishers wake up and see the great marketing possibilities). When you shop for music, whether in person or by mail, you may want to include your child in the buying process. Depending on his age and maturity, give him several choices, and either explain to him or have him read about those particular recordings. You can discuss the contents and the performing artist. Now, more than before, he can be included in the decision process. You must remember to keep this experience a pleasurable one and realize that your child's taste may not be your own. Don't give him a choice if *you've* already decided what he is *going* to have.

At our store, for children eight and up, many parents seem worried that the only things their kids will listen to is music from the pop culture. This may in fact happen with many children; however, many more are still eager to hear music about things that are relevant to their lives and ages. Artists such as Peter Alsop, Dan Crow, Barry Louis Polisar and Joe Scruggs really talk to kids in a way that is direct but never condescending. Children who have been consistently exposed to a variety of musical styles and formats will keep treasuring them as they continue to grow. My two children heard music from many cultures and a variety of performers over the years, and now, as adults, they both have a wide range of musical tastes, as evidenced in their separate massive collections of recordings. This chapter is full of varied styles and musical tastes; there is something for every listener. Many songs deal with topical issues. There are some real treasures here. Enjoy!

## DO:

- Find music that relates to your child's interests.
- Include your child in the buying decisions.
- Talk with kids about the messages in the songs.
- Look for more complex orchestral arrangements and movement activities.
- Look for longer, more substantial lyrics.
- Find humorous recordings.
- Suggest that your child use music either for or as part of a school project.

# DON'T:

- Stop bringing home children's music.
- Give in to the marketers and advertisers.
- Give in on sharing your cultural heritage and musical tastes with your child.
- Forget about classical and folk music.
- Stop singing.
- Forget to look through other chapters for selections of interest to a broad age range.

★★★     **PLUGGIN' AWAY**
        **Peter Alsop**
        **Moose School Records**
        **Cassette**
        **Lyric sheet with guitar chords and activities
          included**
        **Ages 4–10**

Peter Alsop has an incredible rapport with school-age children. His lyrics reflect the humor and concerns that children experience, often touching upon such serious subjects as child abuse and terminal illness. He has a Ph.D. in educational psychology, and his recordings are excellent helps in the transition from childhood to pre-adolescence. Alsop and young friends present thought-provoking and fun songs. Musically, this is one of Alsop's most interesting efforts. The activity sheet gives parents and teachers lots of things to talk about and do with kids. "That's My Thang!" is a wonderful song about things that kids like to do. "Safari" is goofy and gross, sure to bring on a lot of laughs. "If I Was in Charge" expresses both the child's as well as the adult's point of view. "No One's Normal" discusses differences from burping to allergies to missing a little toe. The most poignant song on this recording is "Gotta Lotta Livin' to Do," which describes a child's uncle who is HIV-positive. Peter sings this powerful song with a child, and gives factual information about this horrible virus and about living with and relating to people who have the disease. Sung in a question and answer format, we hear "What Is AIDS? It's a virus bug. What can you do? Well, I give'm a hug. You hug your friend?

Sure, and he hugs me. But aren't you scared? Well, I used to be. . . . Where's the AIDS? It's in his blood. What if he bleeds? We patch him up." I have listened to this song several times and am always moved and impressed with both the accurate and important information disseminated and the sensitivity of the music and lyrics. Ry Cooder accompanies Alsop on this piece, a song that all children and many adults should hear. "Under the Rainbow" is a lovely piece about taking care of the planet. Other songs include "New Games," "High Standards" (about grades), "Hyperactive," "Heal the Bay" (about the environment) and "What If?" Alsop's messages are compelling and passionate.

**IN THE HOSPITAL**
**Peter Alsop and Bill Harley**
**Moose School Records**
**Cassette**
**Lyrics and guitar chords included. Activity**
    **and information book "A Guide for**
    **Parents, Nurses and Others Who Care"**
    **available**
**Ages 3–10**

This is a very important recording. Alsop and Harley have written a story and some songs about what it is like to be in the hospital. Peter comes to visit his friend Bill, who has just had an emergency appendectomy. While there, Peter has an accident that lands him in the bed next to his friend. They meet other young patients with different medical problems. As in both these talented artists' other recordings, the lyrics are poignant, fun and thought-provoking. Musically, they are varied and bear repeated listenings. One of my favorite songs is "If It Doesn't Have Me." Bill wonders what the world is like with him in the hospital. "Is an airplane an airplane if it doesn't have wings? Is a song really there if nobody sings it? If it doesn't have branches, can you call it a tree? Is it really my family if it doesn't have me?" "Let's Face It" is a song about how friendship isn't about how people look. "My Little Clock" is sung to those doctors and nurses who don't take into account a child's questions and needs while performing medical procedures. "Inspection!" makes fun of all those things that one must endure while in the hospital. "A Friend Like Me" is a riotous song that shows how a friend can try to cheer you up. "While I'm Sleepin'" addresses how children can confuse going to sleep with "sleep" as it relates to death. There are a few clever stories, and many more informative, entertaining and sensitive songs. This should be available in every pediatric hospital ward and pediatrician's office. The book, written in cooperation with several medical professionals, has phenomenal information.

**STAYIN' OVER**
**Peter Alsop**
**Moose School Records**
**Cassette**
**Lyric sheet with guitar chords and activities**
    **included**
**Ages 4–10**

This recording contains more songs about self-esteem, communication and topical issues by Peter Alsop and friends. "Bigger, Bigger, Bigger" describes how children sometimes feel overpowered by adults and how talking can sometimes help the situation. "You're Okay" explores the differences and things that are wrong with each of us. "Where Will I Go?" is a song about dealing with death. Although this sounds morbid and strange, it is an issue for children as well as adults, and Alsop treats it with respect. "I Cried" is a tender song about divorce. "Aaargh!" expresses the frustration of feeling that you have to be "good" all the time. Other songs include "If You Love a Hippopotamus," "Us Kids Brush Our Teeth," "No Excuse T'Use Booze," "Dear Mr. President" and "Go To Sleep You Little Creep." Many of Alsop's songs are good for prompting discussions, and his activity guide helps parents and children deal with many topics.

**TAKE ME WITH YOU**
**Peter Alsop**
**Moose School Records**
**Cassette**
**Lyric sheet with guitar chords and activities
   included**
**Ages 4–10**

Alsop presents another lively collection of songs, accompanied
by children's voices, with silly and serious messages. All kinds
of answers to kids' questions are dealt with in "Logical," while
"Take Me with You" gives parents many reasons to *not* leave
the kids at home. In "Animal Crackers," Alsop sings of all the
zany ways these creatures get eaten. "Let 'Em Laugh" teaches
children how to preserve self-esteem. "Letter to Mr. Brown"
describes children's sad feelings that their male teacher can't
hug them or physically touch them (in good ways) anymore,
due to the backlash of the child abuse issue. Other songs
include "Chickens For Peace," "Kid's Peace Song," "It's No Fun
When Ya Gotta Eat an Onion," "He Eats Asparagus," "Irish
Seatbelt Jig" and "Gnarly Dude."

**WHA'D'YA WANNA DO?**
**Peter Alsop**
**Flying Fish Records**
**Cassette**
**Lyric sheet with guitar chords and activities
   included**
**Ages 4–10**

Alsop uses simple musical arrangements and a marvelous
group of children to present these mostly original songs. One
of his more famous songs, "I Am a Pizza," is about imagination. "Bored, Bored, Bored" gives children ideas on how to
keep themselves busy. "No One Knows for Sure" encourages
kids not to give up. It describes some unfortunate situations,
including a child entering a hospital for more tests, but says
"No one knows for sure . . . no one knows for sure." "Don't
Trick Your Dad," a very age-appropriate song, explains why
certain pranks aren't funny. "My Body" is about learning to say
"no." "You Get A Little Extra When You Watch TV!" delivers

an important message about the physical hazards of watching
TV. Two of the more outrageous songs, written by Barry Louis
Polisar (see pp. 179–183), are "I Wanna Be a Dog" and "My
Brother Threw Up on My Stuffed Toy Bunny." Other fun songs
include "Wha'd'ya Wanna Do?" "Slap Hands," "Sandwiches,"
"Yecch!" "Be Gentle" and "Robin."

**HAPPINESS CAKE**
**Linda Arnold**
**A&M Records**
**Cassette/C.D.**
**Lyrics included**
**Ages 3–6**

Linda Arnold and friends provide pleasurable singing and listening. Many songs incorporate lively sounds, such as "Dr.
DoReMi," "Abazaba Scooby Dooby," "Barnyard Talk," "Hippo
Hurray" and "Bumble Bee Boogie." Songs about feelings and
love include "One Earth," "Thank You," "If You're Happy,"
"Love," "There's a Lot of Magic in Tears," "Be a Friend" (sung
a cappella by children), "Happiness Cake" and "Our Family."
"Mamma Don't Allow" is a wonderful traditional song that uses
homemade instruments. (Be sure to see Thatcher Hurd's beautiful book of this song.) Arnold's version of "Puff the Magic
Dragon" is a real treat. Her voice is the perfect pitch for young
voices to sing with, and her musical arrangements are lively
but never overpowering.

**MAKE BELIEVE**
**Linda Arnold**
**A&M Records**
**Cassette/C.D.**
**Lyrics included**
**Ages 3–6**

Linda Arnold's original lyrics and music are built around
themes of imagination and magic. The ideas are interesting, but
Arnold's songs encourage an interaction that makes repeated
listening especially pleasurable. "Boom Boom" is a fun song
about feelings. "Hey Mr. Spider" begins with a spider climbing

on a child and discusses the ways one might deal with it. My favorite song, "Find a Peaceful Thought," has a group of children accompanying Linda with thoughts about what makes them feel good. It's an original and warm song that can stimulate interesting conversation at home or school. Linda's version of "Zip-A-Dee-Do-Dah" is delightful. Other songs include "The Bathtub Song," "Popcorn," "Be Kind to Your Parents," "Tick Tock," "Do You Know What Magic Is?" "Magic Horse," "The Vegetable Lament," "Mommy's Lullaby," "Waiting for Baby" and "Count with Me." The voices of many children, including her daughter Katy, join Linda in this enjoyable recording.

★ ★ ★     **PEPPERMINT WINGS**
**Linda Arnold**
**A&M Records**
**Cassette/C.D.**
**Lyrics included**
**Ages 4–8**

Linda Arnold's lovely voice meshes beautifully with interesting musical arrangements in a lively presentation of imaginative songs. A children's choral group is heard throughout the recording. "Monster Day" is a clever song about silly monsters, sure to appeal to little monster types. In "Pasta" Linda sings about the different kinds of pasta that we eat: tortilini, ravioli, and more. "At the Dinosaurs Baseball Game" gives information about both. "Yam Jam" features fiddle music in a song about a potato head family. Other songs include "Mr. Wizard Lizard," "I Am a Pizza," "Please Please Hercules," "Let's Play," "Treehouse," "Read a Book," "Hello" and "I Wish I Was Magic." Linda's voice is so pleasant to hear, and her daughter Katy has a lovely voice, also. This is an upbeat and very satisfying recording to play at home or in the car. The original lyrics have young children in mind, and the melodies are easy to remember. This is my favorite of Arnold's recordings to date.

**RAINBOW PALACE**
**Linda Arnold**
**A&M Records**
**Cassette/C.D.**
**Lyrics included**
**Ages 4–8**

As you sit and listen to this delightful recording, you may sense that you're hearing the soundtrack of a Broadway play. Arnold's voice and musical style normally lend themselves to this mode, but the songs on this recording are from musical plays or are original pieces with the same flair. The recording opens with an overture and has an intermission at the end of the first side. As in her other recordings, Arnold uses children's voices as accompaniment. The arrangements sound as if a full orchestra were playing. Some of the show tunes are "Do Re Mi," "Heart (You've Gotta Have Heart)," "Oh, What A Beautiful Mornin'," "Captain Hook's Waltz," "Happy Talk" (*South Pacific*), and "I Whistle a Happy Tune." Other songs include "Bravo," "Rainbow Chorus Line," "Quite A Combination," "Big Feet" (a funny song about a child who hasn't quite grown into their feet), "Broadway Banana," "Top Hat, Bow Tie and Tails." A refreshing recording, although many of the songs are not specifically geared to children.

**ADVENTURES ON THE AIR CYCLE**
**Banana Slug String Band**
**Music for Little People**
**Cassette**
**Lyrics included**
**Ages 5–10**

The Banana Slug Band consists of four male musicians, songwriters and educators who have combined their talents to teach science and environmental issues through music. They are accompanied by the Slug Kids, a children's choral group. The songs are fairly long with lengthy introductions. The lyrics carefully explain the different concepts, using upbeat contemporary music. The vocals sometimes sound a bit cluttered, but overall, the recording has great educational value. The songs include "Nature Rap," "Air Cycle Swing," "Brown Air," "Lizards," "Tidepool Boogie," "Big Red Rap," "No Bones Within," "Animals," "Ecology" and "Everything Needs a Home."

**DIRT MADE MY LUNCH**
**Banana Slug String Band**
**Music for Little People**
**Cassette**
**Lyrics included**
**Ages 5–10**

This second recording from the Banana Slugs has less chatter between selections, and the overall quality is somewhat better than on their first offering. Here are more songs that will raise a child's awareness of the world around us, including "Dirt Made My Lunch," "Solar Energy Shout," "Sun, Soil, Water and Air," "Roots, Stems, Leaves," "I'm a Tree," "River Song," "Prayer Song," "Decomposition," "Banana Slug," "Newts, Salamanders and Frogs," "Bats Eat Bugs," "Nocturnal Animals," "Quail" and "With People I Like."

**SLUGS AT SEA**
**Banana Slug String Band**
**Music for Little People**
**Cassette**
**Lyrics included**
**Ages 5–10**

The Banana Slugs sing new songs about animals and issues of the oceans. Musically, this is the most interesting of the recordings by this group. Produced with the help of Project Ocean, this collection of original songs helps young school-age children understand our relationship to the sea and its inhabitants. The songs include "Ocean Communities," "Tidepool Boogie," "Life on the Shore," "Butts Up," "Giant Kelp Forest," "Water Cycle Boogie," "Blue Planet," "Island Rock," "Estuary Life" and "Ocean Rap." A great choice for classroom use.

**WEE SING SING-ALONGS**
**WEE SING AMERICA**
**WEE SING FUN 'N' FOLK**
**WEE SING BIBLE SONGS**
**WEE SING DINOSAURS**
**Pamela Conn Beall and Susan Hagen Nipp**
**Price, Stern, Sloan**
**Cassette**
**Lyric booklet with melody lines and activities
    included**
**Ages 3–8**

These five book and cassette packages follow the formats of
the recordings for younger children by Beall and Nipp. They
are mostly well-known songs performed by adults and children. The booklets contain lyrics and melody lines for the
music, and some include suggested activity ideas. They are a
great bargain, and you get sixty minutes of listening with each
cassette.

*Wee Sing SING-ALONGS* includes "The More We Get Together,"
"Jacob's Ladder," "The Riddle Song (I Gave My Love A Cherry),"
"Kum Ba Yah," "He's Got the Whole World in His Hands," "Make
New Friends" (a round), "Swing Low, Sweet Chariot," "Oh, Su-
sanna," "I've Been Working on the Railroad," "Clementine,"
"Sarasponda," "Now the Day Is Over," "Taps" and many more.

*Wee Sing America* includes "Yankee Doodle," "America The
Beautiful," "The Star Spangled Banner," "You're a Grand Old
Flag," "When Johnny Comes Marching Home," "Marine's
Hymn," "Anchors Aweigh," "John Henry," "Erie Canal," "Git
Along, Little Dogies" and more. There are also spoken pieces:
"Preamble to the Constitution," "Pledge to the Flag," plus
quotes from John F. Kennedy, Thomas Jefferson, Martin Luther
King and Abraham Lincoln.

*Wee Sing Fun 'N' Folk* includes "Jennie Jenkins," "Old Dan
Tucker," "Big Rock Candy Mountain," "Pawpaw Patch," "Little
Red Caboose," "Turkey in the Straw," "Buffalo Gals," "Old Joe
Clark," "Frog Went A-Courtin'" and many more.

*Wee Sing Bible Songs* includes "Jesus Loves the Little Children," "Jesus Loves Me," "Deep and Wide," "The Lord Is My Shepherd," "This Little Light Of Mine," "He's Got the Whole World," "Rise and Shine," "Praise Him, Praise Him," "Who Built The Ark?" "Little David Play Your Harp," "Heavenly Sunshine" and many more.

*Wee Sing Dinosaurs* includes fifty original songs and poems about dinosaurs: "Ankylosaurus," "Big, Bigger, Biggest," "The Brachio Limo," "Dinosaur Ages," "Dinosaur Bones," "Dinosaur Names," "Dinosaur Sounds," "Eggs," "If I Could Be a Dinosaur," "Footprints," "Little Dinosaurs," "My Tail," "Stegasaurus," "Triceratops," "What Happened? Whew!" "Who Named the Dinosaur?" and many more. More Wee Sing recordings are listed on pp. 36–37, 61–62, and 218.

**IMAGINE THAT!**
**Andrew Belling**
**Kid Rhino Records**
**Cassette/C.D.**
**Lyrics Included**
**Ages 4–8**

Belling's melodic voice and clear, imaginative musical arrangements are very inviting. His talents as a composer and songwriter come through on this recording, and many of the songs sound like they've been written for a Broadway musical. The ten original songs have a theme of imagination. One of my favorites is "Kauai Lullaby (Little Sailor)" which is a lovely lilting song that is sure to relax. "Balloonia" is a swaying song about a land where balloons go after they are released into the air. "Magic" is about learning magic tricks and believing. "Tooth Fairy" is about that elusive fairy that comes in the middle of the night and leaves a surprise under the pillow. "Drip Drop" is a gentle song about dressing appropriately for the rain. I found "Be Careful What You Wish For" to be an inappropriate song for kids. The song says that if you wish for something it will come true, and this could be very scary to young children. All children wish for things, and the beauty of wishing and imagination is that it's harmless. This song gives the opposite message and could really stifle a young person. If this recording is about imagination, why include a song that discourages it? The rest of the songs are clever and well-presented.

**SPIN, SPIDER, SPIN—**
  **Songs for a Greater Appreciation of Nature**
**Marcia Berman and Patty Zeitlin**
**Educational Activities**
**LP/Cassette**
**Lyrics included**
**Ages 3–8**

This is a wonderful collection of original songs about all kinds of insects and creepy-crawlies. Berman and Zeitlin have done many recordings together, and this is one of the most popular for older children. The topic is timely and kids really love singing and hearing about all the animals. The two most popular songs, "Spin, Spider, Spin" and "Lots of Worms," are sung in classrooms and homes across the country. The luscious voice of Dave Zeitlin truly enhances the music. Other clever and informative songs include "I Love Lizards," "Mr. Tickles" (about a turtle), "The Little Bird Is Dead," "The Way of the Bees," "Secret Is My Name" (about snakes), "Night Sounds," "Down by the Creek" and "Frogs and Crickets Lullaby." A wonderful recording for children who are interested in animals and nature. Additional recordings by Berman and Zeitlin are on pp. 12 and 62–64.

**BELLYBUTTON**
**Heather Bishop**
**Mother of Pearl Records**
**Cassette**
**Lyrics included**
**Ages 4–8**

Heather Bishop's deep, rich voice sings fun songs for kids with a sense of humor. Some of the sillier songs are "Alligator Waltz," "Bellybutton" and "If You Love a Hippopotamus." "Long Tall Texan" is a women's version of this old rock 'n' roll song. "He's My Brother—She's My Sister" playfully describes siblings that get along. Other songs are "Woodmore Polka," "From the Seed in the Ground," "Boom, Boom," "The Barn Dance" and "Lullaby Medley." Although the lyrics on most of the songs are very amusing, the musical arrangements are sometimes lackluster.

## A DUCK IN NEW YORK CITY
**Heather Bishop**
**Mother of Pearl Records**
**Cassette**
**Lyrics included**
**Ages 4–8**

A duck introduces the songs in this collection of music by Canadian Heather Bishop. Bishop's voice is deep and appealing. The songs are all original, mostly by Connie Kaldor. The sense of humor in this recording is right in sync with this age group. Most of the songs deal with issues familiar to school-age children. Excessive use of the silly duck sound is regrettable, as it is hard to understand and detracts from the music. Songs include "Betty Is Convinced That She's a Buffalo" (about the way children sometimes act), "I Want a Robot," "One Little Nose," "Nice Little World," "Slug Opera," "That Beautiful Tree," "Yakety Yak" (the piece made popular in the fifties), "Duck Rap," "Dancing Fool" and "A Duck in New York City."

## PURPLE PEOPLE EATER
**Heather Bishop**
**Mother of Pearl Records**
**Cassette**
**Lyrics included**
**Ages 4–8**

This is by far the finest recording by Heather Bishop. The musical arrangements are varied and more interesting than her other recordings. Her voice is pleasant and easy to sing with. This collection has many zany songs sure to elicit chuckles. Among the sillier songs are "The Name Game" (the song from the fifties—"banana fana fo fana"), "Purple People Eater" (still popular after all these years), "Oh No Bo" (Bo is a dog) and

"Silly Song" ("Ho Hum the tune is dumb and the words don't mean a thing"). Bishop's versions of "Ghost Riders in the Sky" and "Somewhere Over the Rainbow" are great. Other songs include "The Fairy Song," "Winter Lullaby," "The Man with the Weird Beard," "Always a Mission" and "Sugar Blues." A very satisfying recording.

**COLOR ME WILD**
**Rory Block**
**Alacazam Records**
**Cassette**
**No lyrics included**
**Ages 4-8**

Folksinger Rory Block sings mostly original songs, accompanied by guitar and rhythm instruments. Most are long and tell a story, such as "Football Toad," "Billy the Bad," "Opera Break," "The Magic Pond," "The Bear with No Hair" and "The Monkey and the Horse." I found her vocal pitch a bit low and difficult to sing with. It is hard to understand some of the lyrics and, since there is no lyric sheet included, it is difficult to follow along. Most of the songs have cute lyrics, with Rory and friends portraying different characters. Other songs include "The Papaya People," "Dressed Up," "In the Wild Landscapes," "Your Children and Mine" and "The Doctor's Call."

**PATRIOTIC SONGS AND MARCHES**
**Dennis Buck/Vocals by Al Dana**
**Kimbo Educational**
**LP/Cassette**
**Lyrics included**
**Ages 4-10**

This recording is a collection of the most popular American patriotic songs. Side A has vocals, and Side B features marches with instrumental music only. This recording was produced for classroom use, but is not limited to that use. Despite a children's chorus who joins Al Dana, the arrangements are lackluster, and one doesn't get the sense of "rah rah" that some patriotic music evokes. The marches are also lacking in energy, but would be good marching music for little bodies. The vocals include "America the Beautiful," "Yankee Doodle," "Star Spangled Banner," "God Bless America," "Yankee Doodle Dandy/ You're a Grand Old Flag," "This Land Is Your Land," "America," "My Country 'Tis Of Thee." The instrumental marches include "The Caissons Go Rolling Along," "Stars And Stripes Forever," "Battle Hymn of the Republic," "Hail to the Chief," "Pomp and Circumstance" and five more.

### LET'S CLEAN UP OUR ACT—
#### Songs for the Earth
**Ron Callinan and Ann Shapiro**
**American Melody Records**
**Cassette**
**No lyrics included**
**Ages 4–10**

This duo presents songs on important environmental issues. A great variety of instruments, including banjo, mandolin, bass (played by Phil Rosenthal), banjo, ukulele and conga drums, are put to good use. This is a fine collection of songs, but the singing is unexciting. Included here are Tom Lehrer's "Pollution," "The Garden Song (Inch By Inch, Row By Row)," "Garbage," "You Can't Eat the Oysters," "Habitat," "Who Dunnit," "Mother Ocean," "Clouds," "This Land," "Save What's Left," "Garbage Blues," "Who Will Tend My Garden" and "Let's Clean Up Our Act." This has a decidedly folksy sound. The lyrics to the songs are great and the messages are clear. This recording is recommended for children with good listening skills who are interested in the environment. Teachers will also find this good for classroom use.

### CHILDREN'S ALL-TIME RHYTHM FAVORITES
**Jack Capon and Rosemary Hallum, Ph.D.**
**Educational Activities**
**LP/Cassette**
**Lyrics and Activity Guide included**
**Ages 6–10**

This recording was produced for classroom use; however, there are some great dances and activities that are perfect to use at parties, scout meetings and other times when you need group activity ideas. Both Hallum and Capon are highly respected movement and child development specialists who have worked with children in group settings for many years. This is one of their newer recordings and will bring you many hours of movement and dancing fun. Most of the pieces are sung by either a male or female voice, and a few are instrumental. The musical arrangements are institutional sounding, but the dances represent a variety of cultures and are easy to learn. Music and instructions for many of these popular dances are not readily available, so this recording fills a gap. The activity guide provides suggestions for using these dances with physically challenged children and shows how to adapt the pieces for older children. The dances include "If You're Happy and You Know It," "Chicken Fat" (a physical education classic), "Patty Cake Polka," "Hokey Pokey," "La Raspa," "Limbo," "Bunny Hop" and four more.

★★★    KIDS SONGS—VOL. 1, VOL. 2, JUBILEE AND
            SLEEPYHEADS
            **Nancy Cassidy**
            **Klutz Press**
            **Cassette**
            **Full-color lyrics book included**
            **Ages 4–10**

Although this fabulous series of cassettes comes from a book publishing company, it truly rates among the finest in children's audio recordings. Produced by Ken Whiteley (a member of the Junior Jug Band, and co-producer and performer with Raffi), these are high quality recordings with diverse and lively musical arrangements. Cassidy's voice is deep and rich, the kind that can lull or excite at will. Children often accompany Cassidy. This collection of songs is outstanding. These will probably not be available in record stores, but most bookstores will stock this series. The full-sized book has color illustrations throughout and lyrics and melody line with guitar chords. A real value.

VOLUME I contains twenty-two songs including "Jamaica Farewell," "This Old Man," "Puff (The Magic Dragon)," "This Little

Light," "Wabash Cannonball," "Ting-a-layo," "Baby Beluga," "Kum Ba Ya," "Shake My Sillies Out," "Apples and Bananas" and "Polly Wolly Doodle."

VOLUME II contains twenty-two songs including "She'll Be Coming 'Round The Mountain," "Fooba Wooba John," "The Bus Song," "Ghost Riders in the Sky," "Michael, Row The Boat Ashore," "La Bamba" (her Spanish accent leaves a lot to be desired), "Mail Myself to You" and "He's Got the Whole World in His Hands."

*Jubilee* contains twenty-two songs including "Do Your Ears Hang Low," "Riddle Song," "This Land Is Your Land," "The MTA Song," "Tie Me Kangaroo Down Sport," "Swing Low, Sweet Chariot," "Squirming Worms," "Rubber Ducky," "When the Saints Go Marching In," "Jambalaya," "I Wanna Be a Dog" and "Going to the Zoo."

*Sleepyheads* contains twenty songs including "Amazing Grace," "The Water is Wide," "Greensleeves," "Hobo's Lullaby," "Somos El Barco," "By 'N Bye," "Danny Boy," "Time To Sleep," "Turn Around," "Shenandoah" and "Angels Watching Over Me."

★★★     **FAMILY TREE**
         **Tom Chapin**
         **Sony Kids' Music**
         **Cassette/C.D.**
         **Lyrics included**
         **Ages 4–8**

Famed folksinger Tom Chapin has written and performed some wonderfully creative songs for children. His clear voice and clever arrangements are very appealing. He has a great sense of humor, and the songs invite active participation. "Parade Came Marching" is a cumulative song in the same genre as "She'll Be Coming 'Round the Mountain." The title song is a lovely piece about each person's cultural heritage. "Uh Oh, Accident" is a lively song with humorous words that will appeal to most kids. "Nick of Time" is another song that kids will truly understand. Judy Collins accompanies Chapin on a few of the songs, and their duets are lovely. "Big Rock Candy Mountain" is a classic that doesn't appear on many recordings, and Chapin's version is terrific. "Pretty Planet" is a timely song about ecology. "Shovelling," sung in a blues format with a harmonica, is catchy and singable even if you've never had to shovel snow in your life. This is a recording well worth purchasing. Tom Chapin is great! If he's ever appearing in your town, be sure to take your whole family. He puts on a great show.

**MOONBOAT**
**Tom Chapin**
**Sony Kids' Music**
**Cassette/C.D.**
**Lyrics included**
**Ages 4–8**

This is another fulfilling cassette from folksinger Tom Chapin. Using themes familiar to young children, Chapin has composed some more delightful songs that will engage and entertain children. "The Library Song" is a clever piece about all of the characters in favorite children's books. "The Trail Song" is about a horse named Homesick, a perfect song for young cowboys and cowgirls, sung in true western style complete with yodeling. Learning the states is great fun with "State Laughs" (Ida Ho Ho Ho, Tennessee He He He). Other engaging songs include "Neat Mess," "Happy Birthday" (performed as a waltz), "Don't Play with Bruno," "Sing a Whale Song" and "You'll Come Shining Through." It's apparent Tom Chapin has a great time singing and writing music for children. His enthusiasm is contagious!

**BILLY THE SQUID**
**Tom Chapin**
**Sony Kids' Music**
**Cassette/C.D.**
**Lyrics included**
**Ages 4–10**

Tom Chapin is back with thirteen new songs sure to delight young audiences. Chapin's inviting voice delivers lots of messages about ecology and getting along with people. Rosanne Cash joins Chapin in a beautiful song called "All Of My Friends," which describes the many ways that friends can be there for one another. "The Ghost of Bleakhouse" is a clever song about a ghost who doesn't want to share his house with a group of kids. The children's voices are really cute and the message is about sharing. "You'll Be Sorry" warns a dog about things that he should watch out for. "Bye Bye Dodo" is about animals that are becoming extinct. "I Got The Blues, Greens and Red" is about things not going your way, and the range of emotions that you experience. "Bedtime Round" is a round about procrastinating at bedtime. Other songs include "'Cameling," "Sore Loser," "Happy Earth Day," "The Missing Parade," "City Lullaby" and more. A delightful recording.

★ ★ ★     **MOTHER EARTH**
         **Tom Chapin**
         **Sony Kids' Music**
         **Cassette/C.D.**
         **No lyrics included**
         **Ages 4–6**

In this collection of original songs and ditties from the ever entertaining Tom Chapin, there is an ecological theme, but it never sounds preachy or imposing. Chapin's sense of humor and clever use of the English language are refreshing and sure to please the adults as much as their children. "The Picnic of the World" lists more countries than I could count and asserts that we're all sitting on the same picnic blanket with the same set of problems. It's brilliant! Two songs about water and the sea are "The Wheel of the Water" and "Sailing to the Sea." "Good Garbage" is a witty song about recycling. Chapin has cleverly put the classic story of "Stone Soup" to music. "Cousins" is a riotous look at what can happen when cousins get together. Other ingenious songs include "Mother Earth's Routine," "Two Kinds of Seagulls," "A Song of One," "On My Way to School," "A Capital Ship," "All Through The Night" and "Thanksgiving Day." A brilliant collection from a brilliant lyricist and musician.

**ALLIGATOR IN THE ELEVATOR**
**Rick Charette**
**Pine Point Records**
**Cassette**
**Lyrics and Activity Booklet included**
**Ages 4–8**

Rick Charette has a very smooth voice and sings original music about entertaining things in an appropriate pitch for young children. Unfortunately, many of the songs sound similar, many of the lyrics have forced rhymes, and the musical arrangements are repetitive. The activity booklet is a gem, not only are the lyrics included, but many songs show how to sign some of the words, and lots of craft and activity ideas are given. The songs include "Staple in My Sock," "I Hate to Clean My Room," "I Always Leave the Crust," "Tiger's Cage" and more.

**WHERE DO MY SNEAKERS GO AT NIGHT?**
**Rick Charette**
**Pine Point Records**
**Cassette**
**Lyrics and Activity Booklet included**
**Ages 4–8**

Here are fifteen more original songs by Rick Charette. As in his previous recording, the songs all have a very similar sound. Most of the lyrics are interesting and Charette has a very pleasant voice. One of the high points in the recording is a child from Charette's native Maine country who sings his own original song about his cat named Porky. It's quite clever. The songs include "My Dog," "Waterbed Afternoon," "Missing Sock," "Baxter the Bear," "My Dad," "Broken Donuts" and more. The lyric and activity book is filled with ideas and things to do.

> 1 2 3 KIDS
> Chenille Sisters
> Red House Records
> Cassette
> Lyrics included
> Ages 4–8

Three lovely voices harmonize with upbeat, mostly original songs. The Chenille Sisters, Connie Huber, Cheryl Dawdy and Grace Morand, are a delightful trio. Their orchestrations are lively and refreshing. "The Kitchen Percussion Song" is about making music with things found in the kitchen. "At the Codfish Ball" has a big band and Andrew Sisters flavor. "Singing in the Tub" is a song that will delight young bathers. One of my favorites is "Harmony Song," which typifies their strong vocal abilities. The well-known songs are "I'm Being Eaten by a Boa Constrictor," "The Hokey Pokey" and "Russian Lullaby." Some of the lyrics are a bit forced, but the voices and arrangements are so nice that some of that can be overlooked.

> ★ ★ ★    OOPS
> Dan Crow
> Rounder Records
> Cassette/C.D.
> Lyrics included
> Ages 4–10

Dan Crow is a genuine, talented, and terrific person. He's a singer, songwriter, teacher and performer who travels around the world entertaining children in schools and family concerts. His original songs concentrate on consonant or vowel sounds, with witty lyrics that kids love singing. This recording is a compilation of a recording that Crow produced himself called *Sound Songs*. If Dan is ever in your area, be sure to see him live—there's never a dull moment. The title song, "Oops," is about always dropping things, with a wonderful whiny chorus of "Do I have to pick it up? I don't want to pick it up." "American Gum" is for all those gum chewers, and "My Mouth" is a silly description of things in and around the mouth. "Dogs," which has become a favorite of kindergarten children in our local school district, drones about those wonderful pets.

"Apples and Bananas" is the silly song using all the vowels in the alphabet. "Yambo" tells the story of a nonviolent sweet potato who's not at all like Rambo. Other "sound songs" include "I Had Ham," "Kiss A Cow," "The Beat of All Bugs," "The Ballad of Ruben Rooster" and "Miranda (Was Born In A Barn)." This recording is a fine teaching tool for children who are learning English, as well as entertaining listening for native English speakers.

**WORD FACTORY**
**Dan Crow**
**Sony Kids' Music**
**Cassette/C.D.**
**Lyrics included**
**Ages 6–10**

Previously called "Thunderwear" this recording has been updated with some new songs. In another offering of sound and wordplay songs from Dan Crow, bright and witty lyrics help teach kids about our language with lighthearted humor and fun. Although the recording says for ages ten and up, we've sold this to many happy customers as young as six. The clever verses of "Homonyms" include "I saw Jim in the gym, I heard him sing a hymn." "The Ballad of Collective Nouns" describes "a trip of goats, a knot of toads, and a troop of kangaroos" with a zany musical accompaniment. "Dirty Words" catalogs words like filth, soil, dust, mud, slime, swill and grime. "Madam, I'm Adam" teaches kids about palindromes (words that spell the same thing forwards and backwards) and a mighty guitar accompanies Dan in a get-down version of Preposition Blues." Other extraordinarily clever songs include "Adjectives And Nouns," "The Sandwich" "Screwball (Word Origin Song)," "Beautiful Words v.s. Ugly Words," "I'm A Pronoun" and more. This will bring hours of painless educational fun into your home or school. Dan Crow's holiday recording is listed on pp. 219–220.

**A FRIEND, A LAUGH, A WALK IN THE
  WOODS**
**Dan Crow**
**Sony Kids' Music**
**Cassette/C.D.**
**Lyrics included**
**Ages 4–10**

Here are thirteen more delightful sound songs from Dan Crow. The musical arrangements on this recording are fabulous, and Dan's marvelous wit comes through with his clever lyrics. "A Happy Horse" is sung with a hiccup accompaniment. "The Zucchini Song" tells of all the things that grow in a vegetable garden—tomatoes, zucchini, mushroom, zucchini, pumpkins, zucchini, onions and zucchini. For those of you who have grown zucchini, this song will be particularly relevant and funny. "Walking On My Wheels" is a great song about a child who uses a wheelchair to get around. "Forget It!" bemoans the difficulty of getting a parent's attention. "Haleakala" is a tribute to the volcano in Hawaii. Other fun songs include "Walk Outside," "I Love a Circus," "Blowing Up Balloons," "The Shape of My Shadow," "On The Move" and "To Be A Friend." A fine recording from a master performer.

**DIAMOND IN THE ROUGH**
**Charlotte Diamond**
**Diamond Records**
**LP/Cassette**
**Lyrics included**
**Ages 4–8**

Charlotte Diamond's success with *10 Carrot Diamond* is not repeated on this recording. Her voice is lovely and the musical arrangements are very good, but the majority of the songs are not very interesting. "The Hug Bug" is a cute song about using hugs to make you feel better. "When I First Came to This Land" (by Oscar Brand), "The Foolish Frog" (by Pete Seeger) and "Boa Constrictor" (by Shel Silverstein), all delightfully presented, are great sing-along songs. The "educational songs" such as "Metamorphosis," "The Days of the Week" (in English, French and Spanish), "Goin' Metric" and "What Kind Of Tree

---

Are You?" seem forced. "The Laundry" and "You Never Praise Me Enough" just seem contrived. The French collection included "Collinda" (a Cajun song), "Donne-moi la main" and "La Bastringue." Other recordings by Charlotte Diamond are on pp. 67–68.

**LITTLE HANDS—**
**Songs for and About Children**
**Jonathan Edwards**
**American Melody**
**Cassette**
**No lyrics included**
**Ages 3–6**

This is one of those recordings that you and your children will listen to for years and years. Some of the songs are long and a bit complicated, but they are true to the American folk music tradition and are engaging enough for preschoolers. Edwards' voice is delightful to hear, and the superb musical accompaniments by Phil Rosenthal (see page 210) on the mandolin and banjo are worthy of many repeated playings. The three traditional songs are "Winkin, Blinkin and Nod," "Children, Go Where I Send Thee" (worth the price of the recording!) and "Stewball." Edwards' original pieces include "My Little Girl," "Red Light, Green Light," "Little Hands," "Flies in the Buttermilk" (not the "Shoo Fly Shoo" version), "Give Us A Song," "Old Jim" and "Graceful Lullaby." This recording is an auditory delight.

**GRANDMA SLID DOWN THE MOUNTAIN**
**Cathy Fink and Friends**
**Rounder Records**
**LP/Cassette**
**Lyrics and Activity Booklet included**
**Ages 4–8**

This unique and fun recording features instruments and songs with a country, western and rockabilly sound. Cathy Fink's superb voice is matched only by her banjo playing ability. Children's choral groups and Marcy Marxer join in on many selections. The age range on this recording is very wide. Some of the songs, "Brush Your Teeth," a new and wild version of "The Jazzy Three Bears," "The Cuckoo Rock," "Peanut Butter and Jelly," and "What Does Your Mama Do," are definitely for the younger group, while many of the other songs are targeted at an older crowd. Fink is fond of yodeling, and even includes a "Yodeling Lesson" (ever hear yourself try to yodel? The kids will have a great time!). Yodeling is used in the title song, as well as in "Yodel Polka" and "I'd Like to Be A Cowgirl (But I'm Afraid of Cows)." Other songs include "New River Train," "It's A Shame," "Oh! Susanna," "A Flea and a Fly in a Flue" (a great play on words), "The Cat And the Fiddle/Briar Picker Brown" and "Little Rabbit, Where's Your Mammy?" The musical arrangements and vocals are outstanding. Instruments such as the fiddle, banjo, mandolin, harmonica, kazoo, and pedal steel guitar give this recording a distinctive style. Other recordings by Cathy Fink are on pp. 69–70.

**FOOTE PRINTS**
**Norman Foote**
**Disney Records**
**Cassette/C.D.**
**Lyrics included**
**Ages 3–8**

Another Canadian children's performer is making a big impression on the American children's music industry. Foote's voice is bold, his musical arrangements are delightful, and his original music and lyrics are entertaining. The songs are filled with humor, which may appeal to some younger children, but will definitely engage the post-preschool group. Part of the recording was taped from a live concert, so children's singing and laughing can be heard. "I'm A Book" is a clever song about why books are so wonderful, and "Raining Cats and Dogs" uses this phrase to sing about many breeds of cats and dogs. "Nursery Medley" changes the last lines to some of the well-known rhymes. Some of the other sillier songs include "He Dum Diddle Dum," "Fancy Dinner" (about what all those fancy foods look and taste like to a child), "The Eggplant That Ate Chicago," "Fascination Cafe" and "His Majesty the Baby." Other songs include "Little Armadillos," "Dinosaur and the Progress of Man," "If at First," "Johnny Cut Grandpa's Wood," "Anything Can Happen," "Ahh Song Sing-along" and "Living in a Pumpkin Shell." A decidedly upbeat recording.


> **ALL IN THIS TOGETHER**
> **Candy Forest and Nancy Schimmel**
> **Sister's Choice**
> **Cassette**
> **Lyrics included**
> **Ages 4–10**

The Singing Rainbows Youth Ensemble accompanies Forest and Schimmel in a fine collection of awareness songs about the earth and the environment. The children's chorus is a pleasure to hear, and the musical arrangements are interesting and varied. Kids can learn a lot of interesting facts while singing along with other children. The songs are: "I'm a Reptile" (a very catchy song), "All in This Together," "My Sister's a Whale in the Sea," "Who's Gonna Save the Ark?" "The Clouds," "Must Be Johnny Appleseed," "Home in the Sky," "Eating up the Forest" (the rain forest), "Lambeth Children" (written by Schimmel's mother, Malvina Reynolds), "Beulah the Beast" (a vegetarian beast), "Fix My Dog" and "My Very Tall Friend" (a redwood tree). Two songs speak out against using animals for testing, "Just Like We Do" and "Fancy Face Waltz" (about the Draize Test where rabbits are used to test cosmetics). The messages are clear in this recording, and the musical presentations are very enjoyable. Teachers will find many of the songs useful for the classroom.


> **GOOD MISCHIEF—**
> **Songs and Dances for Children**
> **Gemini**
> **Gemini Records**
> **Cassette**
> **No lyrics included**
> **Ages 4–8**

This is a live recording by a singing set of twins named Sandor and Laszlo Slomovits. Side One is a varied collection of interactive songs with lively collaborations and interruptions from the audience. The twins play fiddle and guitar, and their voices are pleasant. The songs are: "The Marvelous Toy," "Zum Gali Gali" (in Hebrew), "Oh, How Lovely" (a round), "Aiken Drum," "A Place in the Choir," "Lunch" and "I'm Gonna Tell." Side Two is a set of instrumental pieces for listening or creative movement. The songs, played on banjo, fiddle, guitar and pennywhistle, include "Fiddlesticks-Lumberjack," "Merrily Kiss the Quaker's Wife/Haste To The Wedding," "The Halting March," "Westphalia Waltz" and "Simen Tov" (the only vocal piece on this side). If your child isn't into dancing or moving to the music, the second side is a pleasure for listening only.

**GROWING UP TOGETHER**
**Gemini**
**Gemini Records**
**Cassette**
**No lyrics included**
**Ages 4–8**

Gemini's fourth recording for children has some interesting songs with varied musical arrangements, and is by far their best vocal effort. There are children's voices as well as accompaniment from the Chenille Sisters (see page 142). "Hello" is a delightful song about ways people in different countries say "hello." "Just One More" explores the universal desire for that one last cookie, pet, or ride. "Deli" describes the myriad of enticing goodies in the delicatessen. "Right Field" tells the sensitive story of a young boy trying to play team baseball. "Loose Tooth Blues" is a creative song that toothless kids will easily understand. Other songs include "This Little Light of Mine," "Prairie Lullaby," "Why Oh Why" and "Puppy Love."

**PULLING TOGETHER**
**Gemini**
**Gemini Records**
**Cassette**
**No lyrics included**
**Ages 4–8**

This third recording by the Gemini twins is definitely superior to the first two. It is more musically interesting and the recording quality is better. I like their collection of songs, but their versions are sometimes less than exciting. The songs include "Dry Bones," "Michael Row the Boat Ashore," "May There Always Be Sunshine," "Yellow Submarine," "Chiribim," "Skinnamarink," "This Land Is Your Land" and "You Can't Make a Turtle Come Out."

**SWINGIN'**
**Gemini**
**Gemini Records**
**Cassette**
**No lyrics included**
**Ages 4–8**

The knack for selecting songs that really appeal to children is evident in another collection of childhood favorites recorded at a live concert. Gemini's music is varied, using many instruments. The recording quality leaves something to be desired, a drawback perhaps due to the nature of live recording. The songs are "Magic Penny (Love Is Something)," "Old Joe Clark/ Angelina Baker" (with wonderful fiddle accompaniment), "Beans in My Ears," "Apples And Bananas," "Mama Don't Allow" (be sure to see Thacher Hurd's wonderful illustrated version of this book), "There's a Hole in My Bucket," "Skip to My Lou," "Everybody Loves Saturday Night" and more.

★★★ **AMAZING**
**Robin Goodrow and Micheal Goodrow**
**Isn't It Amazing Music**
**Cassette**
**Lyrics included**
**Ages 4–6**

This fine collection of original songs fosters positive self-esteem in children. Robin Goodrow, an Emmy award-winning children's performer, and her brother Micheal, a fabulous musician, have written and produced one of the finest and most original recordings for children! The music is upbeat, professional and exciting. The lyrics speak to children about themselves and others, always with respect and love. "The Power," a song of feeling our inner as well as outer strength, is one that kids really appreciate, both for its lyrics and its musical style. "Rainbow of Colors" (with lead vocals by Kenny Rankin) is a beautiful song about the multiethnic diversity on our planet. "Listen" is a lovely song about hearing the sounds of nature. The title song, my favorite, is a powerful piece about the wonders of people and the planet (with a guest appearance by saxophonist Richard Elliot). "Can't Stop Dancin'" is the appropriate title for a song about different musical rhythms. "Sara, Sara" is a humorous song about an active child who has a hard time sitting still. Other wonderful songs include "Why Does It Have to Hurt So Much?" "Imagination," "Knock Knock," "Hello World," "I'm Cool" and "The Chocolate Pudding Queen." A thoroughly delicious recording! I hope to see more from the Goodrows.

★★★      **YOU'RE IN TROUBLE**
         **Bill Harley**
         **Round River Productions**
         **Cassette**
         **Lyrics included**
         **Ages 4–10**

Bill Harley has a reputation as a superb storyteller and tremendously nice person. On his storytelling recordings, he always includes a couple of original songs. This fine recording is a tribute to his lyrical genius. Harley's understanding of children and their issues and sense of humor is abundantly evident. Not only do his lyrics deal with subjects that are important, but musically he captures the mood with upbeat and contemporary sounds. The title song is an all-too-true piece about a child who decides to cook up a batch of cookies to replace the ones that he shouldn't have eaten off the kitchen table. "Cool in School" is an a cappella song with many voices about peer pressure. The Coasters join Harley's great vocals and finish the song with a musical line from their hit, "Poison Ivy." One of my favorites is a long song called "Dad Threw the TV Out the Window." A father throws the TV away, so that the family can reprioritize their lives. The kids find that they can survive just fine without the tube, and then find Dad secretly watching a TV. One of the children finally throws the

TV out the window. "Family" is a great song about different
kinds of families, some intact, some separated; some traditional, some modern. "I'm Busy" is a funny song about a child
who keeps trying to warn his Dad about some horrible thing
that wants to get into the house, but the father keeps saying
he's too busy. Guess what happens to Dad? Other clever songs
include "No School Today," "If You're Gonna Be a Grub,"
"Moon and Me," "I Don't Believe It," " Watchout," and "When
You Don't Know What It Is." Be sure to listen to Harley's
storytelling recordings. They're great. Other recordings by Bill
Harley are on pp. 207 and 226.


★★★    **50 WAYS TO FOOL YOUR MOTHER**
       **Bill Harley**
       **Round River Records**
       **Cassette**
       **No lyrics included**
       **Ages 4–10**


Bill Harley is a master storyteller, musician and performer. I've
never had the honor of seeing him perform, but I've heard
from many people that he's tops. His humor and sense of
what's real in children's lives is right on target. The musical
orchestrations are fun and the lyrics are first rate. The vocal
intonations and sound effects are great. "There Goes My
Brother Again," is a song that older siblings will find all too
true. "Havin' A Party," is a good old fashioned rock 'n' roll
song about a child who's NOT invited to his parent's party, but
decides to invite himself anyway. "My Dog Sam" concerns a
dog that has died. "When I First Came To This Land" is a traditional song, where kids accompany Harley. "I'm On My Way"
is another traditional freedom song sung with real contagious
gusto. "Under One Sky" tells of all the living things that share
the earth. The title song, sung with Harley slapping and clapping his hands as the only accompaniment, is a riotous song
in which some ingenious ideas backfire when the child realizes
it's Saturday, and not a school day. Harley's energy is
astounding! "Somos El Barco/We Are The Boat," is beautifully
sung in a bilingual format. Other songs are: "Nobody Knew"
and "Mr. Spaceman." This is a phenomenal recording that will
bring your kids hours of entertainment.

## MONSTERS IN THE BATHROOM
**Bill Harley**
**Round River Records**
**Cassette**
**Brief song explanations included—no lyrics**
**Ages 4–10**

Bill Harley's magical style entertains children and parents alike. His marvelous sense of humor and his facility with language make him a delight to listen to over and over again. This recording includes a pair of story songs—"Abiyoyo," the famous story of the giant by Pete Seeger, and "The Freedom Bird," a fun story from Thailand. Most of the songs include guitar accompaniment. As this recording was produced live in an elementary school, children's voices and responses are heard. A few of the songs feature rather elaborate orchestration. Some of the zany songs include "The Billboard Song," a whimsical look at a billboard sign that has several layers of advertising showing through; "I'm Not Small," a great sing-along where children can add their own verses; "Black Socks," about socks that never seem to reach the washing machine; "That's What Friends Are For;" "When I Grow Up," a look at many possibilities of what kids can do later in life, regardless of gender or color; "What's The Matter With You," about differences in people; "Freddy The Fly Eating Frog" and the title song. Bill Harley is a fantastic performer, and his marvelous recordings are a testament to his great love of his work.

★★★     AMERICAN CHILDREN
**Richie Havens, Rory Block, Fred Koller,**
        **Happy Traum, Maria Muldaur, Taj Mahal,**
        **Peter Schickele, Rick Danko and Dave Van**
        **Ronk**
**Music for Little People**
**Cassette**
**No lyrics included**
**Ages 3–10**

A rich and bountiful collection of songs sung by a first-class group of performers. The title song, sung by Richie Havens, talks about all the different cultures that make up our great nation. Rory Block's "Papaya People" is upbeat and delightful. Dave Van Ronk, is his gruff and folksy voice, sings "I'm Proud to Be a Moose." "Jamboree," by Happy Traum, is a silly song sung in duet with Rory Block. Maria Muldaur, in her unparalleled voice, sings "Daydream." "Tyrannosaurus Rex" is a clever song by Peter Schickele. Taj Mahal brilliantly sings "Deva Devalita." Other songs include "Blue Tail Fly" sung by Rick Danko, "Lucky Ol' King" sung by Rory Block, "You Got to Relax" sung by Fred Koller, "I'll Be Your Baby Tonight" sung by Maria Muldaur, and the whole group singing "Kumbaya/ American Children." In addition to great variety of voices and styles, this brilliant recording offers messages of peace, friendship, self-esteem and other positive concepts.

**SONGPLAY HOORAY!**
**Dennis Hysom**
**Sleepwalker Productions**
**Cassette**
**No lyrics included**
**Ages 4–8**

Hysom is an extremely talented writer and performer. His voice is very pleasing and the musical arrangements are varied and interesting. In this recording, he uses traditional Mother Goose rhymes as a base and changes the words into topical lyrics that will appeal to school-age children. They will remember the rhymes and will appreciate the new lyrics. "Old Mother Hubbard" tells of Bob, who needed to get a job, and "The Ballad of Elizabeth Moo" (from "Hey Diddle Diddle") is about a cow who goes into outer space and learns from the man in the moon about keeping the earth and its inhabitants together. Other very clever songs include "Little Miss Muffet (MMMM Berry Pie)," "Jack Be Nimble, Jack Be Fun," "Twinkle Twinkle Little Car," "Pull Yourself Together, Humpty," "Take A Tip From Jack and Jill" and "Ladybug, The Famous Firefighter." A creative recording!

**THE BEST OF BURL'S FOR BOYS AND GIRLS**
**Burl Ives**
**MCA**
**Cassette**
**No lyrics included**
**Ages 3–8**

This is another nostalgic recording by another master of folk music, Burl Ives. Although recorded many years ago, the technical quality is fine and will bring you hours of listening and singing enjoyment. It's nice to hear a real orchestra instead of synthesized sounds. Burl's voice is delightful and pitched perfectly for young singers. The selections include "Blue Tail Fly," "Riddle Song (I Gave My Love A Cherry)," "The Ballad of Davy Crockett," "Polly Wolly Doodle," "Hush Little Baby," "Boll Weevil," "I Know an Old Lady," "Big Rock Candy Mountain," "Aunt Rhody," "The Fox (Went Out On A Chilly Night)," "Shoo Fly" and "Way Down Yonder in the Paw Paw Patch." These favorite songs of more than one generation will delight parents and children alike.

**THE FIFTY STATES**
**Janet and Judy**
**Janet and Judy Records**
**Cassette**
**Lyrics included**
**Ages 4–8**

Janet and Judy are twins who perform regularly in schools and have made several recordings for children. In this one, they take a bus tour through the U.S. using different states as the subjects of their songs. Done with narration and children as an audience, the songs describe sights and historical facts about selected states. The sound is "cutesy," but the information is interesting. Some of the humor may be more appreciated by adults than kids, especially if the listener is unfamiliar with some of the common jokes about certain states. The original songs include "New Yawk, New Yawk," "In the Hills of Tennessee," "Chicago Blues," "North Dakota, South Dakota," "M-i-s-s-i-s-s-i-p-p-i," "T Is for Texas," "Aloha from Hawaii," "Alaska,

Land of the Last Frontier," "On Our Way to the Rocky Mountains" and "Cali-Yeah-Yeah."

**GOOD CLEAN FUN**
**Janet and Judy**
**Janet and Judy Records**
**Cassette**
**Lyrics included**
**Ages 4–8**

This array of songs about friends, fun and staying "clean" is a new format for the twins; there is no story to follow, nor are there children as part of a play. The original and generally upbeat songs are filled with harmony. "Laugh All Your Blues Away," "Good Clean Fun" and "Too Cool" deal with staying away from drugs, cigarettes and alcohol. Other songs include "Party," "Let's Play Ball," "My Best Friend," "Sing a Song," "Dance the Doogie," "Couch Potato" and "Carnival." Of all their recordings, this is the easiest on the ears, not too contrived or full of forced audience participation.

**MUSICAL ALMANAC**
**Janet and Judy**
**Janet and Judy Records**
**Cassette**
**Lyrics included**
**Ages 4–8**

To an audience of children, each introduced by a different character, the twins sing nine original songs about science and nature. Their theme recordings can be useful for teachers who are teaching these particular subjects. The music is interesting and the information contained in the songs is current, but the peripheral elements are a bit overdone. Songs include "Thank A Plant," "Lots and Lots of Animals," "Where Does It Come From," "What's the Weather," "The Sun Story" and "Nine Planets."

**MUSICAL FITNESS**
**Janet and Judy**
**Janet and Judy Records**
**Cassette**
**Lyrics included**
**Ages 4–8**

Eleven mostly original songs about health and nutrition are presented with many spoken introductions and canned children's reactions. While the songs promote healthy eating habits and exercise, the humor makes me uncomfortable because it is so contrived. There is very little recorded music about this theme, and while it may be a bit much all at once, the information and songs are good. Teachers will find this recording of interest for classroom use. The songs include "Four Basic Foods Rap" (sung with a "valley girl" accent), "Keep the Sugar On," "Fruits and Vegetables," "Keep Movin'," "Eat Good Food" and "Get Your Rest and Exercise."

**WORDS 'N' MUSIC**
**Janet and Judy**
**Janet and Judy Records**
**Cassette**
**Lyrics included**
**Ages 4–8**

This, the earliest of Janet and Judy's recordings, has some superb music for kids, but the talking and canned children's laughter tires after repeated listening. The twins have very melodic voices and sing with nice harmonies, but at times they sound too cute. The songs are well conceived and overall the recording is a fun one. Songs include "O Susanna," "Old Dan Tucker" (sung as though they were very old people), "The Purple People Eater," "Herb the Verb," "The Antonym Song," "The New ABC Song" and "Everybody Loves Saturday Night."

**SONGS TO SING**
**Junior Jug Band**
**Pyramid Records/Children's Music Group**
**Cassette**
**No lyrics included**
**Ages 4–8**

The Junior Jug Band is a group of extremely talented Canadian children's performers: Chris, Ken, Jenny and Daniel Whiteley. They have helped to produce and have performed with the best of other Canadian performers, and have here pooled their musical talents to introduce children to a wonderful style of folk tradition. Some of the instruments that they use are harmonica, trumpet, pots and pans, jaw harp, banjo, washtub bass, washboard, cowbells, fiddle, ukulele, clarinet, mandolin, piano, organ and autoharp. This is a wonderful sing-along recording with great sounds and lyrics. The songs include "Muffin Man" (with new lyrics), "Never Swat a Fly," "Shim Sham Shimmy," "Play That Washboard," "Hobo's Lullaby" and "Barnyard Song."

★ ★ ★     **HANS CHRISTIAN ANDERSEN/TUBBY THE**
            **TUBA**
            **Danny Kaye**
            **MCA**
            **Cassette**
            **No lyrics included**
            **Ages 3–8**

This was one of my favorite recordings when I was growing up. Danny Kaye was a prominent performer who gave many programs for and with children. This recording contains selections from one of his movies, *Hans Christian Andersen*. The music and lyrics are still delightful after all these years. Songs from the movie include "I'm Hans Christian Andersen," "Anywhere I Wander," "The Ugly Duckling," "Inchworm," "Thumbelina," "No Two People" (sung with Jane Wyman), "The King's New Clothes" and "Wonderful Copenhagen." Side B has Kaye's famous version of "Tubby the Tuba," a story song that introduces children to the instruments of the orchestra, with

Danny taking all the parts of all the instruments. He's phenomenal! One of Danny Kaye's lifelong projects involved bringing children and classical music together in a fun and exciting way. Two other songs, written by his wife Silvia Fine, are performed with wit and charm: "Uncle Pockets" and "There's a Hole in the Bottom of the Sea" (a cumulative song full of fun). A wonderful nostalgic recording for young and old!

**REALLY ROSIE**
**Carole King**
**Epic**
**Cassette**
**No lyrics included**
**Ages 2½–10**

Take some of Maurice Sendak's delightful stories, rhymes and lyrics and mix them with the music and illustrious voice of Carole King, and you have a delightful recording that is considered a classic. This soundtrack from a TV special, is used by teachers, parents, librarians and others to thoroughly delight children. A fine video version from C.C. Studios is available and highly recommended. The heroine of the musical is Rosie. The stories and music come from the "Nutshell Library" of books by Sendak, which include: "One Was Johnny," a counting rhyme, "Alligators All Around," a clever look at the alphabet, "Pierre," a cautionary tale of a boy who only says "I don't care" and "Chicken Soup With Rice," a brilliant piece about the months of the year. This collection of books should be in every child's library, and this recording belongs there too. Other songs not derivative of the Nutshell Library are: "Screaming and Yelling" (sung with appropriate intonation) and "The Ballad of Chicken Soup" (complete with the appropriate "Oh Vey"). The other songs relate to Rosie's vision of life and her environment: "Ave. P," "Simple Humble Neighborhood," "The Awful Truth," "Such Sufferin'" and the title song, "Really Rosie." This is a recording that has gone out of print several times over the years, but it deserves to be available to every generation. You might want to get one before they decide to take it off the market again.

★★★     **ONE WORLD**
**Lois LaFond**
**Boulder Children's Productions**
**Cassette**
**Lyrics included**
**Ages 3–8**

This is one of those recordings that you wish you had for yourself as a child. LaFond has a sultry, inviting voice that presents incredibly imaginative musical arrangements and creative, original lyrics. The result is a recording that will make you and your children clap, sing, dance and have some great musical times. "I Lost My Shoes," done in a blues style, is about those continually lost items. "Some Days Are Happier than Others" performed a cappella, is a song we can all appreciate. "Part of the Family" talks of all the family folks, and then is sung in French, Spanish, Russian and Japanese. One of the sillier songs is "Wascaway Wabbit," with wyrics by Wois WaFond. "One World" is a call for peace, sung in English, Spanish, Russian, French, Japanese, and Chinese. Other songs include "You Can Dance," "Smile," "Raining Cats and Dogs," "Bokey," "In Control," "The Night Rides in on Ships" and "You Can Be." This recording is sure to bring hours of fun, entertainment, and positive messages to you and your family!

**HOWJADOO**
**John McCutcheon**
**Rounder Records**
**LP/Cassette**
**Lyrics and Coloring Book included**
**Ages 4–8**

*Howjadoo* is a wonderful recording of authentic folk tradition. McCutcheon's voice is a pleasure to hear and easy to sing along with. He is a versatile performer who also plays the hammer dulcimer, fiddle, banjo, guitar, autoharp, jaw harp and spoons. The title song is a Woody Guthrie classic that employs a lot of funny sounds. "Cut the Cake" is a delightful birthday song that begins with a seventh birthday. "Molly and the Whale" is a story in rhymed verse told with Holly Near, followed by a funny song called "Rubber Blubber Whale." I especially like the version of "John Henry" with banjo accompaniment; it's great! "All God's Critters," "Peanut Butter" (along with a spoken story), "Tender Shepherd," "Pap's Billy-goat" and "Father Grumble" are all folk classics. This is a fun-filled recording, sure to appeal to all those with the folk tradition in their background.


★ ★ ★     **MAIL MYSELF TO YOU**
          **John McCutcheon**
          **Rounder Records**
          **LP/Cassette/C.D.**
          **No lyrics included**
          **Ages 4–8**

McCutcheon presents another wonderful collection of traditional and original songs with upbeat, dynamic musical arrangements in a voice pitched perfectly for sing-alongs. The title song, written by Woody Guthrie, is a favorite. Traditional songs sung in nontraditional ways are "Over in the Meadow," "Hambone" (great fun to listen to and to try) and "Sly Little Crow." There are two delightful songs written by kids from Widney High School, "Teddy Bear" (a reggae song) and "New Car." McCutcheon's own songs are "The Awful Hilly-Daddy Willie Trip" (a riotous song about a trip with dad and son), "Old Blair Store" and "Kindergarten Wall." Other songs include "Somos El Barco (We Are The Boat)" in English and Spanish about the relationship between people and the oceans, "Turn Around" (written by Malvina Reynolds), "I'm a Little Cookie" and "Barnyard Dance." The exciting thing about this recording is that children can experience a variety of musical styles and types of songs along with John McCutcheon's delightful voice. A real treat!

★ ★ ★     **SHAKE IT TO THE ONE THAT YOU LOVE THE BEST—Play Songs and Lullabies from Black Musical Traditions**
**Collected and adapted by Cheryl Warren Mattox**
**Warren-Mattox Productions**
**Cassette**
**Lyrics and illustrated songbook included**
**All ages**

One day a beautiful book and cassette package arrived at our store. We were ecstatic when we opened it, listened to the cassette, and examined the full-color booklet. The songbook contains amazing illustrations by Varnette P. Honeywood and Brenda Joysmith, two fine artists. The information listed with each song helps explain where the song has come from and what kind of song it is (line dance, clapping rhyme, etc.), and all the guitar chords are shown. Men, women and children sing this rich collection of cultural songs, although some of the female voices are pitched a bit high. Taj Mahal is featured in "Hambone." The musical styles featured are jazz, reggae, gospel, rhythm and blues, and classical, and represent music and chants from the African, African-American, Creole and Caribbean cultures. The sixteen playsongs include "Loop de Loo," "Little Sally Walker," "Miss Lucy," "Mary Mack," "Bob-A-Needle," "There's a Brown Girl in the Ring," "Down, Down Baby" and "Go in and out the Window." The ten lullabies are "Fais Do Do," "Colas," "All the Pretty Little Horses," "Gone to the Mailboat," "Short'ning Bread," "Kumbaya," "Who's That?" and "Sleep, Baby, Sleep." A real treasure!

    **ANIMAL CRACKERS**
**Mary Miché**
**Star Trek**
**Cassette**
**Lyrics included**
**Ages 3–10**

Any child who likes animals will find this recording great fun. Miché has collected some of the most interesting and entertaining songs about the zoo and pets. Her arrangements are uncluttered, and her voice is fairly high pitched. This is a recording that can be used by teachers in a classroom as well as parents in the home or car. The songs include "Stewball," "My Dog Named Cat," "High Hopes," "Old Blue," "Nine Green Fingers and Forty-Seven Toes," "Puff the Magic Dragon," "Going to the Zoo," "If You Love a Hippopotamus," "Boom Boom It's Great to Be Crazy," "The Dinosaur Song" and "I Wanna Be a Dog." This is a delightful recording.

**EARTHY TUNES**
**Mary Miché**
**Star Trek**
**Cassette**
**Lyrics included**
**Ages 3–11**

This is a wonderful collection of songs about animals, insects, trees and other parts of nature. Miché's voice is basically pleasing, although sometimes pitched a bit high. The musical arrangements are simple and clear. This collection of songs is perfect for kids who are fascinated with creepy-crawlies and other interesting members of nature's family. Many of the songs have factual information. This lively assortment includes "Animal Party," "Spiders and Snakes" (my favorite), "Banana Slug Song," "You Can't Make a Turtle Come Out," "Bug Bits," "Dirt Made My Lunch," "Lotta Seeds Grown," "Six Plant Parts," "Move Over" and "You Big Trees." An educational and entertaining recording.

**KID STUFF**
**Mary Miché**
**Star Trek**
**Cassette**
**Lyrics included**
**Ages 5–12**

This silly selection of songs is sure to tickle funnybones. Using very simple accompaniments, Miché performs some of the funnier songs written for children. Although some are fairly long and the language is definitely for older children, these are the kinds of songs that kids will learn and sing to amuse their friends or present in a school play. Since Miché uses a lot of these songs in school, you can be sure that they represent some of kids' favorite silly songs. "Fried Ham, Fried Ham" is sung in several accents, hillbilly, French, English, kitty (meowing), doggy, piggy and baby. "Sarah Cynthia Silvia Stout" (by Shel Silverstein) is about a child who refuses to take out the trash. "Throw It out the Window" is an old camp song filled with word games. Other songs include "Goo Ga Gee," "The Cat Came Back," "Green And Yeller," "I Wish I Was," "Jenny Jenkins," "Fifty Nifty United States," "Hagdalena Magdalena" (a tongue twister song) and "I Want to Eat Apples and Bananas." This is the perfect recording for a child with a good sense of humor and for scout meetings and classrooms.


**NATURE NUTS**
**Mary Miché**
**Star Trek**
**Cassette**
**Lyrics included**
**Ages 4–10**

*Nature Nuts* is Miché's contribution to the current craze of ecological recordings for children. As in her other recordings, the selection of songs is fabulous and children's voices enhance the tonal quality. Although the musical accompaniments are simple, the songs are contagious and worth repeated listenings. The songs include "All God's Creatures," "Hey Ms. Spider" (by Linda Arnold), "Garbage," "Nature's Niches," "Bats Eat Bugs," "Camp Granada" (the old Allan Sherman classic), "Ally Ally Oxen Free," "Workin' Together in the Sun," "Recycle Blues" and "Pollution" (by Tom Lehrer). A fun and informative recording.

**PEACE IT TOGETHER**
**Mary Miché**
**Star Trek**
**Cassette**
**Lyrics included**
**Ages 3–11**

Mary Miché has collected and sings some of the greatest songs about peace and friendship. The orchestrations are very simple; children's voices are often used and, although Miché's is a bit high pitched on some songs, this is a worthwhile and important recording. Miché works extensively with children in schools and does workshops for teachers. She has a great sense of what works with children of this age. All children (and adults) can learn from the themes presented here. It's not a preachy recording, yet the message of getting along with one another comes through loud and clear. The songs are "Chickens for Peace" (by Peter Alsop), "Use A Word" (by Red Grammar), "The World Is a Rainbow" (by Greg Scelsa of Greg and Steve), "Mir, Peace," "Friends Forever," "Dona Nobis Pacem," "Yambo" (a Dan Crow song), "Down by the Riverside," "I'd Like to Teach the World to Sing," "We Are the World," "Shalom Chaverim," "Let There Be Peace on Earth," "Hands," "Find A Peaceful Thought" (by Linda Arnold), and more. This recording can be very useful to teachers as well as to parents.

★★★     **A KID'S EYEVIEW OF THE ENVIRONMENT**
**Michael Mish**
**Mish Mash Music Records**
**Cassette**
**Lyrics and Activity Guide included**
**Ages 4–10**

Children help introduce each song on this recording by relating their feelings about ecological and environmental issues. Their open and honest discussions speak to children of all ages and set the perfect stage for Mish to follow with some poignant songs. His lyrics are fresh and informative, and his musical arrangements are varied and interesting. Michael's voice is easy to listen to and his diction easy to understand. Children often accompany him with the vocals. This recording has high educational value, but also provides pleasurable listening. It is a very popular recording in our store. I love the song "Write To Your Senator," which tells how our government works; Mish encloses a sample letter for kids to explain their feelings to the elected officials. "Trash in the River" is a catchy tune about how the trash moves around. "Greenhouse" is about the Greenhouse effect. Other topical songs include "Recycle It!" "If You Find a Penny," "Something's Happening," "Oil on the Water" and "My Electric Car." A great recording for the whole family to share. Other recordings by Michael Mish are on page 25.

**WE LOVE THE ANIMALS**
**Michael Mish**
**Mish Mash Music Recordings**
**Cassette**
**Lyrics and Activity Booklet included**
**Ages 4–10**

Michael Mish presents his songs about protecting and caring for the animals in the world. As in his other recordings, the selections are educational and entertaining, and convey a clear message. The songs are clever, with witty and stimulating lyrics and varied musical arrangements. The activity booklet lists ten things kids can do to help save the environment, and also enumerates some endangered animals. Mish is a master of sounds, and the sound effects on this recording are fun. The songs include "Coup de Cluck," "Betsy Bovine," "Dolphin Song," "Charlie the Elephant," "Gorilla Walk," "Harp Seal" and "Bird Song." This recording can be very useful at school as well as home. There are lots of things kids can learn with this toe-tapping tape.

★★★      **I'M BLUE**
         **Michael Mish**
         **Mish Mash Music Records**
         **Cassette/C.D.**
         **Lyrics included**
         **Ages 4-10**

Musically and lyrically, this is a truly great recording. Michael
Mish's devotion to quality children's music and the environment is reflected here. I haven't heard many recordings that
give children an entertaining and educational perspective of
the earth and the solar system the way this one does. Each
song is introduced by a group of children who give their opin-
ions on what something is or what something means. The kids'
answers are delightful and funny. Children often accompany
Mish's magical singing. He uses different musical styles to bring
his message across, as well as lyrics that teach, but never pon-
tificate. "Rockin' to the Sound of Nature" has all the pizzazz of
a great 50's rock song, and encourages kids to listen to the
marvelous sounds that are the wind, rivers and animals. "You
(Are the World to Me)" is a "shooby wa"-type song, complete
with backup singers and a spoken verse (in Platters style) that
is a love song to the earth and all its wonders. "Center Of The
Earth" is a rap explanation of molten lava. "The Solar System"
starts off with a rap sound and then blends into a "soft shoe"
beat. Other songs are "The Earth," "Gravity," "The Moon,"
"Stars Twinkle," "Plant A Tree," and more. This is a superb
recording!

★★★      **ON THE SUNNY SIDE**
         **Maria Muldaur and Friends**
         **Music for Little People**
         **Cassette/C.D.**
         **Lyrics included**
         **Ages 4-8**

Maria Muldaur's voice is warm, loving, inviting and diverse.
The musical arrangements are wonderful, fun and exciting.
Join the marvelous voice and sensational arrangements to an
exotic collection of songs, and you've got a hit! This is one of
those recordings you and your family can enjoy for many

years, as the music is ageless. Muldaur is accompanied on some of the songs by some young friends who add to the merriment. The songs include "Would You Like to Swing On A Star?" "On the Sunny Side of the Street" (in a duet with Fred Penner), "Cooking Breakfast for the Ones I Love," "The Story Book Ball," "Never Swat a Fly" (a funny, sassy song that kids will love), "Melancholy Baby," "Put On a Happy Face," "The Circus Song," "Side by Side" (with Fred Penner), "Mocking Bird Hill," "Coat of Many Colors," "Prairie Lullaby" and "Dream a Little Dream." This tender and nostalgic recording is sure to become a classic!

**IMPROVISE WITH ERIC NAGLER**
**Eric Nagler**
**Rounder Records**
**LP/Cassette/C.D.**
**Liner notes included**
**Ages 4–10**

Eric Nagler is a fabulous, diverse musician from Canada who uses a variety of instruments and imaginative lyrics to entertain and educate children. His assortment of instruments includes banjo, fiddle, spoons, slide whistle, sewerphone and psaltery. Of his several recordings, this is the first to become available in the U.S. Hopefully more will cross the border soon. He often appears on Sharon, Lois and Bram's *Elephant Show* on Nickelodeon. Songs include "Howjadoo" (a Woody Guthrie song), "Mairzy Dotes," "Daddy's Whiskers" (a silly song full of wacky sounds), "Ain't Nobody Here But Us Chickens," "Juba," "The Strangest Dream" (a song about world peace accompanied by The Walton Memorial Church Family Chorus), "Cluck Old Hen" (an old fiddle tune with new words) and "Super Mom." This recording has so many wonderful sounds that children and adults will discover something new with each listening. It may be hard to find this recording, but it's worth the search.

### IN SEARCH OF THE WOW WOW WIBBLE WOGGLE WAZZIE WOODLE WOO
**Tim Noah**
**Noazart Productions—A&M Records**
**Cassette**
**Lyrics included**
**Ages 6–10**

In this musical journey through a child's imagination one has a sense of listening to a production rather than an interactive recording. Noah's original music and lyrics are generally interesting, but require concentration. Songs include "I Can Do Anything," "Little Miracles," "Musty Moldy Melvin," "Big Booger," "Tears on My Toes," "Zoom," "Friends with a Song" and more. Noah's voice is very pleasing and his sense of imagination is creative, although some of the songs sound forced.

### KIDDYWOMPAS
**Tim Noah**
**Noazart Productions—A&M Records**
**Cassette**
**Lyrics included**
**Ages 6–10**

Musically, this recording is superior to the previous one. Noah's voice is clear and gratifying, but some of the lyrics are abstract and hard to relate to. Songs include "Debalexy" (a child who loves to dance experiences the death of a grandmother), "Aunt Ber and Uncle Don," "Ol' Fiddles," "Country Store," "Mud" (a mean hombre), "Giddy Up," "Keep on Keepin' On," "The Great Potato Uprising" and more.

### ★★★  BACKWARDS LAND
**Hap Palmer**
**Hap-Pal Music**
**LP/Cassette**
**Lyrics included**
**Ages 3–6**

When your children have passed the toddler stage having enjoyed Hap Palmer's recordings for younger children, this is a perfect next recording. Hap's understanding of children and their development is again apparent. The title song, sure to elicit some belly laughs, is about a land where everything is backwards ("Eat popcorn in the morning, pancakes in the night/Fly a boat or float your favorite kite"), and "Amanda Schlupp" is a wonderful piece about a little girl who has a terrible time keeping her room tidy. "Helping Mommy in the Kitchen" tells of all those wonderful concoctions that children make, and "Francie Had a Football" is a nonsexist song about girls and boys. Other delightful songs are "If I Had Wings," "When Things Don't Go Your Way," "Teddy Bear," "Chomping Gum," "When Daddy Was a Little Boy" and "Teddy Bear Ball." Hap's voice and musical arrangements are a pleasure to hear again and again. Additional recordings by Hap Palmer are on pp. 48–50, 87–88, 170–173 and 221–222.

**HOMEMADE BAND**
**Hap Palmer**
**Random House**
**Cassette**
**Lyrics and activity ideas with illustrated book**
      **included**
**Ages 4–8**

This creative cassette and book are designed to encourage children to make their own rhythm instruments with materials found around the house. The music and lyrics invite children to play along, while learning tempo, beat and rhythm to songs like "Slow and Fast Song," "Soft and Loud Song" and "Play and Rest." "I'm a Little Woodblock," sung to the tune of "I'm a Little Teapot," describes and uses the homemade instruments including woodblock, tambourine and sticks. "Old MacDonald's Band" is Hap's clever, upbeat version of "Old MacDonald" using the sounds of different rhythm instruments. "Old Fashioned Rock and Roll" is a wonderful rock and roll song using such rhythm instruments as spoons, tambourines and sticks. Hap's imaginative lyrics and lively music make this an excellent recording for active children. Its active listening and participation also encourage language learning for non-English speaking children.

**PRETEND**
**Hap Palmer**
**Educational Activities**
**LP/Cassette**
**Lyrics and activity ideas included**
**Ages 3–6**

Hap made this recording many years ago, but it still endures as an excellent way to involve children in movement and imagination activities. Hap is a movement specialist as well as a fine singer and songwriter, and all of these songs have been "kid tested." One side is sung and the other is instrumental only, permitting the child to create whatever kind of dance the music evokes in them. The vocal side gives children some basic ideas for creating their own movements, reinforced by the tempo and beat of the music. This is a great thing to do with an active child and with children who want to act things out. Songs are "Rag Doll" (this is my personal favorite), "Guitar Player," "The Friendly Giant," "Rushing," "The Clown," "Little Ants," "Motorcycle Racer" (kids love this piece), "Big Heavy Box," "Jumping Frog," "The Bullfight," "The Kite Song" and "Little Elf." A great way for kids to feel good about themselves and their bodies.

**RHYTHMS ON PARADE**
**Hap Palmer**
**Hap-Pal Music**
**LP/Cassette**
**Lyrics and activity booklet included**
**Ages 3–8**

This unique collection of songs introduces young children to the basic concepts of movement, rhythm and beat. You can use this recording with homemade instruments (see *Homemade Band* by Hap Palmer on page 169), pots and pans, or commercial rhythm instruments. The only other instrument your child will need is his body. "The Mice Go Marching" is a song about loud and soft, while "Switch On The Music" and "Roller Coaster" are about fast and slow. "Woodpecker" demonstrates different rhythms and instruments. There are songs to use with other instruments: "Tap Your Sticks," "Bean Bag

Shake" and "Kris Kringle's Jingle Bell Band." Other songs are "Sounds Around The World," "Five" (about meter), "Jingle Bell Bees" and "Mother Goose Has Rhythmical Rhymes." This recording is a magical musical treat for young musicians.


**SALLY THE SWINGING SNAKE**
**Hap Palmer**
**Educational Activities**
**LP/Cassette**
**Lyrics and Activity Booklet included**
**Ages 4–8**

The sequel to *Walter the Waltzing Worm* is *Sally the Swinging Snake* with more creative movement songs to get kids moving and thinking. Hap has a magical musical quality and a true concern for children that is apparent in his recordings. This recording gives children incentive to move and feel good about themselves and their abilities. Songs include "Something Special," "Wiggy Wiggy Wiggles," "Rubber Band Man," "Up and Down a Mountain," "On the Count of Five," "Ride and Swing" and "Everything Has a Shape."


**WALTER THE WALTZING WORM**
**Hap Palmer**
**Educational Activities**
**LP/Cassette/C.D.**
**Lyrics and Activity Booklet included**
**Ages 4–8**

This recording is chock full of movement activities that involve listening as well as activity. Lively music encourages kids to listen to tempo, beat and rhythm, and participate in the singing. "What a Miracle" is one of my favorites about all the body parts and how they can move. "Flick a Fly" uses fine motor muscles as children flick those pesky flies away. "Song About Slow, Song About Fast" gets kids to listen to tempos as they move. Other wonderfully creative songs are "All the Ways of Jumping Up and Down," "Swing, Shake, Twist and Stretch," "Slide Whistle Suite," "A Genius of Course" and "Walter The Waltzing Worm." Although created for classroom use, this is a

wonderful recording to have around your home. It's also great
to use with children who have a limited English vocabulary.


★ ★ ★     **WE'RE ON OUR WAY**
          **Hap Palmer**
          **Hap Pal Music/Kid Rhino Records**
          **Cassette/C.D.**
          **Lyrics included**
          **Ages 4–8**

Hap Palmer's imaginative lyrics and upbeat music are inviting
and easy to sing along with. Not only is he an extremely talented musician/lyricist, but he's also an accomplished dancer,
as evidenced in a song called "Tina Took Her Tap Shoe,"
which is about Tina tap dancing in the aisles of the super-
market. The tapping that is heard is actually done by Hap. "At
The Library" is a guessing song in which kids are given the
chance to sing about all their favorite storybook characters.
"The Things We Like To Do" suggests creative activities with
things readily found around the house. "Teddy Took a Train
Ride" is a clever song about how a teddy bear rides a train,
plane, truck and finally a car to arrive as a birthday gift. "Tiger
with a Toothbrush" is about an imaginary companion who's
there at tooth-brushing time. Other delightful songs include
"Freddy Fuzzywizz" (a teddybear), "Partytime in the Mud,"
"Truck Driver's Song," "We're On Our Way" and "Mrs.
McFritter" (the babysitter). Palmer's effervescent personality
and music demand repeated listenings.


          **WITCHES' BREW**
          **Hap Palmer**
          **Educational Activities**
          **LP/Cassette**
          **Lyrics and Activity Booklet included**
          **Ages 4–8**

This is another of Hap's recordings made for school, but that
also have wonderful applications for home use. The songs,
designed to promote and stimulate language development,
were written with easy-to-learn lyrics and many have an

"Instant Sing Line" repeated several times throughout to give the child a chance to participate immediately. Some of the songs are repeated, but without complete vocals, so that children can insert words of their own. This type of recording is wonderful for children learning English as a second language or for children who need to improve their listening or speech skills. It's also great for just plain sing-along. The title song is a popular Halloween favorite in our store. Other original songs include "Grandma's Farm" (what's on the farm), "Space Explorer," "The Eagle," "Clickity Clack" and "They Go Together."

**ZANY ZOO**
**Hap Palmer**
**Hap-Pal Music**
**LP/Cassette**
**Lyrics included**
**Ages 4–8**

*Zany Zoo* is another winner from Hap Palmer. The songs are filled with exciting language and invite active participation as well as quiet listening. My favorite song, "Amos, the Alligator Dude," takes you on a wild musical and verbal romp. "Got to Hurry Got to Worry Blues" is a song about an all-too-well-known time when Mom and Dad are in a rush. "Amazing," "Friends" and "You Can Do It" help children feel good about themselves and others. One of the more unusual songs is called "Halloween Hanukkah Christmas Ghost" and is about a Halloween ghost who's stayed on through Christmas and Hanukkah. Other inviting songs are "The Clown Song," "The Summer Slumber Party at Sabrina's House" and "Billy Blotsky's Birthday Bash." A interactive recording full of great music.

**BALLOON-ALLOON-ALLOON**
**Tom Paxton**
**Pax Records**
**Cassette**
**Lyrics included**
**Ages 4–10**

The magic lyrics of these twelve zany fun songs from Tom Paxton will bring hours of fun into your home or car with such selections as "At The 'Quarium" (a silly, bubbly song about the aquarium), "Allen Gator" (about a loving alligator), "The Thing That Isn't There" (a spooky sounding song about being afraid), "The Monkies' Baseball Game," "I've Got Measles," " Balloon-alloon-alloon" and the hilarious "Wooly Booger." Paxton's voice is delightful to hear again and again, and his musical arrangements are superb. You'll get many hours of listening pleasure with this recording.

**A CAR FULL OF SONGS**
**Tom Paxton**
**Pax Records**
**Cassette**
**Lyrics included**
**Ages 4–10**

After listening to this recording, you can tell that Paxton has had first-hand experience traveling with children. These orig-inal songs have very catchy tunes that you and your family will learn quickly and be singing in no time at all. This is a perfect recording to use in the car, the plane, the train, the boat or whatever form of transportation you use. Paxton's sen-sitivity and charm comes through over and over again in songs such as "Are We There Yet?" "Dad's Not Lost," "I've Gotta Go," "The Wheels Go 'Round," "This Old Car," "I Spy," "Sleepin' in the Backseat," "Somebody's Hungry," "License Plate" and nine more.

**A FOLK SONG FESTIVAL**
**Tom Paxton**
**Pax Records**
**Cassette**
**Lyrics included**
**Ages 4–10**

This superb collection of America's most popular folk songs is sung by one of America's most famous folksingers. Paxton's musical arrangements are extraordinary and his voice is appealing and inviting. This collection contains "Oh Susanna," "Clementine," "On Top of Old Smokey," "The Riddle Song," "I Ride an Old Paint," "Sweet Betsy from Pike," "Paper of Pins," "The Foggy Foggy Dew," "Springfield Mountain," "Turtle Dove," "Danville Girl," "The Golden Vanity," "Young Man Who Wouldn't Hoe Corn," "In Good Old Colony Days" and "My Little Mohee." This collection is for children of all ages!

★★★     **THE MARVELLOUS TOY AND GALLIMAUFRY**
**Tom Paxton**
**Pax Records**
**Cassette/C.D.**
**Lyrics included**
**Ages 4–10**

Tom Paxton is a legendary folksinger whose wit and wisdom carried many of us through the sixties. His collections of children's songs are unequaled in charm and musical genius. Paxton's voice is as clear and lovely as it was years ago. He's a national treasure! We have had the pleasure of having Tom perform in our store for children from ages one to eighty-five, and everyone had a great time. The title song on this recording is a classic, which many of us have sung among ourselves and with our children. Another classic written by Paxton, "Going to the Zoo," is delightfully presented on this recording. Two special treats are the story songs "Englebert the Elephant" and "Jennifer's Rabbit," each of which are also available in beautifully illustrated book editions. "Come and Play Catch with Me" is a great song sung to a Dad. "My Dog's Bigger Than Your Dog Is" is a "na na na" type song, and "Let's Pretend" is a creative imagination song. Other songs include "The Subway

Song," "Hush-You Bye," "Go To Sleep," "Katy," "Little Brand New Baby," "The Thought Stayed Free," "Grey Mares" and "Fred." This is a wonderful slice of folk music.

**PEANUT BUTTER PIE**
**Tom Paxton**
**Sony Kids' Music**
**Cassette/C.D.**
**Lyrics included**
**Ages 4–10**

Original fun songs are the contents of this Paxton offering. "Great Big Box" is a clever song about curiosity and a certain birthday present, and "ABC" uses lots of words with the letters A, B, and C. Terrific songs about foods are "Ketchup" (a rock-style song sure to elicit more than a few laughs), "Mashed Potatoes," "Peanut Butter Pie" and "Bananas." "Sing, Spider, Sing" is about a child and his dog, and "E I Addie Addie O" is a silly song full of tall tales. Other delightful songs include "A New Baby at Our House," "Dinosaurs at Play," "Lazy, Lazy," "The Magic Whistle," "Plant A Tree" and "One Ship Is Sailing." A delicious recording.

**SUZY IS A ROCKER**
**Tom Paxton**
**Sony Kids' Music**
**Cassette/C.D.**
**Lyrics included**
**Ages 4–10**

Tom Paxton's marvelous voice and lyrics are combined to present 15 bright new songs. The orchestrations are clever and hold up after repeated listenings. Children often accompany Paxton on the vocals. Paxton understands the lives of children, as shown in a great song called "Oops," which deals with all those things that deserve the response of "I'm sorry." "We Have Each Other," my favorite song, is a contagious melodic description of what friendship is all about. "Pretty Clever" is a bouncy song that looks at interesting facts about animals, nature and people. The title song is about a rocker heroine named Suzy. "Ride My Bike" is a song all kids who love to ride their bikes can relate to. Other fun songs include "The Crow's Toes," "The Baseball Kids," "A Giraffe Can Laugh" and "I've Got A Yo Yo." Bravo, Tom Paxton.

**EBENEEZER SNEEZER**
**Fred Penner**
**Oak Street Music**
**Cassette/C.D.**
**Lyrics included**
**Ages 3–6**

This delightful recording, previously entitled "Special Delivery," contains some great musical entertainment. Penner is accompanied here by Ken Whiteley, and their arrangements are great fun. Children's voices also join in the musical merrymaking. The duo uses a wide variety of musical instruments, so repeated listenings are worthwhile. Some of the songs are appropriate for small children, while others work better for older kids. Songs for the younger children are: "There Was An Old Lady (Who Swallowed A Fly)," a rollicking version of "Car Car Song" ("Riding In My Car" by Woody Guthrie), "This Old Man" and "Bon Soir Mis Amis" (Good Evening My Friends). Songs for older children include "Polly Wolly Doodle," "The Old Sow Song" (complete with delightful sound effects), "The Fox," "Mail Myself To You" ("I'm gonna wrap myself in paper, I'm gonna dab myself with glue. Stick some stamps on top of my head, I'm gonna mail myself to you."—a Woody Guthrie classic), "My Grandfather's Clock" and "The Marvelous Toy" (by Tom Paxton). Penner recites a cute poem called "Stars," and the title song, written by Penner, is about a child who's sneezing because he didn't take care to dress for the cold. The musical accompaniment includes violin, mouth trumpet, trombones and some very real sneezes. Other songs are: "Holiday," "Old Chisholm Trail," "I've Got No Strings," "Ba Ba No Ma" (an African song about talking with drums) and "En Roulant" (a French song). A very satisfying recording!

★★★    **PETER, PAUL AND MOMMY**
       **Peter, Paul and Mary**
       **WEA/Music for Little People**
       **Cassette/C.D.**
       **No lyrics included**
       **Ages 3–8**

Once upon a time Peter, Paul and Mary recorded a live concert for children, and the result has become a classic. Their
selection of songs is fabulous and their voices, augmented by
some younger ones, has made this a best-selling recording for
many years. This has the original version of "Puff (The Magic
Dragon)," which many have sung over the years but none the
way they do! Other famous songs include "The Marvelous Toy"
and "Going to the Zoo" (written by Tom Paxton), "The Boa
Constrictor" (written by Shel Silverstein), "It's Raining," "All
Through the Night" (a lullaby), "Day Is Done," "Mockingbird"
and "Make-Believe Town." It's an eclectic group of songs, but
a time-tested hit with children.


       **I WUV YOU**
       **Bonnie Phipps**
       **Golden**
       **Cassette**
       **No lyrics included**
       **Ages 4–8**

Bonnie Phipps was a teacher before she became a performer
for children. In this colorful selection of humorous songs,
Phipps' clear and inviting voice mixes well with innovative
musical arrangements. She sings songs that have clever lyrics
and fun sounds. "Dogs" is a song by Dan Crow, using lots of
D sounds, that kids love to sing. "Iko Iko," a song made popular in the fifties, is full of words with interesting sounds
accompanied by great rhythm. "La Cucaracha" has English
lyrics that don't really relate to the original song, but are sure
to get the attention of the kids. Other playful songs include
"Can You Dig That Crazy Gibberish," "My Belly Button Fell
Off," "Everybody Eats When They Come to My House/A
Chicken Ain't Nothin' But a Bird," "Madelina Catalina" (a real
tongue twister), "B-A Bay," "I'm Popeye The Sailor Man/Sail-

or's Hornpipe," "Halloween Song" and six more. Great for kids who love silly songs.

**CAPTURED "LIVE" IN THE ACT**
**Barry Louis Polisar**
**Rainbow Morning Music**
**Cassette**
**No lyrics included**
**Ages 5–10**

Barry Louis Polisar is a unique musician who performs wild, wacky and sometimes gross songs for school-age children. Nothing is sacred; he sings about all kinds of absurd things. While many adults may find his music strange and at times irreverent, kids love him. He reaches children in their funny-bones and touches on subjects that are often taboo. He accompanies himself on the guitar and sings in a folksy, brash manner. This is a live recording with a group of school children. Some of the songs are a bit off key, but then Polisar never professes to be the world's greatest singer. The fourteen songs on this record are from previous albums. The nice part of this recording is that Polisar explains why he wrote some of these songs. "Early Sunday Morning," "He Eats Asparagus," "Why Can't You Be That Way," "I'm a Three-Toed Triple-Eyed, Double-Jointed Dinosaur," "My Friend Jake," "Thump Thump Thump," "Tomorrow," "Fred," "When the House Is Dark and Quiet," "One Day My Best Friend Barbara Turned into a Frog," "The Apple of My Eye," "I Got a Teacher and She's So Mean," "Shut Up in the Library," "Don't Put Your Finger Up Your Nose" and "Louder" are the tape's contents.

**FAMILY CONCERT**
**Barry Louis Polisar**
**Rainbow Morning Music**
**Cassette**
**Lyrics included**
**Ages 5–10**

Kids thoroughly enjoy listening and singing along with Polisar. A second live recording features some of his more popular songs, including "My Brother Thinks He's a Banana," "I've Got a Dog and My Dog's Name is Cat," "Our Dog Bernard," "My Brother Threw up on My Stuffed Toy Bunny," "Underwear," "I Got A Teacher and She's So Mean," "I Sneaked into the Kitchen in the Middle of the Night," "My Mother Ran Away Today," "When the House Is Dark and Quiet," "Don't Put Your Finger up Your Nose," and more.

**I EAT KIDS—**
   **and Other Songs for Rebellious Children**
**Barry Louis Polisar**
**Rainbow Morning Music**
**Cassette**
**No lyrics included**
**Ages 5–10**

This first recording by Polisar contains the following songs: "He Eats Asparagus," "Why Can't You Be That Way," "I'm A Three-Toed, Triple-Eyed, Double-Jointed Dinosaur," "I Don't Brush My Teeth and I Never Comb My Hair," "My Dentist Is an Awfully Nice Man," "I Eat Kids," "I Need You Like a Doughnut Needs a Hole," "I Never Did Like You Anyhow," "To Mommy," "Shut Up in the Library," "I Don't Believe You're Going to the Bathroom," "I Sneaked into the Kitchen in the Middle of the Night," "Fred," "I Got a Teacher and She's So Mean," "Me and You," "Giggle Tickle Fiddle Little Wiggle Around," "When Suzie Sneezed," "My Friend Jake," "Early Sunday Morning" and "Louder." Don't be afraid to buy these recordings; children really identify with Polisar's humor. Many use his songs for class performances.

**JUGGLING BABIES AND A CAREER**
**Barry Louis Polisar**
**Rainbow Morning Music**
**Cassette**
**Lyrics included**
**Ages 5–10**

I am reluctant to suggest an age range for this recording. Most of the songs relate to how Polisar is coping with being the father of newborn twins. These songs will bring a chuckle to many parents as they recall those first few months of parenthood, but I personally don't think many children will find this recording very interesting unless they are diehard Polisar fans. The songs include "Don't Wake up the Baby (or the Baby Will Get You)," "Diaper Rash (A Monster Song)," "Why Do I Love You?," "Symphony in Why# Major," "What Are We Gonna Do About the Baby?" "As You Sleep So Peacefully (A Father's Day Nightmare)" and "Turkeys in the Straw" (featuring the voice of one of the three-month-old twins).

### MY BROTHER THINKS HE'S A BANANA—
#### and Other Provocative Songs for Children
**Barry Louis Polisar**
**Rainbow Morning Music**
**Cassette**
**No lyrics included**
**Ages 5–10**

This is the second zany collection of original songs from Barry Louis Polisar. It contains the following looney songs: "When the House Is Dark and Quiet," "The Skater Brak Flath Who Lives in the Bath," "One Day My Best Friend Barbara Turned into a Frog," "My Brother Thinks He's a Banana," "Barnyard Stomp," "Our Dog Bernard," "My Name Is Hiram Lipshitz (Oh, To Be a Smith or Jones)," "Tomorrow," "All I Want Is You," "My Brother Threw up on My Stuffed Toy Bunny," "For My Sister, Wherever I May Find Her," "My Mommy Drives a Dump Truck," "Talking," "I Got a Teacher and He's So Boring (Or I Shall Be Free #1–12)," "I Got a Dog and My Dog's Name Is Cat," "But I'm Just Thirteen," "I've Got A Little Sister" and "The Apple of My Eye."

### NAUGHTY SONGS FOR BOYS AND GIRLS
**Barry Louis Polisar**
**Rainbow Morning Music**
**Cassette**
**No lyrics included**
**Ages 5–10**

With each succeeding recording, Polisar's voice improves, his lyrics get stranger, and the kids love him more! This third collection of weirdness includes "Thump Thump Thump," "Hey Jack, What's In The Sack," "You Can't Say PsbPsbPsb on the Radio," "My Name Is Hiram Lipshitz (Jr.)," "With a Giggle and a Hug and a Tickle and a Kiss," "The Man and the Chicken (A Fable)," "Don't Put Your Finger up Your Nose," "I Can't, I Can't," "Mom and Dad Are Always Right," "They Said 'Eat The Broccoli,'" "Never Cook Your Sister in a Frying Pan," "A Brontosaurus with Bronchitis," "Tyrannosaurus Nix," "My Mother Ran Away Today," "The Poetry Lesson: A Tragi-Comedy," "Do This, Do That," "Dad Says That I Look Like Him," "Leroy Is a Late Bloomer," "You're as Sweet as Sugar on a Stick," and "Marching Shoulder to Shoulder." These songs may sound offensive to many adults but, as noted earlier, Polisar is very very popular with the kids.

**OFF COLOR SONGS FOR KIDS**
**Barry Louis Polisar**
**Rainbow Morning Music**
**Cassette**
**Lyrics included**
**Ages 5–10**

In this seventh recording of bizarre songs, Polisar's eighteen songs include "Underwear," "I Forgot," "Hands and Kilometers," "What If a Zebra Had Spots," "Town of Round," "The Chameleon," "I'd Be Me," "Oh No, I Like My Sister," "You'd Better Not Giggle," "Now Don't You Laugh But I'm in Love with a Giraffe," "A Bee Will Sting You," "Five More Minutes" and "Later."

**SONGS FOR WELL BEHAVED CHILDREN**
**Barry Louis Polisar**
**Rainbow Morning Music**
**Cassette**
**Lyrics included**
**Ages 5–10**

This recording contains twenty-five more ridiculous songs that kids love to hear. Polisar's fifth collection includes "I Wanna Be a Dog," "The Bumble Bee Song," "Ellen Grew a Beard,"

"I'm Bored," " I Don't Wanna Go to School," "The AlfaBet Song (A is for Armpit)," "Poor Orville Thlapp," "There's No Substitute for a Cat," "Aunt Anna Came to Our House," "Don't Leave Me in the House Alone" and "The Accident."

### STANLEY STOLE MY SHOELACE AND RUBBED IT IN HIS ARMPIT— and Other Songs My Parents Won't Let Me Sing
**Barry Louis Polisar**
**Rainbow Morning Music**
**Lyrics included**
**Ages 5–10**

The title song gives a clear message of the topics included in this recording. One wonders where Polisar comes up with these titles! Some of the wackier songs include "I Lost My Pants," "Mom Said No, I Said Why," "Marvin Doesn't Like the New Baby," "I Don't Think My Teacher Likes Me," "I'm Standing Naked on the Kitchen Table (Trying to Get Your Attention)," "Go and Hush the Baby," "I'm Late," "Nothing," "Reptile World," "I Love My Daddy" and eight more.

### EVERGREEN EVERBLUE
**Raffi**
**Shoreline/MCA**
**Cassette/C.D.**
**Lyrics included**
**Ages 6 and up**

This recording represents a new style for Raffi. Its songs are geared to older children and adults and have an ecological message. The superb musical arrangements are more expansive than other recordings he has done. The only song that has appeared on other children's recordings is "One Light One Sun." As in his earlier recordings, Raffi's voice is warm and inviting, worthy of repeated listenings. Although very young children should be exposed to the messages of saving our planet, these songs are quite a bit more sophisticated and will probably appeal to older children. Teachers will find many

songs appropriate for classroom use. The new songs are "Big
Beautiful Planet," "Alive and Dreaming," "Where I Live,"
"What's the Matter with Us," "Just Like the Sun," "Clean Rain,"
"We Are Not Alone," "Our Dear, Dear Mother" and "Mama's
Kitchen." Other recordings by Raffi are on pp. 93–98 and 223.

**OLDIES FOR KOOL KIDDIES**
**Re-Bops**
**Re-Bop Records**
**Cassette**
**No lyrics included**
**Ages 3–8**

New versions of classic rock 'n' roll favorites from the fifties
and sixties are sung by adults and children. This is a nostalgic
recording that will bring back many memories for parents and
will expose young children to some of the sillier music of the
past. "The Monster Mash" is great fun, as is "Papa Oom Mow
Mow." Other songs include "Lollipop," "Splish Splash," "The
Loco-Motion," "Duke Of Earl," "I Love Onions," "Alley-Oop,"
"Rockin' Robin," "Blue Moon" and "Little Star." All you need
to add are poodle skirts and Brill Cream.

**SADDLE PALS**
**Riders In the Sky**
**Rounder Records**
**LP/Cassette**
**No lyrics included**
**Ages 4–8**

A rich collection of cowboy songs and ballads sung by the likes
of Ranger Doug, Woody Paul, and Too Slim (better known as
the Riders In the Sky). Using fiddle, guitar, mandolin, harmonica and banjo, these men have chosen a fine selection of
songs, great for imagination time or sing-along. The songs
include "The Old Chisholm Trail," "I'm Going to Leave Old
Texas Now" (with a children's chorus), "Clementine," "Sweet
Betsy from Pike," "Get Along Little Dogies" and seven more.
This recording would be great to use for a cowboy theme

party. Be sure to watch their Saturday morning T.V. show. It's great fun!


**PIGGYBACK PLANET**
**Songs for the Whole Earth**
**Sally Rogers**
**Round River Records**
**Cassette**
**Lyrics included**
**Ages 4–10**

Although the message in this marvelous collection of songs about saving our earth is obvious, the songs never seem preachy or heavy handed. Rogers has a delightful voice, and the musical arrangements are pleasant and varied. Some of the more interesting songs include "Over in the Endangered Meadow" (new words to "Over in the Meadow"), "La Tierra Es Mi Madre (The Earth Is My Mother)" sung in Spanish and English, "K'Ang Ting Song" (a traditional Chinese song with new lyrics), "Garbage," "The Recycle Song" (by Cathy Fink), "What Have They Done to the Rain," "This Land Is Your Land" and "What Did The Dinosaurs Say?" This is a timely recording that can be used as sing-along (the songs are fun to sing), for classroom or teaching purposes or for a great theme party. Rogers is joined by some young voices that enhance the musicality of this very creative recording.


**I'M JUST A KID**
**Rory**
**Sony Kids' Music**
**Cassette/C.D.**
**Lyrics included**
**Ages 4–8**

Rory has a delightful voice that is here combined with upbeat musical arrangements. This collection of original songs is fun to hear and endures repeated listenings. Although there are only ten songs on this recording, they are all quality pieces. Two of my favorites are "My Invisible Band," about playing all the instruments in a band, even though it's invisible, and

"Bubble Bath," an a cappella doo-wa song that is very catchy. "The Ballad of Mr. Toad" tells the story of being shy, and "You're Drivin' Me Crazy!" is told from both the child's and the parent's point of view. "The Incredible Piglets" is about vegetables. Other songs are "The Best You Can Be Is You," "I'm A Kid," "Another Rainy Day," "Dreamwings" and "You're My Friend." This is a pleasant recording with varied musical styles and pleasing vocals.

**LITTLE BROADWAY**
**Rory**
**Sony Kids' Music**
**Cassette/C.D.**
**Lyrics included**
**Ages 4–8**

Rory sings some of Broadway's most famous songs in this well-rounded collection of ten pieces. The musical accompaniments are generally interesting. Her voice often sounds too much like that of a little girl, but overall is very gratifying. Although each side of the cassette lasts only twelve minutes, this nostalgic recording deserves repeated listenings. The songs are "Oh, What A Beautiful Mornin'" from *Oklahoma*, "Put on a Happy Face" from *Bye Bye Birdie*, "I'd Do Anything" from *Oliver*, "I Won't Grow Up" from *Peter Pan*, "Happiness" from *You're A Good Man Charlie Brown*, "Seventy-Six Trombones" from *The Music Man*, "I've Gotta Crow" from *Peter Pan*, "Together, Wherever We Go" from *Gypsy*, "My Favorite Things" from *The Sound of Music*, and "Never Never Land" from *Peter Pan*. This recording provides a wonderful way for your children to experience music from Broadway and perhaps become interested in attending and learning about theater.

**MAKE BELIEVE DAY**
**Rory**
**Sony Kids' Music**
**Cassette/C.D.**
**Lyrics included**
**Ages 4–8**

This recording contains eleven songs mostly about imagination. Rory's voice is very pleasant, although many of the songs sound overly sugar-sweet. Eight of the songs are original. "Noise" is a clever song that encourages children to make the sounds of fire engines, motorboats and a Tarzan yell. "Yuk!" is a song that will appeal to a child's sense of the gross. "Family" is a loving song about individual families and about the families of humanity. The two well-known songs on this recording are "I've Been Working on the Railroad" and "Over The Rainbow." The other songs are "Make Believe Day," "The Pocket Song," "I'm Gonna Be Somebody," "Footprints," "Toys" and "Time for Bed." This recording is not as long as many others, but overall is pleasing to hear.

**FAMILY VACATION**
**Rosenshontz**
**RS Records**
**Cassette**
**Lyrics included**
**Ages 4–8**

What is Rosenshontz? It's the dynamic duo of Gary Rosen and Bill Shontz. They have been performing together since the mid-seventies and are great fun to see and hear. Their mostly original songs are filled with amusing and playful lyrics. Their charm and wit are apparent in their vocal intonations and musical variety. Gary plays guitar, and Bill plays flute, clarinet, and saxophone. This recording is one of their wild and wacky collections of original songs. "Peanut Butter Blues" will appeal to every child and adult who has eaten peanut butter and jelly endlessly for lunch. A song that will either be a reality in your house or an impetus to change is "Daddy Does the Dishes." "Dear Diary" explores the feelings of a child whose mother is going to remarry. "Better Say No" deals with safety. Some of the sillier songs include "Pizza," "Crazy for Dinosaurs," "Goin' Fishin'," "Tooth Fairy," "Family Vacation" and "Snowman." This upbeat recording touches on some delicate subjects in a caring way, and also gives kids a great chance to sing just for fun.

★★★  **IT'S THE TRUTH**
**Rosenshontz**
**RS Records**
**Cassette**
**Lyrics included**
**Ages 4–8**

Rosenshontz keeps writing new children's songs that appeal to
both kids and adults, as demonstrated in this recording that is
so much fun to play. It's hard to describe the wit and crazi-
ness, mixed with love and tenderness, that comes through their
music, but it's there and kids love it. "Don't Bring It Home" is
a funny song about all those things that kids drag into the
house and want to keep. A song that has become their trademark is "Hugga Hugga," a contagious song about hugging. Two
well-known songs, "House at Pooh Corner" (which was a rock
and roll hit sung by Loggins and Messina) and "Somewhere
over the Rainbow," are beautifully done. "One Shoe Bear" is
scintillating, using musical styles and adaptations of songs from
the fifties and sixties. The title song is filled with truths and
untruths that kids will understand. Other songs sure to tickle
the funny bone and make kids think are "Sugar," "Bananas,"
"Security Blanket," "Don't Be a Tease" and "A Good Friend."
Rosenshontz' sense of humor, mixed with great musical talent,
is refreshing and terrific for kids and adults.

**ROCK 'N' ROLL TEDDY BEAR**
**Rosenshontz**
**RS Records**
**Cassette**
**Lyrics included**
**Ages 4–8**

This collection of Rosenshontz's originals is clever and contemporary, with lots of rock 'n' roll music for children. "The
Rosenshontz Rap" is an autobiographical selection about the
two performers and all the funny ways people pronounce their
name. "Do Be Do Good" promotes doing good deeds in a rock
'n' roll style. "Bobo and Fred" describes a lazy man and his
dog Bobo. "Go for It" is about giving things your best shot. A
very touching yet upbeat song, "The Best That I Can," is a

musical tribute to children with different disabilities. "Mr. Stringbean" asks kids to consider before listening to everything that other people tell them. Other songs are "The Circus Is Here," "Little Light Of Mine," "Rock 'n' Roll Teddy Bear," "Billy Don't You Cry Now" and "Quiet Time."

> **SHARE IT**
> **Rosenshontz**
> **RS Records**
> **Cassette**
> **Lyrics included**
> **Ages 4–8**

*Share It* presents more humorous and fun songs from Gary Rosen and Bill Shontz. You can always count on terrific singing and interesting musical arrangements with these two performers. There's also a delightful children's chorus. These guys are great at making silly sounds, as shown in "Sounds from A to Z." While one sings the letters of the alphabet, the other sings the corresponding sounds in this wonderfully frenetic song. This is followed by "Pet Sounds," sung in a rock and roll style, with more animal sounds than you can imagine. They do a great version of "Garbage," the ecology song. The title song has an important message for children and adults. "Eat It Up (Just One More Bite)" is about that eternal problem at dinner time. They do a rollicking version of "Who's Afraid of the Big Bad Wolf?" Other songs are "Happy Place," "Sleep Sleep," "The Mandolin Song" (instrumental), "The Music Store," "Going Away" and "Gonna Have a Good Time." It's always a pleasure to hear these two great performers.

> **TICKLES YOU**
> **Rosenshontz**
> **RS Records**
> **Lyrics included**
> **Cassette**
> **Ages 4–8**

This was recorded live, so you'll hear many children's voices, both singing and giggling. Their version of "Teddy Bears

Picnic" is great. "Imagination" is a song about the power of
children's minds at work. "It Takes Two to Make One" cleverly describes how it takes two people or animals to create a
new one. "Sam, The Tickle Man" will elicit many giggles.
"These Are the Questions" is a wonderful song that asks "Can
a clock tell time? Is the sun ever cold? Do fish ever see the
sky?" "I Wish I Was" explores the silly fun in pretending to be
different kinds of animals. Other songs include "A Beautiful
Day," "The Garden Song (Inch by Inch)," "Life Is," "It's OK,"
"Sing a Happy Song," "Hey, We'll Fill the World with Love,"
"One Sweet Song" and "Hippopotamus Rock." This recording
is sure to bring hours of listening fun.

**UH-OH**
**Rosenshontz**
**RS Records**
**Cassette**
**Lyrics included**
**Ages 4–8**

This sixth recording from the zany Rosenshontz group features
twelve upbeat songs. Combining wit and musical talent, these
two guys bring hours of listening fun to you and your children.
"Brothers and Sisters" is one of those songs that realistically
looks at the sibling situation: "My sister's a twerp! She drinks
all my soda with a slurp and a burp." "On the Funny Farm"
details the mixed-up sounds and things that occur on this
strange farm. "What a Wonderful World" explores friendship,
peace and saving the planet. "Sunday Morning," about getting
everyone up and going, is a song all parents and children can
appreciate. Other fun songs include "Uh Oh," "Jenny the
Bubble Gum Queen," "Mister Penn," "Look Ma No Hands,"
"Accentuate the Positive," "Tiny Toes," "Bugs" and "Swinging."

**CHICKENS IN THE GARDEN**
**Phil Rosenthal**
**American Melody**
**Cassette**
**Lyrics included**
**Ages 4–8**

Traditional and original songs are sung in country-western style. Rosenthal has a wonderful voice, and his versions of classic songs are sung in a key that facilitates singing along with him. The instrumentation is country but uncluttered. The lyrics of some of the traditional songs are for older children, but the songs are fun and can definitely be used with younger children. All are well presented. Traditional songs include "Down in the Valley," "The Crawdad Song," "The Cannonball," "The Little Chickens in the Garden," "Twenty Froggies Went to School," "The Little Black Bull" and a musical version of "Calico Pie" (by Edward Lear). Some of Rosenthal's original songs include "The Swimming Hole," "Old Dog" and "Bluegrass Makes Me Tap My Toes" (and it really will!). This is a fun collection with a great sound.

**DADDYSONGS**
**Kevin Roth**
**Sony Kids' Music**
**Cassette/C.D.**
**Lyrics included**
**Ages 4–8**

Kevin Roth's voice is tremendously inviting, and the mostly original songs represent a look at parents and children. Three of the well-known songs are a medley of "It's Raining, It's Pouring/I Can See Clearly Now," "My Girl" (the song made popular in the 60's) and "This Old Man" with a new arrangement and delightful new nostalgic lyrics ("This old man he played two, I loved him, he loved me too—This old man he played three, he sang the sweetest songs to me . . ."). "Waltzing with Bears" will get you waltzing along with Roth as he sings about his Uncle Walter who dances at night with the bears. "Ice Cream Man" is a child's plea to his dad to buy him ice cream from the ice cream truck. "Playing Right Field" is a song about being picked last for a baseball team. "Rainbows" is a beautiful song, with music by Beethoven and lyrics by Roth, that describes all the wonders that nature has to offer and that we have to preserve. A few of these songs are really for the adult who's watching his children growing or who's viewing his own relationship with his father, but overall this is a top-quality recording with the message of love. Other recordings by Kevin Roth are on pp. 28–29, 101–102, and 224.

## DINOSAURS, DRAGONS AND OTHER CHILDREN'S SONGS
**Kevin Roth**
**Marlboro Records**
**Cassette**
**Lyrics included**
**Ages 4–8**

This is a fabulous collection of upbeat songs about dinosaurs and large monsters. Roth's voice is enticing, and his orchestral arrangements are sufficiently interesting and varied that one doesn't get bored after repeated listenings. The songs are long enough to hold older children's attention and fun enough for young children to savor. All were written by Roth except "Puff the Magic Dragon," which is beautifully sung in duet with its author Peter Yarrow. My favorite song is "Dan's Dinosaur Galore," about how and where to buy dinosaurs. There are new versions of old favorites such as "Dry Bones" (adapted from "Dem Bones," "Your toe bone's connected to your foot bone," etc.), and "Down by the Bay" (a rollicking, wacky new version that will elicit great giggles). Many songs are laced with imagination and fantasy such as "The Dragon Song," "The Funny Man," "The Cave Man and The Big Feet" and "The Singing Dragon." Others, such as "Dinosaur Rap," "The Little Lizard" and "Mr. Sun, Sun" are based on factual information and presented in a fun and interesting way. This recording provides a great introduction to dinosaurs and dragons.

**THE SECRET JOURNEY**
**Kevin Roth**
**Marlboro Records**
**Cassette**
**Lyrics included**
**Ages 4–8**

This collection of mostly original songs written and beautifully
sung by Kevin Roth is primarily about animals and nature. The
animals are "Little Piggy," "The Unicorn," "The Turtle and the
Hare," "Mr. Bed Bug," "The Mermaid Song" and "The Puffed-
up Frog." Some of the message songs include "The Wonder
Song," "The Secret Journey," "Bear Lovin'," "Sam," "You've
Got to Have Love" and "Autumn To May." While this collection of songs is interesting, some of his other recordings have
more pizzazz and are less esoteric. This is the kind of recording
I might play for quiet time listening and relaxing.

**IN A CHILD'S HEART**
**Bob Schneider**
**Golden**
**Cassette**
**No lyrics included**
**Ages 4–8**

In these upbeat, original songs by Bob Schneider, variety of
musical arrangements is the hallmark, which makes the songs
fun to hear again and again. Schneider's sense of humor is
apparent in songs like "No, No, No," which is about no, maybe
and yes, and "Funky Expressions." Some children's solos are
spotty, such as on "Just Like You." "Busy, Busy, Busy" is a
fast-paced song about the things that can keep a child occu-
pied (such as chores). Other songs include "Feelings and Emotions," "What Are You Wearing Today?" "Going on Vacation," "All Day Long" and more. Generally, this is a pleasing
recording.

**JUST FRIENDS**
**Bob Schneider**
**Golden**
**Cassette**
**No lyrics included**
**Ages 4–8**

These twelve original songs by Bob Schneider employ a variety
of musical styles and arrangements. Schneider's voice is generally very pleasing. Many of the lyrics are clever and will
appeal to a child's sense of humor, as in "I Don't Know," which
uses a great children's chorus to sing the title over and over
in excellent harmony. "Heebie Jeebies" is about being afraid
of things. "Lazy Day" says it's okay to have one of these occa-
sionally. "Got a Hat Hat" is a wild song to sing. Some of the
songs use steel drum as background, which is great fun. Other
songs include "It's a Holiday," "The Nothing Song," "Going to
the Movies," "Goodbye Song" and "Gotta Believe."

**PLAYING BASEBALL**
**Bob Schneider**
**Golden**
**Cassette**
**No lyrics included**
**Ages 4–8**

For any child who loves baseball, this recording will be a hit.
There are songs about the players (which can all too quickly
become outdated), the umpire, the mechanics of the sport, the
coach, and even the vendors in the stadium. Schneider's voice
is pleasant and most of the kids who accompany him are fun
to hear, although a few are off key. The musical styles are
diverse and colorful. Some of these lively original songs are
"De Ump," "Ball Girl," "Run Do Run," "Grump in a Slump,"
"Baseball Hall of Fame," "Third Base Coaches' Dance," "Play
by Play," "Food Vendor's Round," "Spring Training Delight"
and five more. This is a unique recording.

**ABRACADABRA**
**Joe Scruggs**
**Educational Graphics Press**
**LP/Cassette**
**Lyrics included**
**Ages 3–8**

Joe Scruggs' mellow voice and superb sensitivity to children is disseminated in thirteen delightful original songs. "Justin," a warm and loving song about a best friend moving away, will comfort children who experience this loss. "Rocking Chair" is a comforting song that talks of being hugged and rocked in moments of fear. What's that magic word children are supposed to use when asking for something? It's *not* "Abracadabra," but Scruggs turns the "please and thank you" issue into a comical song. Other fun songs from a kid's point of view are "I'm Too Full for Broccoli," "Bubble Gum" (about stepping on that dreaded stuff), "School Glue" (about moderation when using glue for projects) and "Zip Zip" (sometimes children are told to zip their lips, but Joe says he's never seen a zipper in a mouth). A wonderfully scary song for Halloween is called "Everybody Freeze," is great for active participation and movement. "I Had A Dream" uses sound effects to invite children to move and imitate the sounds of different kinds of machinery (robot, washing machine, popcorn maker, etc.). Other songs include "Red Rover," "Nursery Rhymes" (we're never too old), "ABC" and "The Train Song." There's never a dull moment when Joe Scruggs is around. More recordings by Joe Scruggs are on pp. 102–103 and 225.

★★★     **BAHAMAS PAJAMAS**
**Joe Scruggs**
**Educational Graphics Press**
**LP/Cassette**
**Lyrics included**
**Ages 4–6**

This is another collection of exciting and innovative songs from the impressive Joe Scruggs. Imagine some singing birds who incorrectly hear and incorrectly echo Joe's words to a love song, creating the witty, silly title song that is sure to spark belly laughs. "The Gingerbread Man" takes that classic tale and converts it into a story about trying to catch a child who doesn't want to put on his pajamas. "Star Sun," sung in a cowboy ballad style, cleverly cautions children about overexposure to the sun. "New Baby" addresses feelings of anger, frustration and finally acceptance of a new sibling. The feelings and emotions expressed in this song are some of the most realistic I've heard in music. "Whole Bed," sung to the tune of "He's Got the Whole World in His Hands," salutes the joys of having the whole bed to oneself. A jubilant round combines "Swing Low Sweet Chariot" and "She'll Be Coming Around the Mountain." As usual, the orchestrations and accompaniments are lively, original and exciting. Other fun songs include "Humpty Dumpty" (a song about safety), "Baby Busy Box Band," "He's Got Hopes and He's Got Dreams" (a troll song about doing what you want with your life), "Halloween Night" (scary and fun), "Peas Porridge Hot" (a new Scruggs version), "Bathtime Blues" and "Almost Home." This collection is a sure hit with the young and the not so young.

★ ★ ★   **DEEP IN THE JUNGLE**
**Joe Scruggs**
**Educational Graphics Press**
**LP/Cassette**
**Lyrics included**
**Ages 4–8**

The continually creative Joe Scruggs has provided another winning recording. As in his other recordings, the length of some songs is more appropriate for older children, but I have friends whose preschoolers absolutely adore this recording. The title song is a clever adaptation of a popular song about two self-assured monkeys and a crocodile. It's musical arrangement and vocals are spectacular! "Read a Book" is a salute to literacy, and "Grandmas and Grandpas" is a loving song dedicated to all those nonjudgmental, caring and cuddling grandparents. "Eency Weency Spider" has some new contemporary verses that will make kids giggle. Other humorous songs include "Skateboard" (buying Mom a skateboard for her birthday), "Rock and Roll MacDonald" (a contemporary success story based on the classic "Old MacDonald"), "By the

Way" (a song about parents and kids and procrastination) and "Take a Nap" (about who ends up taking a nap at nap time). The six other songs are "Aunt Lucy," "Who Knows?" "Green Peas," "Refrigerator Picture," "Pour on the Sugar" and "Put Your Thumb in the Air." This is a super recording, filled with originality, imagination, love and respect. Joe also appears on a video called "Joe's First Video," which is great fun.


**EVEN TROLLS HAVE MOMS**
**Joe Scruggs**
**Educational Graphics Press**
**LP/Cassette**
**Lyrics included**
**Ages 4–8**

This great group of original witty songs that deal with life from a child's point of view is wonderfully presented by Joe Scruggs. The concepts in these songs are generally for a slightly older age group than those on some of his previous recordings, but young children will also enjoy this collection. "Chicken Wings" is a sensitive story song about a child who's not particularly athletic. "First Day" talks of that dreadful teary first day of school, but it's not the child who's crying, it's the mom. "Flying 'Round the Mountain," based on "She'll Be Comin' 'Round the Mountain," is a wacky song about a retired woman and her plans to keep herself busy. This is actually a wonderful song for adults who have friends or relatives about to retire. I'm not sure that kids will relate to this one, but it is a clever song. The title song deals with kids wishing they could be dragons, giants and trolls so they don't have to do the awful things that adults make them do, like brushing their teeth, going to school and cleaning their rooms. Scruggs explains that even these creatures have routines and responsibilities. My favorite song is "Twilight Zone Home," which cleverly talks about how things are always strangely disappearing. Other imaginative songs include "Nuke It" (about a microwave dad), "They Must Have Had Kids," "Inappropriate," "Swing and Sway" (an animal movement song), "Talking Toy Box" and "Where Angels Sleep."

**AMERICAN FOLK SONGS FOR CHILDREN**
**Mike and Peggy Seeger**
**Rounder Records**
**3 LPs or 2 Cassettes**
**No lyrics included**
**Ages 4–10**

This double volume recording contains ninety-four of the most
popular American folk songs, as well as some that are less well
known. The Seegers use mandolin, banjo, fiddle, guitar and
other folk instruments. The singing and instrumentation are
very clear. This collection of songs is not necessarily just for
children, and can be enjoyed by adults who want a well-
rounded folk music experience. Some of the songs are "Jim
Along Josie," "Billy Barlow," "Pick a Bale of Cotton," "Who's
That Tapping at the Window?" "There Was a Man and He Was
Mad," "Old Joe Clark," "Juba," "Frog Went A-Courtin'," and
"She'll Be Coming 'Round The Mountain." There is also a songbook, *American Folk Songs for Children* (published by Doubleday) available with all the music and verses to these songs.

**ABIYOYO AND OTHER STORY SONGS FOR**
   **CHILDREN**
**Pete Seeger**
**Smithsonian/Folkways**
**LP/Cassette/C.D.**
**Lyrics included**
**Ages 3–8**

This classic recording has been a favorite for years. Side A
contains two fairly long story songs, written or adapted by Pete
Seeger. These pieces are stories that are partially spoken and
partially sung. "Sam, the Whaler" (11 min. 25 sec.) tells the
story of a poor young boy who wants to go out whaling. He
gets a job as part of the crew and finally makes enough money
to eat to his heart's content. (This was written long before
whales became an endangered mammal.) The title song, "Abiyoyo" (9 min. 45 sec.), is based on an African folk tune. Pete's
story centers around a giant who is terrorizing a village in
which a young boy and his magician father live. When the boy

is finally able to make the giant lay down, the magician father makes Abiyoyo disappear and the village is saved. There is a wonderfully illustrated book, published by Macmillan, of this story available. It has become a classic Pete Seeger story. Side B contains other nighttime theme songs that were written mostly by Seeger. Some are perfect for young children as well as this older group. They include "Sweet Little Baby," "Sweepy, Sweepy, Sweepy," "Where Are My Pajamas?" "Green Grass Grows All Around" and "One Grain of Sand." Seeger is a master storyteller and singer. Other songs by Pete Seeger are on pp. 14, 104–107, 116, and 210–211.

**WHAT'S IN THE SEA?—**
    **Songs About Marine Life and Ocean**
    **Ecology**
**Lois Skiera-Zucek**
**Kimbo Educational**
**LP/Cassette**
**Lyrics and Activity Book included**
**Ages 4–8**

This much-needed recording fills a gap in children's music. Basic, important facts and information about aquatic life are presented in an upbeat, entertaining and catchy format. Men's, women's and children's voices inform listeners about whales, plankton, the Green Bay Estuary, penguins, pollution, manatees and more. There are thirteen songs in all, some better than others, but overall the collection is well presented. The musical accompaniment depends heavily on synthesizer, which gets a bit repetitive, but the variation in singers holds your attention. Parents and teachers can get a lot of mileage out of this recording. Songs include "Some Fish Swim in School," "The Emperor Penguin's Picnic," "S.C.U.B.A. Machine," "The Little Tiger Shark," "Dancing Dolphins," "The Pinniped Polka," "A Whale Vacation," "Predator/Prey" and "Mama Manatee."

**SAVE THE ANIMALS, SAVE THE EARTH—**
**Songs About Endangered Animals and the**
**Earth**
**Lyrics and music by Lois Skiera-Zucek—**
**Various performers**
**Kimbo Educational**
**LP/Cassette**
**Lyrics included**
**Ages 4–8**

Thirteen original songs that give information about animals that are in danger of becoming extinct and things people can do to preserve them and the earth. The lyric sheet includes a few lines of introductory material that help explain the context of each song. The musical arrangements use synthesized sounds, and the vocals are a bit uneven, but the content is very interesting and important. Children's voices are often included as well. Teachers will find this very useful for classroom use, and parents can use this to help children focus on the crucial issues. Some of the songs invite kids to get involved in letter writing and fund raising. Songs include "It's Everyone's World," "I Live in the Zoo," "The Animal Alphabet Song" (lists endangered species), "The Rainforest," "What Can I Do?," "The Wetlands," "In the Jungle Tonight" and more.

**KID POWER**
**Jonathan Sprout**
**Sprout Records**
**Cassette/C.D.**
**Lyrics included**
**Ages 5–8**

Jonathan Sprout's original music is uplifting and clever; the musical arrangements have a contemporary sound. His lyrics relate to issues in school-age children's lives. "Stuck with the Dishes" is about how a child procrastinates about having to do the dinner dishes. "I Want To Know" is a cute piece that asks "why" about things such as "when will tomorrow be today?," "whose fault is an earthquake?" and "what kind of person invented the spoon?" "Stand Up" is a plea for people to stand up and be counted so that there may be food for the hungry and resolution to fighting. Every child can relate to "Loose Tooth." Other songs are "A Better Place to Live," "He Likes to Bark," "Somewhere Deep Inside," "Dance," "My Bicycle" and three more. An upbeat recording. More recordings by Jonathan Sprout are on pp. 29–30.

**ON THE RADIO**
**Jonathan Sprout**
**Sprout Records**
**Cassette**
**Lyrics included**
**Ages 5–8**

This recording wants you to believe that you're listening to a radio show for kids. The announcer gives a brief introduction to most of the songs. The music generally has a rock sound. Sprout has a pleasant voice and his original lyrics tend towards the humorous, although some are a bit forced and preachy. "Wordworm" gives words and then synonyms such as feeble and infirm and trinket and trifle. "Braces" tells of the good things that these intrusive devices will do for your mouth and smile, and how to care for them. "The Shower Song" is about an adult who learns to love showering too much. "Do What You Say You'll Do" deals with being honest. I like Sprout's *Kid Power* much more than this recording, both in terms of lyrics and musical style. Other songs include "Litterbug," "Day Is Done," "I Don't Wanna Go Home," "Friends," "Just a Dream" and more.

★★★  **ALL FOR FREEDOM**
**Sweet Honey in the Rock**
**Music for Little People**
**Cassette**
**Lyrics included**
**Ages 4–10**

Sweet Honey in the Rock is an incredible quintet of African-American women: Bernice Johnson Reagon, Evelyn Maria Harris, Ysaye Maria Barnwell, Aisha Kahlil, and Nitanju Bolade Casel. Their a cappella arrangements are powerful and encourage hand clapping, moving and singing along. "The Little Shekere" is a rap-type original song about how a squash gourd becomes the Shekere instrument. The classic "Little Red Caboose" is incredible in that the group harmonizes to make the sound of the train whistle, and when you hear it, it sounds like the real thing. The vocals also include the sound of the train on the track. No instruments, just voices. The traditional "Cumbayah My Lord, Cumbayah" is hauntingly beautiful. "Juba" is a traditional African-American game song, performed with powerful energy. Other traditional songs with new and exciting arrangements include "Silvie" ("Bring me a little water, Silvie"), "Make New Friends" (a round), "Amen," "Meeting at the Building" (a spiritual), "Everybody Ought to Know What Freedom Is," "So Glad I'm Here," and "If You're All for Freedom" plus five more. This great recording is for children of all ethnic backgrounds.

**SHAKE SUGAREE**
**Taj Mahal**
**Music for Little People**
**Cassette**
**No lyrics included**
**Ages 4–8**

Taj Mahal has long been a folk favorite, and this superb recording will bring his talent into your child's life. Using guitar, mandolin and harmonica, Mahal brings a variety of musical styles into your home. His husky voice sings "Funky Bluesy ABC's," "Talking John Henry," "Shake Sugaree," "Quavi, Quavi" (West African), "Brown Girl in the Ring" (Caribbean), "Little Brown Dog," "Light Rain," "Fishin' Blues" and "A Soulful Tune," where Mahal accompanies himself with hambone-style clapping. An instrumental version of "Railroad Bill" is delightful.

**ALL OF US WILL SHINE**
**Tickle Tune Typhoon**
**Tickle Tune Typhoon Records/Music for Little**
    **People**
**LP/Cassette**
**Lyrics included**
**Ages 4–8**

Tickle Tune Typhoon is a mixture of many voices, male and female. This, their third recording, contains songs about friends, caring, nature and bodies. There are several movement-oriented songs including "Hokey Pokey" and "East/West" where children twist, fly, clap, strut, point and boogie to the East and then to the West. Other pieces focus on feelings, like "Everyone Is Differently Abled," "We've Got the Whole World in Our Hands," "All Of Us Will Shine" and "Let's Be Friends." Listeners learn about bodies in "Pearly White Waltz" and "My Body Belongs to Me." Other songs are "Twinkle Twinkle Little Star," "Let the Sun Shine Forever" (sung in Russian and English), "There Is a Fine Wind Blowing," "Flowers" and "Bicycle Cowboy." As in their other recordings, Tickle Tune Typhoon has a theatrical sound, reminiscent of soundtracks. A holiday recording by Tickle Tune Typhoon is reviewed on pp. 225–226.

**CIRCLE AROUND**
**Tickle Tune Typhoon**
**Tickle Tune Typhoon Records/Music for Little**
    **People**
**LP/Cassette**
**Lyrics included**
**Ages 4–8**

This mostly original music is upbeat and carries educational and ecological messages for kids. Tickle Tune Typhoon is exuberant and prolific, and you can feel the energy generated. "Tree Dancin'" is a waltz that encourages creative movement, and "Vegaboogie" is a clever song about vegetables. "Hug Bug" supports emotional expressiveness, suggesting that kids show their love with a hug. "Bear Hunt" tells the story of a bear chase, including the fears to be overcome. This can also be

played out by listeners as a game. "We Circle Around" is based
on an Arapaho song. Other songs include "Sneakers," "Dinosaurs," "Magic Penny," "Clap Your Hands" and "The Monster
Song." Many of these songs are very long, and might not be
suitable for children with very short attention spans.

**HEARTS AND HANDS**
**Tickle Tune Typhoon**
**Tickle Tune Typhoon Records/Music for Little
    People**
**LP/Cassette**
**Lyrics included**
**Ages 4–8**

The full sound of Tickle Tune Typhoon returns with mostly
original music that explores feelings and self-esteem. One of
my favorite songs, with new arrangements by the group, is
"Sing When the Spirit Says Sing." It's robust and easy to get
involved with. "Words" is a great song whose narrator deals
with name calling by saying "I will not take these words inside,
I will not let them hurt my pride." "Uh Huh" is a song about
exaggeration that kids can thoroughly appreciate. They do a
nice version of "De Colores" in both Spanish and English.
Other songs include "Over The Rainbow," "Shine Out," "Har-
vest Blessing," "Sacred Trees," "I Believe in Me," "Grammar
Rapper" and "Boo Boo Boogie." The group has a unique sound
and a large group of fans around the country. Their songs promote a positive self-image in children and a positive look at
the global environmental situation.

**HUG THE EARTH**
**Tickle Tune Typhoon**
**Tickle Tune Typhoon Records/Music for Little
    People**
**LP/Cassette**
**Lyrics included**
**Ages 4–8**

This collection centers around the unifying themes of saving
the planet and feeling good about oneself. The group's vocals

are fun to listen to and sound almost like a theatrical production. I love their version of "Kye Kye Kule," a musical chant from Ghana. It's a wonderful song to use with children; they are simultaneously learning another language and moving their bodies. Another great piece, "A Place in the Choir," presents the different groups of the human vocal range (soprano, alto, tenor, bass). "The Family Song" is a modern view of non-stereotyped family life. Other songs include "Garbage Blues," "Oh Cedar Tree," "If You're Happy," "Knickerbocker," "Super Kids," "Skin" (under our skin, we're all the same) and "Thanks."

**BARLEY BREAD AND REINDEER MILK**
**Dave and Helene Van Manens**
**People Records**
**Cassette**
**No lyrics included**
**Ages 3–6**

This is a collection of mostly original songs that deal with getting along with others and creating a peaceful world. The lyrics are good, although sometimes a bit forced. Both singers have very pleasant voices and children often accompany the Van Manens. This is a recording that has wonderful messages that children need to hear. "People" is about the ways different people live around the world; what they eat, how they dress, etc. "Imagine a Peaceful World" is a catchy song that describes how kids will someday have the power to change the ways of the world. "I Want To Sing" is a melodic song done in three-part harmony with some kids. It's really fun. There are a few songs ("Warm Fuzzies," "I Love My Home" and "Take A Walk") whose forced lyrics didn't appeal to me. Other songs include "Mairzy Doats," "Under One Sky," "Peace Will Come" and three more.

**WE RECYCLE**
**Dave and Helene Van Manens**
**People Records**
**Cassette**
**Lyrics included**
**Ages 4–8**

Although the theme of this recording is positive and important, most of the songs have tired and forced lyrics. The Van Manens vocals are very nice and the children who often accompany them are great. One of the stronger songs is called "Family Tree," It explains how we may be different outwardly, but inside, we are all people who want to be happy and free. Other songs are "Cold Pricklies" (this is a term that reflects bad or uncomfortable feelings and is the opposite of "warm fuzzies"), "Warm Fuzzies Revisited," "She's My Dog," "We Are Flowers" (a song about looking for world unity), "I'm Angry," "Earthkeeper," "Going to My Garden," "What Is Peace?" and "I Went For A Walk."

**FOR OUR CHILDREN**
**Various Artists**
**Disney Records**
**Cassette/C.D.**
**Lyrics included**
**Ages 5–10**

This recording by all-star performers was made to benefit the Pediatric AIDS Foundation. The music is fun to hear, although many of the songs are not really "children's" songs; some are geared to very young children, while others are about adults looking at childhood. This is a nostalgic recording to play and save for future generations. Some of my favorite selections are Bob Dylan singing "This Old Man," Little Richard singing one of the most electric versions ever of "Itsy Bitsy Spider," Bette Midler singing "Blueberry Pie," Bruce Springsteen singing "Chicken Lips and Lizard Hips," Meryl Streep singing "Gartan Mother's Lullaby" and James Taylor singing "Getting to Know You." Other pieces are "Give a Little Love" by Ziggy Marley and The Melody Makers, "Cushie Butterfield" by Sting, "Mary Had a Little Lamb" (a new version) by Paul McCartney, "The

Ballad of Davy Crockett" by Steven Bishop (it's too bad they chose this song from the Disney Library since it makes reference to "Injuns"), "Autumn to May" by Ann and Nancy Wilson, "Child of Mine" by Carole King, "Tell Me Why" by Pat Benatar, "Good Night My Love (Pleasant Dreams)" by Paula Abdul, "Golden Slumbers" by Jackson Browne and Jennifer Warnes, "A Child Is Born" by Barbara Streisand, "Blanket for a Sail" by Harry Nilsson, "A Medley of Rhymes" by Debbie Gibson, "Country Feelin's" by Brian Wilson, and an instrumental piece called "The Pacifier" by Elton John. The proceeds from this recording go to benefit a formidable foundation, run by Elizabeth Glaser, that works overtime to help in pediatric AIDS research.

★★★     **I'M GONNA LET IT SHINE—**
        **A Gathering of Voices for Freedom**
        **Various Artists—Produced by Bill Harley**
        **Round River Productions**
        **Cassette**
        **No lyrics included**
        **All ages**

Although not specifically for children, these songs represent America's struggle for freedom and the well-being of her people. The singers, of all ages and ethnic backgrounds and from different parts of the country, are active in making the world a better place in which to live. Some are professional singers, and others just love to sing. The project began when they came together to celebrate Martin Luther King's Birthday. This is a fine collection of songs, and, in my opinion, children of all races, ages and backgrounds will truly be enriched by this recording. Songs include "Get on Board, Children," "Hold On (Keep Your Eyes On The Prize)," "Oh Freedom," "Tsenzenina," "This Little Light," "If You Miss Me from the Back of the Bus," "I'm On My Way," "Come By Here" (sung to the tune of "Kum Ba Ya"), "Sing Mandela Gree," "One Little Step Towards Freedom," "We Shall Overcome" and seven more. Bravo to Bill Harley for producing this marvelous recording. Other recordings by Bill Harley are on pp. 150–151.

## 208 GROWING UP WITH MUSIC

**JOURNEY INTO SPACE**
**Various Artists**
**Kimbo Educational**
**LP/Cassette**
**Lyrics and Activity Booklet included**
**Ages 4–10**

These original songs are sure to please even the youngest of space explorers. Factual information is presented in a fun and lively format. Although originally done for schools, this recording is very appropriate for use at home. Children will learn about planets, spacecraft, gravity, and many other space concepts. The singers are both male and female, and the musical arrangements are very simple. There is an activity and lyric booklet that is helpful in stimulating further education. The songs include "Rocket Rock," "The Planet Song," "Moon Rock Rock," "Weightless Workout," "Footsteps on the Moon," "Gravity," "My Space Suit" and "Is Anybody Else Out There?"

**KIDDIN' AROUND VOLUMES I AND II**
**Various Artists**
**Music for Little People**
**Cassette**
**Lyrics with Volume II only**
**Ages 3–10**

These two samplers are compilations of songs from different recordings by various artists. *Volume I* features various artists who record on different record labels, while *Volume II* consists of performers who record on the Music for Little People label. This is a wonderful way to hear many different recording artists and new songs on one cassette.

VOLUME I includes "Rainbow Plant" and "My Blanket Is the Sky" by Jim Valley, "I Wanna Try It" and "Logical" (one of my favorites) from Peter Alsop, "Rapp Song" and "With Two Wings" by Red Grammar, "Crosspatch" and "Hey Diddle Diddle" by Dennis Hysom, "Make Believe," "Teddy Bear," and "Find a Peaceful Thought" by Linda Arnold, and "Kye Kye Kule" and "We've Got the Whole World in Our Hands" by Tickle Tune Typhoon.

VOLUME II includes "Quackity Yakity Bop," "Little White Duck" and "A Fly Walked into a Grocery Store" from the Yakity Yakity Bop recording, "General Store," "Peaceable Kingdom" and "When It's Dark In The Night" by Kathi and Milenko, Nancy Rumbel and Friends, "The Belly Button Song" and "Colors" by Michele Easton-Cortwright, "Jump into the Circle," "Rain Song" and "Jump Down" by Lisa Monet and "Guavi, Guavi" and "Little Brown Dog" by Taj Mahal.

**KIDS SING AMERICA**
**Various Artists**
**Brentwood Music**
**Cassette**
**Lyrics included**
**Ages 4–10**

A children's chorus sings seventeen songs about America and patriotism. The voices are very pleasant, but the arrangements are not terribly creative. It is, however, a good recording with well-known songs. Teachers will find all this patriotic music very useful. The songs include "This Land Is Your Land," "You're a Grand Old Flag," "Yankee Doodle," "America the Beautiful," "Erie Canal," "God Bless America," "This Is My Country," "Home on the Range," "My Country 'Tis Of Thee," "The Star Spangled Banner," "Battle Hymn of the Republic" and "I Pledge Allegiance" (spoken). This is one of a very few similar recordings. We get many requests for patriotic music, and this is as good a collection as any I've heard.

**ONCE UPON A DINOSAUR**
**Various Artists**
**Kimbo Educational**
**LP/Cassette**
**Lyrics included**
**Ages 4–10**

Will dinosaurs ever go out of fashion? Not according to all the people who sell dinosaur-related material. This is an upbeat educational recording about different kinds of dinosaurs and the times in which they lived. It was originally produced for classroom use, but is also appropriate for home. Children's voices help describe data about the giants of the past. The songs have factual information performed in a variety of musical styles. The children's voices are clear and easy to understand. This is a must if your child has any interest in dinosaurs. The songs are "Fossil Rock," "The Stegosaurus," "My Pet Tyrannosaurus," "The Plant Eaters," "The Reptile Rap," "The Brachiosaurs' Song," "The Meat Eaters," "Where Have They Gone," "Big Bad Al" and "Dinosaur Dance."

**ONE WIDE RIVER**
**Various Artists**
**American Melody**
**Cassette**
**Lyrics included**
**Ages 4–8**

Mandolins, banjos, guitars, fiddles, cello, keyboards, bass and harmonicas accompany several artists as they perform original and traditional music and stories. Many of the songs are quite long, but very easy to hear. The recording includes "The Owl and the Pussycat" sung by Phil Rosenthal, "The Haying Song" by Dave Mallett, "Grandmother Rosie and Her Ducks" told by Barbara Reed, "Shenandoah" sung by The Smith Sisters, "The Garden Song" by Dave Mallett, "Get Up and Bar the Door" by Jonathan Edwards and "One Wide River" by Phil and Naomi Rosenthal. A great advantage of this recording is that children get to experience several voices and styles.

★ ★ ★    **PEACE IS THE WORLD SMILING**
**Various Artists**
**Music for Little People**
**Cassette/C.D.**
**Lyrics included**
**Ages 3–10**

This is a collective effort by a wonderful group of performers whose lyrics and music celebrate a world in which peace prevails and people live together in harmony. Linda Arnold's "Find a Peaceful Thought" uses children's definitions of peace, and

Taj Mahal's "Everybody Is Somebody" is a self-esteem booster. "Hug The Earth," by Tickle Tune Typhoon, is an ecological song. "Aiye Mire" is a story chant by Babatundi Olatunji, the great African percussionist. Pete Seeger sings "If I Had a Hammer," and "Voices," which encourages listening to different generations and heritages, is sung by Holly Near. "On Children" has lyrics by Kahil Gibran and is sung by Sweet Honey in the Rock. Other songs include "Kid's Peace Song," "The Planet Is Our Family," "Turn the World Around," "The Whale Gulch Rap," "Peace Is the World Smiling," "We Love Our Home" and "Make Peace." There are also some great poems read by children. A minimum of $1.30 for each recording sold is contributed to an organization called 1 Percent For Peace.

**ROUNDER KIDS**
**Various Artists**
**Rounder Records**
**Cassette**
**No lyrics included**
**Ages 4–10**

This fine collection includes the various artists who record on the Rounder Record label. It is a wonderful way to have a mixture of voices and musical styles on one recording. If you particularly enjoy one of the performers, you can then purchase one of their recordings. John McCutcheon sings "We Are The Boats/Somos El Barco" and "Howjadoo," Cathy Fink sings "Alphabet Boogie" and "Grandma Slid Down the Mountain," Dan Crow sings "Oops!" Mike and Peggy Seeger sing "She'll Be Coming 'Round the Mountain," Riders in the Sky sing "Yippie-Yi-Yo and Away We Go," Marcy Marxer sings "Jump Children," Bessie Jones sings "Way Go, Lily," and Marcia Berman, Dan Crow, Uncle Ruthie Buell, J. P. Nightingale and Fred Sokolow sing "Chanukah At Home." A wonderful collection of fine children's music.

### DOC WATSON SINGS SONGS FOR LITTLE PICKERS
**Doc Watson**
**Alacazam Recordings**
**Cassette**
**Liner notes, but no lyrics included**
**Ages 4–10**

This live concert recording brings a slice of Americana into your homes or cars. Doc Watson's sense of humor and phenomenal guitar playing skills are a delight to listen to. Although there is no lyric sheet, Watson has included some notes telling where he learned the songs. These songs are story-type songs directed at children old enough to follow the story line. Some of the more well-known pieces include "The Riddle Song (I Gave My Love a Cherry)," "John Henry," "Froggy Went A-Courtin'," "The Crawdad Song," "The Green Grass Grew All Around" and "Little Liza Jane." "Talkin' Guitar" is a great piece where Watson uses his guitar to imitate the sounds of the lyrics. "Sing Song Kitty" is wonderfully silly and full of funny, tongue-twisting words. "Mama Blues," an instrumental piece, features a harmonica that sounds like it's saying "mama." The other two songs are "Mole in the Ground" and "The Tennessee Stud." A fine way to introduce children to American folk music.

# *Holiday*
# *Recordings* ♫‥

Listed in this chapter are some of the many recordings available for the different holiday celebrations. The ones described here are specifically for children. Some of the songs for young audiences explain the meaning of the holiday, while others represent the feelings and traditions of the season. Record stores everywhere have traditional music available seasonally, and you can choose from the performers that you enjoy most.

I feel that sharing music at the holidays is an important way of keeping your cultural traditions alive. My family heard music about holidays that we never formally celebrated, and we learned how others observe special days. We learned Christmas carols and Hanukkah songs, listened to the *Messiah* and klezmer music. It was always a time to feel involved with many cultures and peoples. Children love to be part of a celebration, and most of these recordings will give them the feeling of being able to participate. You can start listening to the songs anywhere between one and three weeks before the actual holiday, so that your child has time to learn his favorite songs. Children hear lots of holiday music in school, but some of the more unusual holidays are represented in these recordings.

It's interesting to note that, while many of the recordings have definite Christmas titles, some of them also include one or two Hanukkah songs. I've made it a point to list those songs, so it's a good idea to read through all the titles. Recordings in other sections also contain one or possibly two songs that relate to the holidays, but listed below are the ones that are specifically geared to holidays or holiday seasons.

The question most frequently asked regarding seasonal recordings relates to age appropriateness. Most of the recordings aren't geared to any particular ages (I've noted the exceptions), but rather to the whole family. Since these are used only once a year, you'll be coming back to each one year after year. Many of these songs have religious roots and were intended for listeners of all ages. In modern times many of these songs have become somewhat disassociated from their origins. During the holidays, our customers want to know which recordings feature religious music, as some want to hear traditional church music, while others are looking for a more secular selection. I've identified individual recordings as one or the other in this chapter.

Many families have musical traditions they follow at holidays that really don't necessarily relate to widespread religious or secular traditions. A friend of mine tells me that *Man of La Mancha* has become an Advent tradition in her family for reasons no one can recall. Each year a teacher I know buys any new holiday recording available for her third grade class. They talk about similarities and differences in holiday customs: the different names for Santa Claus, the different spellings of "Hanukkah," and words that we traditionally associate with Halloween. Holidays are a great time for families and friends to sing together. Don't miss this opportunity to share in the festivities.

## DO:

• Share music from other cultures.

• Sing as a family, in the car and at home and school.

• Listen to some classical music.

• Discuss the meanings of the different holidays and find songs that reinforce those conversations.

• Start listening to recordings three weeks before the holiday.

• Ask your child to teach you and the rest of the family their favorite holiday songs from school.

# DON'T:

- Be afraid to start your own "quirky" holiday music traditions.

- Exclude your cultural and or religious heritage. Make this a time of renewal.

### CELEBRATE WITH CINDY—VOLUME I—
#### Jewish Holiday Music for Children
**Cindy Paley Aboody**
**Koleet Productions**
**Cassette**
**Lyrics booklet included**

Cindy Paley Aboody's voice is clear and perfectly pitched for young children. There are simple explanations in English of the mostly Hebrew songs, which will be helpful for the very young and will reinforce concepts for the older children. There are songs for many holidays, including Rosh Hashanah, Yom Kippur, Chanukah and Sukkot. This is a nice way to have a musical overview of the Jewish holidays. Children accompany Cindy on many of the songs. The songs in Hebrew include "Tapuchim U'Dvash," "Shana Tova," "Sisu V'Simchu," "Chag Yafe" and "Shlomit Bona Sukkat Shalom." Some of the songs in English are "The Latke Song," "I Have a Little Dreidel," "Oh Chanukah," "These Are the Days," "This Is What We Need to Build a Sukkah" and "The Dreidel Song." A very satisfying recording.

### CHANUKAH—A SINGING CELEBRATION
**Cindy Paley Aboody**
**Cindy Paley Aboody**
**Cassette**
**Lyrics included**

Aboody introduces each song with an explanation of it's meaning, and then beautifully presents the music of Chanukah. Most of the songs are sung in Hebrew, although four are in English only ("Light One Candle" written by Peter Yarrow, "The Latke Song," "Eight Candles" written by Malvina Reynolds and "Eight Days of Chanukah," sung to the tune of "Those Were the Days"). Others are sung in Hebrew and English. All songs are shown in the lyrics booklet in both Hebrew and English transliteration. The songs include "Chanukah Chag Yafe," "Mi Y'malel," "Blessings Over the Candles" (in Hebrew), "Maoz Tsur (Rock Of Ages)," "Chanukah Oh Chanukah," "Hava Narimah," "Banu Choshech," "Ner Li" and "Lichvod Hachanukah."

### SHABBAT SHALOM
### Cindy Paley Aboody
### Cindy Paley Recordings
### Cassette
### Lyrics included

Cindy Paley Aboody is a Jewish music educator in Los Angeles, and her extensive work with children is apparent in her simple, clear presentations. Her voice is pleasing, and the songs are appropriate for preschool as well as older children. She briefly explains the songs and their meanings before singing them. Many children's voices are used as well. The lyric booklet presents both English and Hebrew. This is a wonderful recording for children. Songs include "Hayom Yom Shishi/Shabbat Shalom," "Chiribim," "Candle Blessings," "Shalom Aleichem," "Mother's Gone a Marketing/I Have a Little Challah/The Sabbath Table," "Mizmor Shir," and "L'cha Dodi."

### A SINGING SEDER
### Cindy Paley Aboody
### Cindy Paley Aboody
### Cassette
### Lyrics included

Cindy Aboody's lovely voice graces this delightful singing celebration of the Pesach (Passover) meal, the Seder. Most of the songs are sung in Hebrew by Aboody, and the Kiddush is recited by Cantor Herschel Fox. A few of the songs are sung in English ("The Ten Plagues" and "Go Down Moses"). The booklet shows the lyrics written in Hebrew and English transliterations. Each song is preceded by a short explanation. The musical arrangements are very nice, and often children's voices accompany Cindy's. This recording provides a splendid way to teach your children the music of this special holiday. Songs include "Simcha Raba," "Hin'ni Muchan Um'Zuman," "Avadim Hayinu," "V'hi She'amda," "Dayenu," "Halleluyah," "Chasal Sidur Pesach," "Chad Gadya" and "Ki Hine Hastav Avar" and "Echad Mi Yodea?"

**MOSTLY MATZOH**
**Fran Avni**
**Music for Little People/Lemonstone Records**
**in Canada**
**Cassette**
**No lyrics included**

Fran Avni tells the story of Passover and then sings songs of this holiday season. Most of the songs are original and sung in English, but some of the traditional songs like "Dayenu" are sung in Hebrew. Avni's voice is very pleasant, and the children's chorus is inviting. The orchestrations are very simple. This recording could be of use to families or teachers who do not know much about Pesach but want to expose children to this important event in Jewish culture. The songs include "What If?" "Yocheved's Lament," "Slaves," "Hurry Up," "The Miracle," "Mah Nishtanah," "The Matzoh Boogie," "The Saga of Baby Moses" and "Wandering."

**CHRISTMAS MAGIC**
**Joanie Bartels**
**Discovery Magic**
**Cassette**
**Lyrics included**

This is another magical recording from the talented Joanie Bartels. Her inviting voice and interesting musical accompaniments make this a wonderful holiday recording. The songs are perfect for sing-along or just for listening pleasure. This collection includes "Santa Claus Is Coming to Town," "Jingle Bells," "Up on the Housetop," "Rudolph the Red Nosed Reindeer," "Jingle Bell Rock," "All I Want for Christmas (Is My Two Front

Teeth)," "Winter Wonderland," "Rockin' Around the Christmas Tree," "Have Yourself a Merry Little Christmas," "I Want a Hippopotamus for Christmas" and "Sleigh Ride." A delightful Christmas recording. Other recordings by Bartels on pp. 11, 35–36, and 58–60.

**WEE SING FOR CHRISTMAS**
**Pamela Conn Beall and Susan Nipp**
**Price, Stern, Sloan Publishers**
**Cassette**
**Lyrics and Activity Booklet included.**

A full sixty minutes of Christmas fun and songs are sung by different adult's and children's voices. The songs are divided among three sections. Here We Come A-Caroling includes "Deck the Halls," "We Wish You a Merry Christmas," "Jingle Bells," "The First Noel," "Joy to the World," "Away in a Manger," "Silent Night," "The Twelve Days of Christmas," "O Christmas Tree" and four more. The Birthday of a King includes "Fum, Fum, Fum," "The Little Drummer Boy," "Where Is the Baby?" "March of the Kings," "Children, Go Where I Send Thee," "What Child Is This," "Go Tell It on the Mountain" and fifteen more. Here Comes Santa Claus includes "Must Be Santa," "Up on the Housetop," "Little Bells of Christmas" and five rounds, five fingerplays and nine more songs. Although this is a very complete collection of songs, the vocal quality is spotty and not very interesting. Other Wee Sing recordings are listed on pp. 36–37, 61–62 and 131–132.

**CHRISTMAS TREE**
**Rick Charette**
**Pine Point Records**
**Cassette**
**Lyrics and Activity Booklet included**

This recording primarily contains original songs by Rick Charette, with his mellow and easy-to-listen-to voice. The songs sound very similar and don't offer much variety for your children. It's always nice to have some new songs for the holidays, but many of these do not bear repeated listening. The traditional songs are more interesting to hear again and again. The activity book includes recipes, sign language directions and craft ideas for Christmas. The original songs include "Shining Star," "Christmas Tree," "Christmas Day Is Coming," "It's Snowing" and "Best Part of Christmas." The traditional songs include "My Dreydl" (for Chanukah), "Santa Claus Is Coming to Town," "Mary Had a Baby," "Jingle Bells," "Up on the House-top," "Silent Night" and "All Through The Night." Additional recordings by Charette are on page 141.


**SANTA SONGS**
**Dan Crow**
**Sony Kids' Music**
**Cassette/C.D.**
**Lyrics included**

Dan Crow's charm and wit overflow in this delightful holiday recording. As he does in his live concerts, Dan interacts exten-sively with children and delights even the youngest. His voice is inviting, and it's easy to sing with him. Crow combines orig-inal selections with some of the more traditional Christmas songs. I loved "Santa Claus in Santa Fe" which uses English and Spanish to describe how two cultures combine at Christmas. "I'm an Elf" is a clever piece about the tremendous amount of work that these poor little things do each year. "Santa Claus Ho Ho" is a great piece about the different mean-ings and names for Santa Claus around the world. Other songs include "Santa Claus Is Coming to Town," "Rudolf the Red Nosed Reindeer," "Up on the Housetop," "I Saw Mommy Kissing Santa Claus," "Jingle Bells" and "All I Want for Christmas" (sung with a lisp). This is a wonderful recording to share with family and friends. More Dan Crow recordings are on pp. 142–144.

★ ★ ★　**CHANUKAH AT HOME**
**Dan Crow, Marcia Berman, Uncle Ruthie**
**Buell, J. P. Nightingale, Fred Sokolow**
**Rounder Records**
**Cassette/C.D.**
**Lyrics not included**

This is my favorite Chanukah recording for several reasons.
First, the combination of voices and musical styles is exciting.
Second, the songs are accessible to children of many ages.
Third, this is a recording that many non-Jewish families use to
teach their children about this holiday. Not all of the performers are Jewish, which supports the notion that sharing
music from all cultures with your children can be educational.
Some of the songs are sung in Hebrew, but the majority have
some English parts. This is a wonderful recording for families
who want their children to learn some factual information
about Chanukah, as well as some of the traditional music from
the holiday. There are even a few original songs that are
delightful. I can't praise this recording enough! Songs are "Chanukah, Oh Chanukah," "Kindle a Candle of Light," "Chanukah
Blessing" (all in Hebrew), "Khanekah," "Chanukah at Home,"
"Chag Yafe," "Family Time," "The Dreydl Song," "Rock Of
Ages (Maoz Tsov)," "Mi Yemaleil," "Ner Li," "Sevivon,"
"Together" and "Eight Candles."


**FRANCINE SINGS A KEEPSAKE OF FAVORITE**
**HOLIDAY SONGS**
**Francine Lancaster**
**Lancaster Productions**
**Cassette**
**Lyrics included**

The strength of this recording is the collection of songs and
the holidays represented. Lancaster's voice is very high and
sometimes difficult to listen to. The lyrics unfortunately are
hard to understand because she sings in an operatic fashion.
The holidays and songs are: Thanksgiving: "Over the River,"
"We Gather Together," "Thanksgiving Prayer," "For the Beauty
of the Earth"; Hanukkah: "O Hanukkah," "My Dreydl," "The
Latke Song," "Song for Hanukkah," "Instrumental Medley";

Christmas: "Jingle Bells,""Deck the Halls," "Away in a Manger"; and New Year's: "Wassail Song" and "The Old Year Now Away Is Fled." A very unsatisfying recording.


### HOLLY DAZE
**Mary Miché**
**Star Trek**
**Cassette**
**Lyrics included**

Mary Miché has done many fun recordings for children, and this one is no exception. She has gathered some of the more entertaining songs for Halloween, Thanksgiving, Hanukkah, Christmas, New Year's, and Martin Luther King's Birthday. She always sounds like she's having fun when she sings. Her constant work with children helps her know what works with kids from four to ten. This is a great tool for classrooms, playgroups and homes. The songs include "The Haunted House," "The Pumpkin Man," "Grandma's Feather Bed," "Raindrops on Roses," "The Thanksgiving Song," "Hava Nashira," "The Marvelous Toy," "Jingle Bell Rock," "Christmas Dinner," "Ding Dong Diggidy Song" and "The Dream of Martin Luther King, Jr." Other recordings by Mary Miché are on pp. 161–164.


### HAP PALMER'S HOLIDAY MAGIC
**Hap Palmer**
**Kids USA**
**Cassette**
**Lyrics included**

Hap's alluring voice and original lyrics are a welcome treat for the Christmas/Hanukkah season. There are some traditional songs such as "Rudolph the Red Nosed Reindeer" and "We Wish You a Merry Christmas." "Jingle Bells/Jingle Song" is a clever new movement version of the classic song: "jingle hands, jingle arms, jingle legs and feet." Hap's original songs are delightful and very creative. "Felíz Navidad/Merry Christmas" is a song of peace and love. "Angel Band" is a catchy counting song about ten little angels. "The Merry Hula" is a tropical holiday song. The other songs are "Merry

Christmas Santa," "Caroling, Caroling," "What A World We'd Have," "Things I'm Thankful For" and "The Baby's Carol." Side A of this recording is sung, and Side B is instrumental only, which can be used as back-up while your children sing. This is a pleasing and refreshing recording. Hap Palmer's other recordings are described on pp. 48–50, 87–88 and 168–173.

★★★        **A CHILD'S CHRISTMAS**
            **Tom Paxton**
            **Pax Records**
            **Cassette**
            **Lyrics included**

If you are bored with the same old holiday music year after year, then this recording is a must. Paxton's original songs are filled with love and the feelings of Christmas. The orchestrations are full and varied, and Paxton's voice is rich and inviting. These are songs that should and could become classics. As a lyricist, Paxton is tops. The songs include "Reindeer on My Roof," "How Many Cookies Can Santa Claus Eat?" "Christmas Stocking," "The Marvelous Toy," "I Hope Daddy Likes His Tie," "The Candy Cane Tree" and "I Know Why There's Christmas." A real delight! More Tom Paxton on pp. 174–177.

★★★        **THE SEASONS: A FAMILY CHRISTMAS**
                **CELEBRATION**
            **Fred Penner**
            **Oak Street Music**
            **Cassette/C.D.**
            **Lyrics included**

Penner's voice is rich and full and perfect for holiday singing. This unique recording includes songs from many cultures, many sung in their native languages. This is a delightful way for you and your children to experience the holiday season in the ways celebrated by others around the world. There is even a Hanukkah song, "Mao Tzur (Rock Of Ages)" sung in Hebrew. The instrumentation is faithful to the culture represented. Although some of the songs are original, they are easy to learn and sure to please the whole family. Penner uses a children's chorus on many of the songs, which gives added appeal. Love and warm feelings come through on this recording. Songs include "Children Go," "O Tannenbaum," "Cantate Domino," "A' Soalin," "Away in a Manger," "Liese rieselt der Schnee (Softly Falls The Snow)," "Il est Né le divin Enfant (The Divine Infant Is Born)," "Dnas' Pohyooshcha (Let Us Sing and Rejoice Today)," "The First Noel," "Deck the Halls," "Rudolph The Red Nosed Reindeer," "Jingle Bells," and "White Christmas." Other recordings by Fred Penner are on pp. 90–93 and 177.

## RAFFI'S CHRISTMAS ALBUM
**Raffi**
**Shoreline/MCA**
**Cassette/C.D.**
**Lyrics included**

Raffi's contribution to the holidays is primarily comprised of traditional songs that will appeal to children and adults of all ages. Raffi's soft, inviting voice and lovely orchestral arrangements suitably reflect love and giving. Ken Whiteley accompanies Raffi on many of the songs, which is an added treat. The traditional songs include "Frosty the Snowman," "Up on the Housetop," "Jingle Bells," "The First Noel/Deck the Halls," "Rudolph the Red Nosed Reindeer," "Silent Night/Away in a Manger," "We Wish You a Merry Christmas," and "There Was a Little Baby." Some of the original and non-traditional songs are "Petit Papa Noel," "Every Little Wish," "Old Toy Trains," and "Must Be Santa." This is a charming holiday recording. Other recordings by Raffi are on pp. 93–98 and 183–184.

## ALL ABOUT HANUKKAH IN STORY AND SONG
**Margie Rosenthal and Ilene Safyan—**
**Story narrated by Peninnah Schram**
**Kar-Ben Copies**
**Book and Cassette—Lyrics and Illustrations**

This is a really nice package for Hanukkah. Rosenthal and Safyan, both cantors in Portland, Oregon, have beautiful voices.

Each song is explained first, giving the child an idea of why and when the songs are sung. The songs are appropriate for all ages, but the book is a little long for very young children. The pieces include "The Story of Hanukkah," "O Hanukkah," "Candle Blessings," "Ma'oz Tsur," "Mattathias Bold," "Who Can Retell?" "Chanukah, Chag Yafeh," "Shine Little Candles," "Oco Kandelikas," "The Dreidel Song" and "Light One Candle." This is a very satisfying recording.

**THE TOYMAKER'S CHRISTMAS**
**Kevin Roth**
**Sony Kids' Music**
**Cassette/C.D.**
**Lyrics included**

Roth's voice is warm and mellow in this collection of mostly original music for the Christmas season. The arrangements are very simple but often unimaginative. If you like Roth's other recordings, this could be a fine holiday selection. The songs include "The Snow Bunny," "Rudolph, the Red Nosed Reindeer," "Simple Gifts," "The Toy Maker," "Jungle Bells," "Frosty the Snowman," "Up on the Housetop/Deck the Halls," "It's Christmas Time Again" and "The Orphan Boy." Additional recordings by Kevin Roth are on pp. 28–29, 101–102 and 191–193.

★★★    **HOLIDAYS AND SPECIAL DAYS**
**Greg and Steve**
**CTP/Youngheart**
**LP/Cassette/C.D.**
**Lyrics included**

Greg and Steve produce high-quality recordings that keep kids listening and moving. This one is full of funky music, original lyrics and activities for holidays throughout the year. In keeping with their rock style, there is a song called "If You Feel Like Rockin'" to get your body movin'. "The Party Line" is a movement song, much like a line dance, using famous nursery rhymes. The three traditional songs are "Jingle Bell Rock," "Peter Cottontail" and "This Land Is Your Land." Greg wrote a beautiful song called "A Man Named King" sung to the tune of "Michael Row The Boat Ashore." "Love Is" sums up the way Greg and Steve feel about people. Other songs are "Somebody's Birthday," "Happy Thanksgiving to All," "Goodbye and Farewell," "Music Makes the World Go 'Round" and "Halloween on Parade." An upbeat recording for home or school. Be sure to see other recordings by Greg and Steve on pp. 73–78, and 118.

★★★    **MERRY CHRISTMAS**
          **Joe Scruggs**
          **Educational Graphics Press**
          **Cassette**
          **Lyrics included**

Joe Scruggs' voice is soft and mellow, and conveys good feelings to the listener. He uses simple but very satisfying musical arrangements. As with other recordings by Joe Scruggs, many songs are original and very clever. "Christmas in July" is about all the holiday hype that starts six months before the actual day of Christmas. "Trouble with Elves" is a topical song about how the elves can't keep up with modern technology. "Miss Gripola" is about people who complain about what they get for Christmas. Some of the traditional songs include "Jingle Bell Rock," "Rudolph the Red Nosed Reindeer," "Silent Night," "We Wish You a Merry Christmas," "Jingle Bells" (with additional lyrics by Scruggs), "Santa Claus Is Coming to Town," "Frosty the Snowman," "Up on the Housetop" and "Away in a Manger." This exceptional recording will be a big hit with kids from three to eight. More recordings by Joe Scruggs are on pp. 102–103 and 195–197.

          **KEEP THE SPIRIT**
          **Tickle Tune Typhoon**
          **Tickle Tune Typhoon Records/Music for Little**
            **People**
          **Cassette**
          **Lyrics included**

A collection of new and traditional Christmas music plus one Chanukah song, "Chanukah," sung in both English and

Hebrew. The group has a lovely sound, with beautiful harmonies and rich musical accompaniments. Some of the a cappella pieces are fabulous. My favorite new composition is called "Peace Child," a terrific song about making the world safe for the children. Other songs include "Jingle Bells," "Deck the Halls," "Silent Night/Snowflake Waltz," "Christmas Town," "Little Drummer Boy" (a musical treat) and "This Little Light of Mine." This recording is sure to be enjoyed for years. Other recordings by Tickle Tune Typhoon are on pp. 203–205, 208, and 210–211.

★★★    **A CHILD'S HOLIDAY**
**Various Artists**
**Alacazam Records**
**No lyrics included**
**Cassette/C.D.**

A fabulous group of children's recording artists and other singers have each contributed one song to this Christmas recording, resulting in a great variety of voices and musical arrangements. I enjoyed this recording so much that I took one home for my own collection. "When Jesus Was A Kid" by Peter Alsop is a thought-provoking, timely song about what Jesus might have been like as a kid and how the meaning of Christmas must allow a child to be a child—another Alsop treasure! Sally Rogers sings "P Is for Peace," a delightful song that spells out the message of getting along with one another. Tom Paxton's original "Reindeer on My Roof" is one of my favorite soon-to-become-classic Christmas songs. Tickle Tune Typhoon sings, "This Little Light Of Mine" with a child and adds some new verses. Bill Harley's comic "Get Me out of Here" is about Santa getting stuck in the fireplace. John McCutcheon's "Calling All the Children Home" (accompanied by Tom Chapin) is a gift to children of the world: Moishe, Sipho, Isabel, Kim, Red Hawk, Johnny, Patty and Rob. Ella Jenkins' interactive song "It's A Holiday" is about all the things we do at Christmas. Lui Collins sings "Blessed," about all the things that surround us. This is a recording full of fun and thought-provoking songs.

**CHRISTMASTIME FOR KIDS**
**Various Artists**
**Brentwood Music**
**Cassette**
**No lyrics included**

Thirty favorite songs are sung by a children's chorus. The children's voices are a delight to hear, and they invite others to join. The orchestrations never eclipse the children's voices. Some of the favorites are "We Wish You a Merry Christmas," "Angels We Have Heard on High," "Frosty, the Snowman," "Felíz Navidad," "Joy to the World," "All I Want for Christmas Is My Two Front Teeth," "Over the River and Through the Snow," "Jingle Bells," "Go Tell It on the Mountain," "Hark! The Herald Angels Sing," "Rudolph, the Red Nosed Reindeer," "Children, Go Where I Send Thee," "It Came Upon a Midnight Clear" and "Santa Claus Is Coming to Town." I'm always partial to children's choruses for Christmas music, and this is a great one. Teachers will also find this a delightful recording to use in the classroom.

**A HANUKKAH SING-ALONG FOR KIDS**
**Various Artists**
**Brentwood Music**
**Cassette**
**Lyrics included**

A children's chorus sings the favorite songs of Hanukkah. This recording has a split-track format, which means that by turning stereo balance to the left, you hear only the instruments, and if the balance is turned to the right you hear only the voices. When the balance is in the middle, both can be heard. This could be useful for classroom use or other teaching purposes. The chorus is very pleasant. Although most of the songs are sung in Hebrew, some have the English translations. This same group does a *Shabbat Sing-Along* and a *Passover Sing-Along* (see pp. 228–229). The songs are "Y'Mé Hanukah," "Hanukah/ Mi Y'malēl," "Sov, Sov, Sov/My Dreidel," "Haneyrot Halalu," "My Candles," "Hanukah Blessings," "Ma' Oz Tsur (Marcello/ Ma' Oz Tsur, Traditional),'' "S'Vivon," "Y'Ladim Baneyrot," "Listen and Follow Me," "Mer Li," "Kemah, Kemah,"

"Hanukah, Hanukah," "Mi Ze Hidlik," "Al Hanisim," and "Shine Little Candles."

**HALLOWEEN FUN**
**Various Artists**
**Kimbo Educational**
**Cassette**
**No lyrics included**

Although this recording was done for the educational market, it definitely can be used at home, particularly if you're planning a Halloween party. Most of the songs are original, and they are sung by both men and women. The orchestrations use synthesized sounds and are rather ordinary. "The Halloween Sound Effects" is quite good, including the scary sounds that kids love to hear. The other well-known songs are "The Monster Mash," "Theme from *The Alfred Hitchcock Hour*" and "The *Ghostbusters* Theme." The original songs include "Scary, Scary Halloween," "The Pumpkin Patch Polka," "We Don't Want a Monster in Our House" and "Are You Ready For Halloween?" This is a mediocre recording, but it is one of the few that is easily available.

**A PASSOVER SING-ALONG FOR KIDS**
**Various Artists**
**Brentwood Music**
**Cassette**
**Lyrics included**

In another split-track recording, a children's chorus sings Passover songs in English and Hebrew. This is a good recording for use at home or in group settings. The children's voice are clear. The songs include "Ma Nishtana (The Four Questions)," "Avadim Hayinu," "Hin'ni Muchan," "Dayenu," "Ki Lo Na'Eh," "Adir Hu," "Echod Mi Yodea," "Chad Gadya" and "Hal 'Luya." A very pleasant recording.

### A SHABBAT SING-ALONG FOR KIDS
**Various Artists**
**Brentwood Music**
**Cassette**
**Lyrics included**

A delightful children's chorus performs songs of the Sabbath in Hebrew and English on a split-track recording where you can hear voices alone, music alone, or the music and voices together. This offering is appropriate for home or group use. The songs include "Nerot Shabbat," "L'Cha Dodi," "Shalom Aleichem," "Kiddush," "Kah Ribon Olam," "Shabbat Shalom," "Shavu'a Tov" and "Adon Olam."

# *Introduction to Classical Music* ♫..

When I was in elementary school, we learned a song sung from Beethoven's Ninth Symphony. It wasn't until Junior High that I discovered the tune's origin and learned about its composer. Classical music is a treat that everyone should experience at some point in their lives. There is nothing quite like sitting in a concert hall and hearing a full orchestra fill the room and your soul with pure and harmonious sounds. Even if your personal taste does not favor classical music as a steady diet, it is definitely something that your children should be exposed to on some level. So many parents express their reluctance to play classical music at home; there seems to be a snobbish attitude associated with it, and some people are hesitant to share this aloof format of music with their children. Many say they want to expose their children to classical music, but since they themselves know nothing about it, they're unsure of what to choose. There are many ways to approach this. One is to decide (perhaps with your child) which instruments you particularly like, and then choose a concerto featuring that instrument or a composer who favors certain parts of the orchestra. If you need guidance on finding these selections, call your local classical radio station or local music store and ask for some help. Another way is to start by listening to a version of *Peter and the Wolf*, which highlights the different instruments, and then go on from there. You can also choose to learn about a composer's life, and then listen in more detail to his or her complete works. Additionally, many local orchestras perform for children. If there's one in your town, be sure to check it out.

In this chapter, I've listed several pieces of classical music that were done specifically to teach children about the instruments in the orchestra and give them a sample of the richness of the music of classical composers. There are some wonderful recordings that share this experience with children, and you can choose which recording you like, depending on the narrator. I have also listed here some excellent recordings that introduce children biographically to the composers and their music. Since many school districts throughout the country have cut their fine arts programs, this is a way for you to share this musical magic with your children at home. Teachers will also find many of these recordings helpful in classroom setting.

I've listed several versions of Prokofiev's *Peter and the Wolf*, only naming the narrator, the orchestra and what piece is performed on Side 2, except where more explanation is needed. The orchestral arrangements are varied, but all have fine tonal quality. The introduction to the composers is listed by production company, since each company uses a slightly different format in it's presentation. As you listen to this music, you might casually mention the name of the selection or the composer. Kids retain information this way. Most of the recordings are appropriate for all ages—infant through adult.

It is impossible to list all the classical music that is available. If you like certain pieces or composers, go to your local audio store and purchase a cassette or C.D. There are no rules here. Music should be played to be enjoyed, and if you have favorites, your child will benefit from hearing them. I have several parents who have told me that classical music is their music of choice at home. They say that even though the children listen to other things, they have developed their own classical tastes from just hearing it played in the background. Just as with other types of music, make this a stress-free, pleasurable time.

## DO:

- Choose music that appeals to your own taste.

- Include your child's taste in your shared listening time.

- Attend local orchestral presentations for children.
- Tell your children what they're hearing.

## DON'T:

- Be intimidated by some of the snobbish attitudes about classical music.
- Be afraid to call local classical radio stations for suggestions.
- Limit your purchases to music geared only to children.

★★★     **BERNSTEIN'S FAVORITE CHILDREN'S CLASSICS—PETER AND THE WOLF**
**Narrated by Leonard Bernstein**
**New York Philharmonic, Leonard Bernstein conducting**
**Sony**
**Cassette/C.D.**

Side A also includes *Young Person's Guide To The Orchestra* (Britten), narrated by Henry Chapin. Side B contains *Carnival of the Animals* (Saint-Saens/Ogden Nash), also narrated by Bernstein.

This classic recording has been recently re-released and is a must!

**PETER AND THE WOLF PLAY JAZZ**
**Narrated by LeVar Burton**
**Various Artists**
**Jazz Cat Productions**
**Cassette**

Side B: *Cool Mother Goose Suite* featuring Carmen McRae. Produced by Jon Crosse (see *Lullabys Go Jazz*), this is a jazz version of Prokofiev's classic piece that takes place in Central Park with a street-smart child named Peter. Jazz aficionados will love this clever recording.

**PETER AND THE WOLF**
**Narrated by Dom DeLuise**
**Little Orchestra Society**
**MusicMasters**
**Cassette/C.D.**

Side B: *Gerald McBoing Boing*, written by Gail Kubik and Dr.
Seuss, narrated by Carol Channing, accompanied by the
orchestra. It's the story of a man who imitates all kinds of
sounds. Also, *A Zoo Called Earth*, written and narrated by
Peter Schickele, the creator of P.D.Q. Bach. Here children can
imagine what aliens from another planets might think of planet
earth in this very entertaining piece.

**PETER AND THE WOLF**
**Narrated by Brandon De Wilde**
**Vienna Pro Musica, Hans Swarowsky**
**conducting**
**Allegro Music**
**Cassette**

Side B: *Young Person's Guide to the Orchestra* (Britten).

**PETER AND THE WOLF**
**Narrated by Sir Alec Guiness**
**Boston Pops Orchestra, conducted by Arthur**
**Fiedler**
**RCA**
**Cassette/C.D.**

Side B: *Carnival of the Animals* and *The Nutcracker Suite*.
Guiness' narration is delightful!

★★★ **PETER AND THE WOLF**
**Narrated by Itzhak Perlman**
**Israel Philharmonic, Zubin Mehta conducting**
**EMI/Angle**
**Cassette/C.D.**

Side B: *Carnival of the Animals* (Saint-Saens/Ogden Nash)
Perlman and Mehta are magical together.

**PETER AND THE WOLF**
**Narrated by Cyril Richard**
**Philadelphia Orchestra, Eugene Ormandy**
        **conducting**
**Columbia/Odyssey**
**Cassette**

Side B: *Young Person's Guide to the Orchestra* (Britten). Richard's English accent is a delight to hear.

**PETER AND THE WOLF**
**Narrated by Sting**
**Chamber Orchestra of Europe, Claudio**
        **Abbado conducting**
**Duetsche Grammophon**
**Cassette C.D.**

Side B: *Overture on a Hebrew Theme* (Prokofiev). This recording is also available with Spanish narration by José Carreras.

**PETER AND THE WOLF**
**Dave Van Ronk**
**Alacazam**
**Lyrics included**
**Cassette/C.D.**

This unique version of *Peter and the Wolf* is not for traditionalists, as Van Ronk uses a jug band as his orchestra. Peter is a fiddle, Grandpa is a mandolin, the duck is a kazoo, the bird is a penny whistle, the cat is a clarinet, the hunter is guitar and low voices represent the wolf. The accompaniment includes a washboard, jaw harp, washtub bass and a jug. Side B has Van Ronk singing "Teddy Bear's Picnic," "Swinging on a Star," "Mairzy Doats" and other songs. The booklet includes melody lines, the text to *Peter and the Wolf* and creative ideas for activities. A real folk version.

PETER AND THE WOLF
**Narrated by Jonathan Winters**
**Philharmonia Orchestra, Efren Kurtz**
   **conducting**
**EMI/Angel**
**Cassette/C.D.**

Side B: *Carnival of the Animals* (Saint-Saens/Ogden Nash),
Winter is delightful and adds a special spark.

★★★     CLASSICAL KIDS SERIES
         **Produced by Sue Hammond**
         **The Children's Group**
         **Cassette/C.D.**
         **Activity Booklet included**
         **Ages 4–10**

This superb collection of recordings narrates the stories of
composers' lives, told from a child's perspective. As the story
of each composer is being told, many of his pieces are being
played. Each recording gives a child exposure to music, a bit
of history and a fine dramatic reading. This series should be
in every home and school. The production is excellent and the
narration is creative and endures repeated listenings. Besides
those listed below, more are due in the future. You'll want to
collect all of this continuing series.

MR. BACH COMES TO CALL—
**A Tale of Wisdom and Enchantment**

Mr. Bach appears in the living room of eight-year-old Elizabeth
(who is practicing the piano) with his magic orchestra and a
boy choir. Pieces include Minuet in G, First Movement of
Orchestral Suite No. 3, Third Movement of Brandenburg Concerto No. 5, Second Movement of Flute Sonata in C, The Goldberg "Variations," "We Hasten" from Cantata No. 78, Chorale
Preludes, "Allein Gott" and many more.

## BEETHOVEN LIVES UPSTAIRS

Young Christoph and his uncle exchange letters about Christoph's boisterous new neighbor, Mr. Beethoven. The story ends with Christoph attending the premier performance of the famous Ninth Symphony. Pieces include Second Movement of Symphony No. 7, First and Second Movements of Symphony No. 5, Second Movement of Piano Sonata Op. 14 No. 2, "Moonlight," Violin "Spring" Sonata, Piano Concerto No. 1 and Shepherd's Theme from Symphony No. 6.

## MOZART'S MAGIC FANTASY—
### A Journey Through *The Magic Flute*

Live the tale of *The Magic Flute* as young Sarah and the dragon explore from the domain of the Queen of the Night through Sarastro's castle. The two help Prince Tamino find his Princess Pamina and also help Papageno (the bird-man) find his Papagena. Words are included to many of the arias. Pieces include "O Help Me (Zu Hilfe)," "You Must Journey (O zitt're nicht)," "Let Us Hurry (Schnele Fusse)" and "Oh, My Heart Is Broken (Ach, ich fuhl's)."

## VIVALDI'S RING OF MYSTERY

Katarina, a young violinist, arrives at the Pieta orphanage in Venice, Italy, where Vivaldi is the music director. A ring is her only clue to her family's heritage, and with the help of Giovanni, a gondolier, she searches throughout Venice for answers about her past. Some of the thirty pieces include *The Four Seasons*, Guitar Concerto, Piccolo Concerto and Double Trumpet Concerto.

**THE INSTRUMENTS OF THE ORCHESTRA**
**Narrated by Richard Maltby**
**Remex Music**
**Cassette**
**No lyrics included**
**Ages 4–10**

Maltby discusses the different instruments in the orchestra and each instrument then plays a solo; however, there is no indication of the pieces being played. A group of singers plays a silly Simon Says game preceding each family of instruments in a format that sounds very dated. The concept of this recording is good and the instrumental pieces are well performed, but the overall presentation is lackluster. This recording is also more difficult to locate than others.

**THE CLASSICAL CHILD I AND II**
**Ernie Mavrides**
**Sophia Sound**
**Cassette**
**No notes included**
**Ages 2–10**

The modern sound of synthesized instruments is used to perform some of the most recognizable pieces of classical music. These have a very "new age" sound and will make many classical music purists crazy. Although not my personal favorites, I can understand how some might find this sound interesting. The author's note suggests this style as a way to expose young children to classical music. The pieces are excerpted from the original. These recordings are interesting, but if you want to give your child a classical music experience, why not use recordings that use the orchestral instruments?

VOLUME I includes Sonata in C (Mozart), Symphony No. 6 (Beethoven), Sarabande (Bach), Symphony No. 9 (Beethoven), Canon in C (Pachebel), Sonata No. 11 in G (Haydn) and Prelude in E Minor (Chopin).

VOLUME II includes music by Bach, Haydn and Mozart.

★★★   HANS CHRISTIAN ANDERSEN/TUBBY
        THE TUBA
**Danny Kaye**
**MCA**
**Cassette**
**No lyrics included**
**Ages 3–8**
**See entry on pp. 157–158.**

**THE ORCHESTRA**
**Narrated by Peter Ustinov**
**Toronto Philharmonic Orchestra, Walter**
  **Babiak conducting**
**Mark Rubin Productions**
**Cassette**
**Ages 4 and up**

This introduction to the instruments and music of the orchestra is beautifully narrated by the great Peter Ustinov. Children experience the feelings of abstract music in pieces such as "William Tell" Overture (Rossini), Symphony No. 5 (Beethoven), Norwegian Dance No. 2 (Grieg), or concrete imagination in such pieces as *Peter and the Wolf* (Prokofiev) and "Orpheus in the Underworld—Can Can" (Offenbach) and are then told how a composer works. Ustinov discusses tempo, rhythm and harmony. The String Family selections includes Symphony No. 9 (Beethoven), Cello Concerto in C Major Op. 101 (Haydn) and *Carnival of the Animals* (Saint-Saens). The Woodwinds Family pieces include "Carmen Suite" (Bizet), "Mother Goose Suite" (Ravel) and "Stars and Stripes Forever" (Sousa). From the Brass Family comes "Midsummer Night's Dream" (Mendelssohn) and "Tubby the Tuba" (Kleinsinger). There is a short "Variation for Percussion" for the Percussion Family. Special Instruments include Piano Concerto No. 5 (Beethoven) and "Dance of the Sugarplum Faries" from *The Nutcracker* (Tchaikovsky). Because Ustinov goes into great detail explaining the instruments, the conductor and the composer, this recording is better suited to a child with good listening skills. It's an important cassette that parents and teachers will enjoy. There is also a video available from Alacazam.

**MUSIC MASTER SERIES**
**Various Narrators**
**Allegro**
**Cassette**
**Ages 6–10**

This series of recordings has been available for many years. The eighteen different recordings give children a glimpse of the music and times of famous classical composers. They are well narrated, although sometimes the text is a bit dry. The pieces played are listed on the cassette insert and reflect some of the more famous works by those composers. The selections are long, and therefore are generally not for very young children. We like to recommend that people buy these for children who have already expressed an interest in learning about classical music and the composers, or for children who might want to do a school report. These are relatively inexpensive and may be more accessible than some of the other recordings. They are good informational tapes that cover many of the composers that other companies don't examine. Three of the recordings discuss two composers per tape. The composers are Bach, Mozart, Chopin, Mendelssohn, Schubert, Schumann and Grieg, Handel, Beethoven, Haydn, Wagner, Vivaldi and Corelli, Dvorak, Tchaikovsky, Brahms, Strauss, Foster and Sousa, Berlioz and Verdi. These make a nice series to collect!

# French and Spanish
# Recordings ♫..

Having raised my two children in Mexico, I was able to experience firsthand the importance of music when learning a second language. My sons' first language was Spanish, and through the recordings that I bought (Pete Seeger, Hap Palmer, Ella Jenkins, Danny Kaye, etc.), I found that their ability to form sentences, rather than just words, was greatly increased through these musical experiences. They began to incorporate the rhythm of the language through music, and it gradually worked its magic into their everyday speech patterns. Later, working as a bilingual teacher in Los Angeles, I again found the same thing to be true. Children who needed to learn English or Spanish greatly benefited from a musical enrichment program. It made learning fun and painless. We are never too old to learn another language, and today, living in the United States, it's almost imperative that we speak English, Spanish and perhaps Japanese. Children's music is the most natural way to learn another language or reinforce a native tongue. The lyrics tend to repeat many of the words, and the concepts are not veiled or ambiguous. The sentence structures are clearly defined and not much slang is used. I can recall singing songs in Hebrew, French, Spanish and other languages as a kid, and to this day I remember what they mean, even though I am not fluent in all those languages. These experiences also enhanced my cultural upbringing and helped me become aware of others. One of the beautiful things we can share with each other and our children is our own cultural history. I have tried to highlight songs from varied cultures in many of the previously mentioned recordings in this book. The few recordings listed below are specifically in either French or Spanish. I have not listed recordings that are only used as language aid; there are many of those available for children. These are musical recordings that reflect a cultural experience and that can be used to teach the language, reinforce the language, or just as pure singing and listening entertainment.

I am constantly surprised at the number of parents who are looking for music in French and Spanish. One customer told me that his wife is French speaking, and that they were always looking for good French tapes for their young boys. He was pleased with the ones I sent him and has me scouting out more for their library. We cannot keep enough Spanish-language recordings in our store. These are not exclusively sold to people who speak Spanish; there are families who want their kids to hear and experience a language that encompasses many aspects of our daily life in Los Angeles. I also get calls from publishers of books and recordings asking about materials that might be translated into Spanish. Even if you live in an area where French or Spanish is not common, your children will surely benefit from hearing stimulating recordings in these two important cultures and languages.

## DO:

- Expose your child to music from other cultures.

- Use music as a fun and natural way to learn another language.

- Reinforce your cultural heritage through music.

- Share these recordings with your child's school.

## DON'T:

- Make learning a language a stressful thing.

- Limit yourself and your children to music sung only in English.

**UN REGALO DE ARRULLOS—**
**A Child's Gift Of Lullabyes**
**Vocals by Tanya Goodman**
**Cassette**
**Lyrics included**
**Infant–6**

This Spanish-language version of *A Child's Gift Of Lullabyes* (see page 19) is a much needed tape, since there is so little available in Spanish for children in this country. Goodman's voice is truly lovely and her pronunciation is adequate, although it's obviously not her native language. The translations to these original songs are forced and almost too literal. It is a shame that the producers didn't use native Spanish singers and try to translate in a more rhythmic fashion.

★★★     **HELLO, BONJOUR**
**Alain Le Lait**
**Polyglot Tots Productions**
**Cassette**
**Lyrics in English and French included**
**Ages 2–10**

This is a truly delightful recording of original children's music, with each song sung in both English and French. As I was sitting and listening to this recording again, I found myself actually singing some of the verses in French, and I speak *no* French at all. The tunes are short and very melodic with nice musical arrangements. The lyrics are creative and lively; the female voice sings in English, and the male voice sings in French. Most of the songs are geared to children between two and five, but the educational language learning value is also appropriate for much older children. This marvelous recording may be hard to find, but it is worth the search. The songs (I'm listing them in English only) include "Funny Face," "The Rooster," "The Duck and the Spider Bug," "One Cookie for You and Me," "Let's Be Friends," "What's the Color of Your Eyes?" "Brother John (Frère Jacques)," "Goodnight," and "Seven Ravens." This is an excellent example of how music can assist in learning another language.

**FAR AWAY ACROSS THE SEA**
**Alain Le Lait**
**Polyglot Tots**
**Cassette**
**Lyrics in English and French included**
**Ages 2–10**

Alain's tender voice is delightful to hear in both English and French. His musical arrangements are varied and clear enough that you hear all the words of the songs. This collection of mostly original music is a wonderful follow-up to *Hello, Bonjour*. Because of the bilingual format of these recordings, your ear just lets you move right into the next language in a natural way—an appealing way to learn French from English or English from French. The original songs are listed here in English "Mr. Butterfly," "The Colors of Summer," "The Rain Song," "I Brush My Teeth," "What I Like," "Hide and Seek," "How I Love You," "Golden Sun," "Goodbye" and more. The two traditional songs are "The Wheels on the Bus" and "Head and Shoulders."

**SOYONS AMIS**
**Alain Le Lait**
**Polyglot Tots**
**Cassette and Activity Book**
**Lyrics in English and French included**
**Ages 2–10**

In the third of Alain's recordings, he has included an activity book that will help children interact with the fine music they're hearing. Unlike the other recordings, this is sung exclusively in French, although the English translations are given. Alain's voice is inviting and pleasant; he is accompanied by a children's chorus. The lyrics use a lot of repetition, which is important for young children. Alain's recordings are a great treasure. The songs included are: "Les Poissons," "Les Oiseaux," "Les Lapins," "Frère Jacques," "Les Dinosaures," "J'aime Les Fruits," "Bonjour!," "Dans Le Ciel," "Avec Un Gros Nez," "J'ai Faim," "J'ai Soif," "Sept Alouettes," "Posé Sur Une Branche," and five more.

**SONGS IN SPANISH FOR CHILDREN**
**Martita, Jesus de Jerez and Juan Rojas**
**CBS Records**
**Cassette**
**No lyrics included**
**Ages 2½—6**

This recording has been available for over twenty years. I originally bought this treasure in Los Angeles for my children in Mexico at a time when little was available there. We used it both at home and at the nursery school where I worked. Over the years we have sold many copies at the store, and it still is a great collection of songs in Spanish. The voices are clear and easy to understand, and the orchestrations are interesting. Unfortunately, a lyric sheet is no longer enclosed. These are all well-known songs that will be recognized in many Spanish-speaking countries. Some of the fourteen songs are "El Barco Chiquitito," "A La Víbora De La Mar," "Los Meses Del Año," "Desde México He Venido," "Mi Granja," "El Zapatero," "La Rana," "Arrurru,"and "Los Quehaceres De La Semana."

★★★　　**RECORDINGS BY JOSÉ-LUIS OROZCO**
**José-Luis Orozco**
**Arcoiris Records**
**LP/Cassette**
**Lyrics and Activity Sheets in English and**
**　　Spanish included**
**Ages 3–10**

José-Luis has been a folksinger and performer for many years, and luckily he now lives in the United States and works with teachers and children all over the country. He has a degree in multicultural education. I have had the pleasure of seeing him share his musical magic with children and adults. Everyone raves about his talent as a singer, about his charisma as a performer and about his charm as a person. The following three recordings are truly special. They represent music, tongue twisters, Christmas songs, rhymes, games and lullabies from all over Latin America. These are our most popular recordings in Spanish, and both teachers and parents rave about them. José-Luis accompanies himself on the guitar; his voice is clear and inviting. There are some original songs on these recordings and some update verses to old favorites. I've listed in Spanish all the pieces on each recording. These are recordings to treasure!

VOLUME I contains "De San Francisco He Venido," "Chocolate," "Coco," "Las Vocales," "Arrullo," "Pin Una," "Sana, Sana," "Noche Buena," "Las Posadas," "Aserrin," "La Media," "Naranja," "Tengo Manitas," "Vamos A Cantar," "Acitrón," "Guantanamera," "De Colores," "Mi Gallo," "Pimpón," "Erre Con Erre," "Caballito Blanco," "Mi Conejito," "El Burrito Enfermo," "Santa Ana," "Campana Sobre Campana," "San Severino," "La Pulga De San José," "Duerme Negrito," "La Comadre Juana," "Buenos Días," "Los Pollitos," " La Casa De Peña" and "El Buque De Papel."

VOLUME II contains "Las Hormigitas," "Tipitin," "Un Ratoncito," "El Jarabe," "El Tepíc," "Atole," "Te Decía," "El Palomo," "La Diana," "Si Pancha Plancha," "Sun, Sun, Ba, Ba, E," "Los Elefantes," "Barquito De Papel," "Las Mañanitas," "Las Estaciones," "Pablito," "La Víbora De La Mar," "La Tablita," "Marcelino," " El Gavilan Pollero," "Al Ánimo," "El Barquito," "La Burrita," "Arrullo," and "Navidad Campesina."

VOLUME III contains "La Bamba" (with some new original verses), "Juanito," "Dos Manitas," "El Gato," "Naranja Dulce," "La Villa," "La Granja," "El Rabo Del Burro," "Dormir," "Las Mañanitas Tapatias," "Paz Y Libertad," "Al Tambor," "La Araña Pequeñita," "Los Camotes," "Perejíl," "De San Diego A San Francisco," "El Coquí," "Cielito Lindo," "Vamos A La Mar" and "Viva Mi Barrio."

> **ARRULLOS DE AMOR**
> **Karen Taylor-Good**
> **Brentwood Music**
> **Cassette**
> **Lyrics in Spanish included**
> **Infant–6**

This is a beautiful collection of original lullabies sung in Spanish. Taylor-Good's voice is lovely and soothing. The orchestrations sometimes overpower her voice, but all in all this is a very pleasant recording. Side B is instrumental only, so that you can sing along. This is a wonderful way to expose your child to loving lullaby music in Spanish. The ten songs include "Cierra Tus Ojos," "Hora De Dormir," "Cálmate," "Duerme Bebé," "Mami Esta Aquí" and "Meceté, Nena."

### SONGS IN FRENCH FOR CHILDREN
**Lucienne Vernay with Les Quatre Barbus**
**CBS Records**
**Cassette**
**Lyrics in English and French included**
**Ages 2–10**

Vernay's soft, clear voice is a lovely way to hear the beauty of the French language. The orchestrations are not extravagant but perfectly acceptable. Other singers, male and female, sing a few of the selections. This recording has been around for many years, and continues to be very popular. The songs include "Sur le pont d'Avignon," "L'alouette," "Le Petit train," "Picotin," "Mon père avait 500 coutons," "La Fourmi," "L'Abeille et le papillon," "La Cane de Jeanne," "La Petite Marie," "As-Tu vu la casquette?" "La Ferme de Zephirine," and ten more songs.

### LOS NIÑOS CANTAN ALABANZAS
**Various Artists**
**Brentwood Music**
**Cassette**
**No lyrics included**
**Infant–10**

A children's chorus sings the religious songs of Christmas in Spanish. The group is from Mexico, and sounds great. This is not a recording to learn Spanish, however; the majority of the songs have a religious theme. This is a split-track recording where you can listen to the voices alone, the accompaniments alone, or both together. A few of the thirty songs are "Toca Tu Arpa Davíd," "Kum Ba Yah," "Díos Bueno Es," "Tengo Paz Como Un Río," "Hay Poder En El Nombre De Cristo," "Tengo Un Hogar En Gloria," "Alelu Aleluya" and " Ven A Mi Ser."

# Resources for Children's Recordings ♫..

First and foremost, I recommend that you check with your local music and children's book stores. Many stores stock children's recordings and others are happy to special order them for you. There are a limited number of mail order sources that carry an extensive selection of recordings, and countless others that seem to carry only a few. Listed below are the resources that carry a wide range of musical recordings for children. These businesses can supply you with music by a wide variety of artists from various publishers. They are all reputable and will try to accommodate your musical needs. Call them for a catalog or to place an order.

Alacazam
P.O. 429
Waterbury, VT 05676
Tel: (800) 541-9904
Fax: (802) 244-6128

Children's Book & Music Center
P.O. Box 1130
Santa Monica, CA 90406
Tel: (301) 535-0264

Chinaberry Books
2780 Via Orange Way, Suite B
Spring Valley, CA 91978
Tel: (800) 776-2242
Fax: (619) 670-5203

Educational Record Center, Inc.
3233 Burnt Hill Drive, #100
Wilmington, NC 28403
Tel: (800) 438-1637

Linden Tree
170 State Street
Los Altos, CA 94022
Tel: (415) 949-3390

Music for Little People
P.O. Box 1460
Redway, CA 95560
Tel: (800) 346-4445
Fax: (707) 923-3241

For further information, write to the author at:
P.O. Box 1130
Santa Monica, CA 90406

# Index of Artists

Abdul, Paula, 207
Abell, Timmy, 57
Aboody, Cindy Paley, 215–17
Albert, Christine, 68
Alda, Alan, 114, 115
Allen, Lillian, 116
Alsop, Peter, 86, 122, 123–26, 208, 226
Arkin, Alan, 57
Arkin, Jeremy, 57
Arnold, Linda, 127–29, 208, 210
Arthur, Bea, 115
Avni, Fran, 217

Babysitters, the, 57–58
Ballingham, Pamela, 9–11
Banana Slug String Band, 86, 129–132
Baron, Laura, 16–17, 38–39
Baron Folk, the, 30, 35
Bartels, Joanie, 11, 35–36, 59–60, 217–18
Beall, Pamela Conn, 36–37, 61–62, 218
Belafonte, Harry, 114
Belling, Andrew, 132
Benatar, Pat, 115, 206
Benson, George, 118
Bergman, Steve, 12
Berman, Marcia, 12–13, 62–64, 133, 211, 219

Bernstein, Leonard, 232
Bessette, Mimi, 13, 30
Bishop, Heather, 133–35
Bishop, Steven, 206
Block, Rory, 135, 153
Boone, Debby, 65
Bowen, Judy, 30
Brand, Oscar, 14
Brooks, Mel, 114, 115
Browne, Jackson, 206
Buck, Denis, 135
Bueffel, Elaine, 45
Buell, Uncle Ruthie, 211, 219
Burton, LeVar, 232

Cafra, Pat, 14–16
Callinan, Ron, 136
Campagne, Carmen, 21–22, 30
Capon, Jack, 136–37
Cappelli, Frank, 66–67
Cassidy, Jack , 115
Cassidy, Nancy, 137–38
Cavett, Dick, 115
Cerf, Christopher, 115
Channing, Carol, 114
Chapin, Tom, 138–40, 226
Charette, Rick, 141, 218–19
Cheney, Martha, 48, 49
Chenille Sisters, 142, 148
Coasters, the, 150

251

# Index of Song Titles

Ladybug, The Famous Firefighter, 153

La Ferme de Zephirine, 246

La-La Man, 88

Lambeth Children, 147

Land of Nod, 23

Land of the Silver Birch, 72

Lapins, Les, 243

La Pulga de San Jose, 245

Las Posadas, 245

Later, 182

Latke Song, The, 215, 220

Laugh all Your Blues Away, 86, 155

Laundry, The, 145

Lavender's Blue, 30, 35

Lazy, Lazy, 176

Lazy Day, 194

L'Cha Dodi, 216, 229

Leatherwing Bat, 105

Left and Right, 88

Leroy Is a Late Bloomer, 182

Let 'Em Laugh, 126

Let Everyone Clap Hands Like Me, 84

Let's all Clap Our Hands Together, 87

Let's Be Friends, 203, 242

Let's Be Together Today, 99

Let's Clean Up Our Act, 136

Let's Face It, 124

Let's Go Riding, 72

Let's Make a Circle, 67

Let's Play, 128

Let's Play Ball, 155

Let's Pretend, 175

Letter Song, The, 78

Letter to Mr. Brown, 126

Let There Be Peace on Earth, 164

Let the Sun Shine Forever, 203

Let Us Come In, 106

Let Us Hurry (Schnele Fusse), 236

Library Song, The, 139

License Plate, 174

Lichvod Hachanukah, 216

Liese rieselt der Schnee (Softly Falls The Snow), 223

Life on the Shore, 130

Lightly Row, 119

Light One Candle, 215, 224

Light Rain, 202

Like Me and You, 96, 97

Limbo Rock, 59, 137

Lindsey's Bakery, 67

Lion Sleeps Tonight, The, 79

Listen, 73, 150

Listen and Follow Me, 227

Listen and Move, 77

Listen to the Blue Grass, 100

Litterbug, 201

Little Ants, 170

Little Armadillos, 146

Little Bells of Christmas, 218

Little Black Bull, The, 105, 191

Little Boy Blue, 17, 49

Little Brand New Baby, 176

Little Brown Dog, 30, 202, 208

Little Bunny Foo-Foo, 45

Little Chickens in the Garden, The, 191

Little David Play Your Harp, 132

Little Dogies, 105

Little Drummer Boy, The, 218, 226

Little Elf, 170

Little Hands, 145

Little Light of Mine: *See* This Little Light of Mine

Little Liza Jane, 93, 100, 105, 212

Little Lizard, The, 192

Little Miracles, 168

Little Miss Muffet, 49, 109, 153

Little Peter Rabbit, 36, 86

Little Piggy, 193